# Contextualizing Global Flows of Competency-Based Education

The new comparative research in this volume explores the global flow of competence-based education, curricular policy, and frameworks for instructional practice. Taking critical perspectives, the chapters trace the pathways through which educators and policy actors adopted and reshaped competence-based education as promoted by the OECD, the World Bank, and the European Union.

The authors ask: What purposes do competence-based educational reforms serve? How are competence-based models internationally deployed and locally modified? What happens as competence-based reforms get re-contextualized and contested in particular cultural, social, and political contexts? In their nuanced examination of these global flows, the authors theorize how competence-based reform strategies variously produce hybridity, silent borrowing, "loud borrowing," and new social imaginaries. Although entangled with other "hot topics" in educational research—skills and dispositions for citizenship and employment; higher-order and critical thinking; and socio-emotional learning—competence itself has multiple, fluid meanings. The authors dissect this polysemy while documenting the pivotal role of key actors in the development, design, and deployment of reforms in diverse international contexts.

*Contextualizing Global Flows of Competency-Based Education* will be a key resource for academics, researchers, and advanced students of comparative education, educational research, curriculum studies, sociology, and education leadership and policy. This book was originally published as a special issue of *Comparative Education*.

**Kathryn Anderson-Levitt** is Professor Emerita of Anthropology at the University of Michigan–Dearborn, USA, and also taught in UCLA's Department of Education 2011–2019. Her books include *Teaching cultures* (2002) and *Local meanings, global schooling* (2003).

**Meg P. Gardinier** is a global education policy researcher, instructor, and manager. She has published on issues such as education in post-communist Albania; teachers as agents of change; and the policy influence of the OECD. She is currently based in Washington DC, USA.

# Contextualizing Global Flows of Competency-Based Education

Polysemy, Hybridity and Silences

*Edited by*
**Kathryn Anderson-Levitt and Meg P. Gardinier**

LONDON AND NEW YORK

First published 2024
by Routledge
4 Park Square, Milton Park, Abingdon, Oxon, OX14 4RN

and by Routledge
605 Third Avenue, New York, NY 10158

*Routledge is an imprint of the Taylor & Francis Group, an informa business*

Introduction, Chapters 2–6 and 8 © 2024 Taylor & Francis
Chapter 1 © 2020 Andreas Nordin and Daniel Sundberg. Originally published as
Open Access.
Chapter 7 © 2020 Armend Tahirsylaj. Originally published as Open Access.

With the exception of Chapters 1 and 7, no part of this book may be reprinted or
reproduced or utilised in any form or by any electronic, mechanical, or other means,
now known or hereafter invented, including photocopying and recording, or in
any information storage or retrieval system, without permission in writing from the
publishers. For details on the rights for Chapters 1 and 7, please see the chapters'
Open Access footnotes.

*Trademark notice*: Product or corporate names may be trademarks or registered
trademarks, and are used only for identification and explanation without intent to
infringe.

*British Library Cataloguing-in-Publication Data*
A catalogue record for this book is available from the British Library

ISBN13: 978-1-032-56380-0 (hbk)
ISBN13: 978-1-032-56382-4 (pbk)
ISBN13: 978-1-003-43524-2 (ebk)

DOI: 10.4324/9781003435242

Typeset in Myriad Pro
by codeMantra

**Publisher's Note**
The publisher accepts responsibility for any inconsistencies that may have arisen
during the conversion of this book from journal articles to book chapters, namely
the inclusion of journal terminology.

**Disclaimer**
Every effort has been made to contact copyright holders for their permission to
reprint material in this book. The publishers would be grateful to hear from any
copyright holder who is not here acknowledged and will undertake to rectify any
errors or omissions in future editions of this book.

# Contents

| | |
|---|---|
| *Citation Information* | vii |
| *Notes on Contributors* | ix |

Introduction—Contextualising global flows of competency-based
education: polysemy, hybridity and silences     1
*Kathryn Anderson-Levitt and Meg P. Gardinier*

1   Transnational competence frameworks and national curriculum-making:
the case of Sweden     19
*Andreas Nordin and Daniel Sundberg*

2   The introduction of competence-based education into the compulsory
school curriculum in France (2002–2017): hybridity and polysemy as
conditions for change     35
*Pierre Clément*

3   Knowledge for the elites, competencies for the masses: political theatre of
educational reforms in the Russian Federation     51
*Elena Aydarova*

4   Curricular design for competencies in basic education in Uruguay:
positions and current debates (2008–2019)     67
*Eloísa Bordoli*

5   Moral priority or skill priority: a comparative analysis of key competencies
frameworks in China and the United States     83
*Li Deng and Zhengmei Peng*

6   21st century skills in the United States: a late, partial and silent reform     99
*Kathryn Anderson-Levitt*

7   What kind of citizens? Constructing 'Young Europeans' through loud
borrowing in curriculum policy-making in Kosovo     115
*Armend Tahirsylaj*

# CONTENTS

8   Imagining globally competent learners: experts and education policy-making beyond the nation-state      130
*Meg P. Gardinier*

*Index*      147

# Citation Information

The chapters in this book were originally published in the journal *Comparative Education*, volume 57, issue 1 (2021). When citing this material, please use the original page numbering for each article, as follows:

**Introduction**
*Introduction contextualising global flows of competency-based education: polysemy, hybridity and silences*
Kathryn Anderson-Levitt and Meg P. Gardinier
*Comparative Education*, volume 57, issue 1 (2021) pp. 1–18

**Chapter 1**
*Transnational competence frameworks and national curriculum-making: the case of Sweden*
Andreas Nordin and Daniel Sundberg
*Comparative Education*, volume 57, issue 1 (2021) pp. 19–34

**Chapter 2**
*The introduction of competence-based education into the compulsory school curriculum in France (2002–2017): hybridity and polysemy as conditions for change*
Pierre Clément
*Comparative Education*, volume 57, issue 1 (2021) pp. 35–50

**Chapter 3**
*Knowledge for the elites, competencies for the masses: political theatre of educational reforms in the Russian Federation*
Elena Aydarova
*Comparative Education*, volume 57, issue 1 (2021) pp. 51–66

**Chapter 4**
*Curricular design for competencies in basic education in Uruguay: Positions and current debates (2008–2019)*
Eloísa Bordoli
*Comparative Education*, volume 57, issue 1 (2021) pp. 67–82

## Chapter 5

*Moral priority or skill priority: a comparative analysis of key competencies frameworks in China and the United States*
Li Deng and Zhengmei Peng
*Comparative Education*, volume 57, issue 1 (2021) pp. 83–98

## Chapter 6

*21st century skills in the United States: a late, partial and silent reform*
Kathryn Anderson-Levitt
*Comparative Education*, volume 57, issue 1 (2021) pp. 99–114

## Chapter 7

*What kind of citizens? Constructing 'Young Europeans' through loud borrowing in curriculum policy-making in Kosovo*
Armend Tahirsylaj
*Comparative Education*, volume 57, issue 1 (2021) pp. 115–129

## Chapter 8

*Imagining globally competent learners: experts and education policy-making beyond the nation-state*
Meg P. Gardinier
*Comparative Education*, volume 57, issue 1 (2021) pp. 130–146

For any permission-related enquiries please visit:
http://www.tandfonline.com/page/help/permissions

# Notes on Contributors

**Kathryn Anderson-Levitt** is Professor Emerita of Anthropology at the University of Michigan–Dearborn, USA, and also taught in UCLA's Department of Education 2011–2019. Her books include *Teaching cultures* (2002) and *Local meanings, global schooling* (2003).

**Elena Aydarova** is Assistant Professor at the University of Wisconsin–Madison, USA. Her interdisciplinary scholarship examines global neoliberal transformations in education through the lens of equity, diversity, and social justice. She has recently published *Teacher Education Reform as Political Theater: Russian Policy Dramas* (2019).

**Eloísa Bordoli** is Professor and Researcher at the faculty of Educational Humanities and Sciences of the Universidad de la República, Uruguay. Her current lines of research are policies of educational inclusion and curricular policy.

**Pierre Clément** is Assistant Professor at the University of Rouen Normandy, France. He holds a PhD in sociology and teaches educational sciences. He is interested in sociology and history of education and in political sociology.

**Li Deng** is Associate Professor of the Institute of International and Comparative Education at the Faculty of Education at East China Normal University, China. Her areas of interest are comparative studies, education policy, and Shanghai education reform experiences.

**Meg P. Gardinier** is a global education policy researcher, instructor, and manager. She has published on issues such as education in post-communist Albania; teachers as agents of change; and the policy influence of the OECD. She is currently based in Washington DC, USA.

**Andreas Nordin** is Professor of Education at Linnaeus University, Sweden. His main fields of research are comparative and international education, education policy, and curriculum theory with a special focus on the complex interplay between national and transnational policy arenas. He is the co-editor of the book *Transnational Policy Flows in European Education*.

**Zhengmei Peng** is Professor and Director of the Institute of International and Comparative Education at the Faculty of Education at East China Normal University, China. His areas of interest are comparative studies, education policy, and educational philosophy.

**Daniel Sundberg** is Professor of Education at Linnaeus University, Sweden. His main field of research is comparative and historical perspectives on education reforms, curriculum, and pedagogy. His recent publications deal with curriculum theory and policy studies in terms of understanding and explaining curriculum change in the complex interconnections of transnational, national, and local curriculum and classroom arenas.

**Armend Tahirsylaj** is Associate Professor of Education at Norwegian University of Science and Technology (NTNU), Trondheim, Norway. His research focuses on curriculum theory, Didaktik/Bildung, education policy, teacher education, international large-scale assessments, and international comparative education. His latest publications have examined teacher autonomy and responsibility across Didaktik and curriculum traditions and the role of transnational and national education policies on mastery of key competences within national contexts.

# Introduction—Contextualising global flows of competency-based education: polysemy, hybridity and silences

Kathryn Anderson-Levitt and Meg P. Gardinier

**ABSTRACT**

This essay introduces the special issue on competencies or 'twenty-first century skills' as learning goals promoted by the OECD and other international organisations. The studies in this issue trace pathways through which competency-based approaches have been incorporated into national reforms, and explore how reform advocates, policy makers, educators, and experts have imagined 'key competencies' for compulsory education. Cases examine reforms in particular countries – Sweden, France, Russia, Kosovo, the United States, Uruguay, and China – as well as conceptualisations of competencies, 'civic competencies' and 'global competence' shaped by international experts. Based on these studies, this essay argues that the concept of competencies, central to the development of the OECD Programme for International Student Assessment (PISA), is a polysemous notion that has led to hybrid forms of discourse and policy implementation. It also highlights the significance of reform *processes* and specific *actors* in diverse settings, illuminating the complexity and contingency of competency-based reforms.

## Purpose and rationale

This special issue presents a comparative perspective on the transnational and localized flows of competency-based education reforms over the last three decades. Competencies, also sometimes called 'twenty-first century skills', are often referred to as a combination of skills, dispositions, and knowledge that learners are said to need in order to be productive workers and good citizens. Varying organisations have articulated lists of competencies and 'key competencies' which include, for example, 'the ability to use language, symbols and text interactively' (OECD 2005), 'digital competence' (European Commission 2006), 'critical thinking and problem solving' (P21 2016), 'the ability to relate well to others' (OECD 2005), a 'sense of initiative and entrepreneurship' (EC 2006), and 'creativity and innovation' (P21 2016).

The special issue is comprised of six analytic country case studies, one comparative study, and one theoretical essay. The cases presented explore how reform advocates, policy makers, educators, and experts have imagined and enacted competencies within curriculum policies, reforms, and assessments in diverse contexts. The research presented here focuses on primary and secondary education and excludes vocational education, higher education, and teacher education, each of which has its own distinct history with competency-based reforms. In compulsory education, competencies are generally cast as broad learning goals, and thus fall within the domains of curriculum and assessment.

### Why research on competencies?

Due to the international prevalence of competencies in curriculum policy debates, the time is ripe for critical and comparative perspectives on competency-based reforms. The introduction of competencies as curricular learning goals has taken place in several dozen nations and other polities, as discussed below. Yet the peer-reviewed literature on competency-based reforms is relatively slim compared to a much more extensive grey literature on the topic (Tahirsylaj and Sundberg 2020). Although several comparativist scholars have examined competency-based reforms (e.g. Hartong 2014; Morgan and Shahjahan 2014; Lightfoot 2015; Morgan 2016; Jules and Sundberg 2018; Li and Auld 2020; Pagliarello 2020), comparativists need to pay more attention to competency-based reforms and the notion of key competencies for several reasons, as discussed below.

First, advocates of competencies often propose them as one part of a standards-based curriculum (e.g. Sundberg and Wahlström 2012), and standards are seen by some analysts as part of a 'Global Education Reform Movement' that facilitates assessment and thus makes accountability possible in decentralising systems (Sahlberg 2016).

Second, major international organisations actively promote competency-based reforms, including the OECD (e.g. OECD 2019), UNESCO (e.g. Marope, Griffin, and Gallagher 2017), the World Bank (Aydarova 2020; World Bank 2018, 102ff) and the European Commission (EC 2006).

Third, as implied by the first point, competencies often play a role in assessment. In particular, the OECD's Programme for International Student Assessment (PISA) aims to assess competencies developed by 15-year-olds in over 75 countries (and ultimately many more through PISA for Development [Li and Auld 2020]). Although the OECD began developing PISA in the late 1980s by focusing on language arts and mathematics (Salganik et al. 1999), it soon launched a multi-year effort to 'define and select' competencies 'beyond reading, writing and computing' (Salganik et al. 1999, 2). Since 2003, each cycle of PISA has included 'innovative assessments' addressing a 'a much wider range of competencies' (OECD 2005, 3), such as critical thinking and problem-solving, financial literacy, collaborative problem solving and global competence. The close link with PISA and standardized assessments connects competencies with comparative studies of New Public Management, particularly management by measurement (see for example, Grek 2009; Møller and Skedsmo 2013; Clément 2020). Likewise, comparativists seeking to understand PISA as a tool of global governance would do well to examine how the OECD has built the notion of competencies into PISA and has encouraged countries through various mechanisms, including its country reports, to incorporate competencies in their curricula as learning goals (Martens and Jakobi 2010; Takayama 2013).

Finally, reformers link competencies to several other issues of interest to comparativists. Skills and dispositions that occur on many lists of competencies (e.g. solving complex problems) represent higher-order thinking, and many reformers believe they require learner-centred pedagogy, another reform idea debated extensively by comparativists (e.g. Schweisfurth 2013; Tabulawa 2013). Lists of competencies also include intrapersonal skills and dispositions, such as emotional intelligence or socio-emotional learning, and interpersonal skills (e.g. OECD 2019), both of interest to comparativists (e.g. Levin 2012).

### *Goal*

The authors in this issue look at the phenomenon of competencies from different theoretical frames and through different analytical lenses to take a critical perspective on this idea as it travels. In understanding its movements, the authors theorise processes, discussing how competency-based reforms are alternatively re-contextualized, appropriated, and/or contested. Several authors direct our attention to the role of key actors in these processes and their results, including instances of hybridity, silent policies, tactical borrowing and loud borrowing. Ultimately, the issue as a whole sheds light on the following concerns: Who is promoting competency-based education in various contexts and for what purposes? And how are various actors' interests engaged through the process of advocating for – or contesting – competency-based reforms?

This Introduction, after noting the terminological ambiguity of competence/competency and debates about why competency-based reforms are needed, tracks the historical and geographic scope of this phenomenon, briefly introduces each article, and then highlights themes discussed across multiple articles: polysemy of the notion of competency; hybridity in actual reforms; and complexities and contingencies revealed by an analytic focus on particular policy processes and key actors. It concludes with suggestions for further research with a focus on the question of who benefits from competency-based reforms.

## The productive plasticity of competence/competency

The terminology around competencies is fluid and its 'productive plasticity' (Bajaj 2014) makes the term available to be used strategically. Throughout the special issue, and likewise in a comprehensive research review (Tahirsylaj and Sundberg 2020), authors indicated a lack of agreement on the terms and their meanings. Regarding the term itself, some English-language texts use the word 'competence', some use 'competency', and some use both. For some, *competence* refers to a broad concept while *competencies* refer to particular abilities (Rychen 2001, 3); for others, *competence* is the more specific or concrete word, while *competency* is the broader concept (Salas-Pilco 2013, 11). Moreover, both 'competence' and 'competency' collapse into a single word in Romance languages (e.g. *compétence* in French, *competencia* in Spanish).

Given the lack of agreement on terminology, in this special issue we treat 'competence' and 'competency' as equivalent and authors use whichever term best fits the literature they cite. In this Introduction, we use the term 'competencies' to refer to skills (knowing *how to*) and dispositions (being *ready to*), noting that this meaning encompasses any knowledge (knowing *that*) required to apply one's skills in a particular situation or context. However, we will not attempt to define competencies precisely. As researchers, we acknowledge the divergent meanings and recommend close attention to how authors use terms such as *competence, competency, competencies, skills,* and related terms in other languages across different regions (e.g. Halász and Michel 2011). For example, see Nordin and Sundberg (2020) on how the Swedish term *förmågor*, glossed as 'abilities', has been used. Rather than assume a unitary or consistent meaning, we should investigate meaning, usage, and contextualisation of competencies as part of our comparative education research.

### What problems do competency-based reforms solve?

At another level of 'productive plasticity', it is difficult to pin down what problem competency-based approaches are meant to solve. A seminal text published by UNESCO emphasised that dispositions and skills like collaborativeness and critical thinking were needed to enable individuals to be better citizens in increasingly multicultural democratic societies (Delors 1996). OECD recently added to that rationale by stressing the need to prepare citizens who can address environmental emergencies facing the globe (OECD 2019). However, the rationale that originally justified OECD and World Bank interest in competencies – and the rationale that appears most often in the research literature (Tahirsylaj and Sundberg 2020) – is economic. It is the argument, in line with a human capital theory, that in the new 'global knowledge economy', citizens must be prepared in schools to exercise interdisciplinary skills – twenty-first century skills' – that are increasingly demanded of workers and professionals for the sake of their own individual success as well as the prosperity of national economies (Robeyns 2006).

In response to the 'new economy' argument, some analysts argue that 'twenty-first century skills' are not really new, but rather are 'dimensions of human competence that have been valuable for many centuries' (Pellegrino and Hilton 2012, 53). The only clear novelty among them is digital information literacy. What some analysts see as new in competency-based reforms, rather, is the expectation that *all* students, not just children of the elite, should develop higher-order thinking skills (e.g. Pellegrino and Hilton 2012). Yet observational studies have demonstrated that 'low-wage service workers' and laborers like plumbers and electricians already practice skills like collaboration, creativity, and critical thinking on the job (e.g. Hilton et al. 2010, 4; Rose 2004). Perhaps the actual novelty is that citizens should now learn these skills *in school* rather than at home, in the community, or on the job. However, some critics counter, first, that schools have been teaching certain skills such as literacy and communication all along and, second, that at least some teachers already teach higher-order thinking, at least to some extent, through seemingly teacher-centred pedagogies (e.g. Barrett 2007; Zhao 2019). Advocates of competency-based reforms reply by arguing that, nonetheless, many teachers in many parts of the world lack the training for teaching 'transferable skills' (UNESCO 2014).

Meanwhile, at a practical level, there is one problem that competency-based reforms clearly was meant address – a measurement problem. If one accepted the need for large-scale international assessments, then assessing a common set of competencies rather than knowledge bound to variable national curricula seemed as if it would solve the 'problems of comparability' that plagued earlier cross-national assessments (Morgan 2012, 52). That solution depends, however, on the contested premise that particular competencies can be measured convincingly (e.g. Engel, Rutkowski, and Thompson 2019).

## The scope of competency-based reforms

Drawing on reports of competency-based curriculum reforms in different polities (including subnational units like Quebec), Anderson-Levitt compiled Table 1 to illustrate their historical and geographical scope. (For additional references and details, see the table in the online Appendix.) Importantly, Table 1 refers only to policies or reports of policies, not actual implementation, and it may not capture all the policies that were later rescinded or dramatically revised. The table identifies over 60 polities said to have established some kind of competency-based reform in elementary and/or secondary education. However, diffusion around the world has not followed an even pace or even geographic distribution. Table 1 suggests that competency-based education reforms have strongly influenced European countries (also the source of most research on competencies [Tahirsylaj and Sundberg 2020]), peaking in the early 2000s. Competency-based educational policies have been embraced by some African countries, apparently peaking around 2010 (or perhaps earlier, as we know in many cases only that policies were adopted some time before 2013). Competency approaches have affected the Australian states and some Canadian provinces, touched the United States lightly, and seemingly had a spotty effect in Latin America and Asia. There are also countries that have instituted competency-based education but later stepped back from some or all of the reform. For example, Sweden partly unravelled its earlier competency-based approach in 2011 (Nordin and Sundberg 2020), while England replaced its competency-based curriculum in 2014 (Marope, Griffin, and Gallagher 2017, 51). Japan (OECD 2012), Poland (Wiśniewski and Zahorska 2020), and the Flemish community of Belgium (Loobuyck 2020) are also said to have shifted back towards more discipline-focused curricula.

While this reform movement does not seem to touch all parts of the world equally (cf. Högberg and Lindgren Forthcoming), some might argue that it is nonetheless part of a Global Education Reform Movement emphasising standardisation and accountability (Verger, Parcerisa, and Fontdevila 2019). However, the strong participation of Western Europe countries but apparent retraction by England and the relatively weak engagement of the United States (Anderson-Levitt 2020) contrast with the argument that other aspects of the Global Education Reform Movement were embraced by England and the United States but resisted to some extent by Western European nations (Sahlberg 2016).

## The studies in this issue

In this issue, we present the articles in a sequence that showcases both their geographic and conceptual relationship to each other. For instance, the first three papers highlight competency-based reforms embedded in European national contexts and the fourth illustrates some interesting parallels in Uruguay. The fifth paper is the comparative case study of China and the US, and the sixth provides additional historical and political context in the US case. The last two papers delve into analyses of particular competencies: civic competencies in Kosovo's curriculum, and global competence in the OECD's 2018 PISA innovative assessment.

6 CONTEXTUALIZING GLOBAL FLOWS OF COMPETENCY-BASED EDUCATION

**Table 1.** Reported competency-based reforms in compulsory education

| Reform Years | Europe | Outside Europe |
|---|---|---|
| 1993–94 | Finland[a]<br>Netherlands[b]<br>Sweden[c] | Botswana[d] |
| 1995–1999 | Austria[a]<br>Belgium (Flemish community)[e]<br>Belgium (French community)[f]<br>German states[a]<br>Ireland[a]<br>Malta[a]<br>Poland[a] | Mauritania[g]<br>Japan[h] |
| 2000–2004 | Czech Republic[a]<br>England, Wales, Northern Ireland[i]<br>Greece[a]<br>Hungary[a]<br>Lithuania[a]<br>Portugal[a]<br>Scotland[j]<br>Switzerland (Francophone)[k]<br>Turkey[l] | Tunisia[m]<br>Algeria[m]<br>Cameroon[n]<br><br>Quebec, Canada[o] |
| 2005–2009 | England (revisions)[a]<br>France[p]<br>Italy[a]<br>Luxembourg[a]<br>Northern Ireland (revisions)[a]<br>Slovakia[a]<br>Spain[a]<br>Wales (revisions)[a] | Benin[m]<br>Cape Verde[m]<br>Gabon[q]<br>Senegal[r]<br>Tanzania[s]<br><br>Djibouti[m]<br>Republic of Korea[l]<br>Sri Lanka (maths grades 6–9 only)[t]<br><br>Guatemala[u]<br><br>Australian states[v]<br>New Zealand[w] |
| 2010–2014 | *England returns to more focus on subject knowledge,* [x]*2014*<br><br>*Sweden returns to more focus on subject knowledge, 2011*[c]<br><br><br>Estonia[y]<br>Kosovo[z]<br>Russia[aa] | Burkina Faso[m] before 2013<br>Burundi[m] before 2013<br>Central African Republic[m] before 2013<br>Chad[m] before 2013<br>Comoros[m] before 2013<br>Congo (DRC) [m] before 2013<br>Guinea[m] before 2013<br>Madagascar[m] before 2013<br>Ivory Coast[m] before 2013<br><br>China[bb]<br><br>*Japan returns to more focus on traditional curriculum*[cc]<br><br>Mexico[h]<br><br>Alberta, Canada[dd]<br>British Columbia, Canada[dd]<br>Ontario, Canada[dd]<br>Saskatchewan, Canada[dd]<br>United States (41 states of 50)[ee] |

*(Continued)*

## Table 1. Continued.

| Reform Years | Europe | Outside Europe |
|---|---|---|
| 2015–2019 | *Belgium (Flemish community) partly reverses teaching of transversal skills, 2018*[e] | Kuwait[ff] |
| | | Brazil[h] |
| | *Poland partly reverses teaching of transversal skills, 2016*[h] | Peru[h] |
| | | Uruguay[gg] |

[a]Gordo et al. (2009)
[b]Trier (2003)
[c]Nordin & Sundberg (2020)
[d]Tabulawa (2009)
[e]Loobuyck (2020)
[f]Mangez (2008)
[g]Roegiers (2008)
[h]Reimers (2020)
[i]Hodgson and Spours (2003)
[j]Priestley and Humes (2010)
[k]Houchot et al. (2007)
[l]Ananiadou and Claro (2009)

[m]Lauwerier and Akkari (2013)
[n]Charton (2014)
[o]Mathou (2018)
[p]Clément (2020)
[q]Nnang (2013)
[r]Thiam and Chnane-Davin (2017)
[s]Mkimbili and Kitta (2019)
[t]Egodawatte (2014)
[u]Asturia and Mérida (2007)
[v]Savage and O'Connor (2015)
[w]New Zealand (2007)
[x]Marope, Griffin and Gallagher (2017)

[y]Estonia (2011a, 2011b)
[z]Tahirsylaj (2020)
[aa]Aydarova (2020)
[bb]Deng and Peng (2020)
[cc]OECD (2012)
[dd]Burns (2017)
[ee]Anderson-Levitt (2020)
[ff]Kuwait (2015)
[gg]Bordoli (2020)

In the first paper, Andreas Nordin and Daniel Sundberg analyse how Swedish reformers, navigating between a transnational context of competency-based education dominated by the OECD and shifting national pressures, creatively retranslated the OECD's framework, moving away from a previous curriculum organised around interdisciplinary competencies toward a hybrid curriculum incorporating competencies into subject matter goals.

Next, Pierre Clément exposes how the 'fundamentally polysemic nature' of the notion of competencies permitted political actors with opposing agendas to agree to redesign France's curriculum around competencies in 2005; he also shows how tensions created by that reform led, under a new political regime, to a more radical reform in 2015.

In the third paper, Elena Aydarova demonstrates that in Russia, reformers appropriated the language of competencies to normalise a bifurcated system, with subject matter content for the elite and competencies for the masses.

In the fourth case study, Eloísa Bordoli demonstrates how teachers contested the 2016 reform of Basic Education in Uruguay, a hybrid model putting subject matter content and competencies in tension.

In the next paper, Li Deng and Zhengmei Peng examine a different kind of hybridity in their comparison of reform movements in China and the United States. They illustrate how Chinese reformers integrate Confucian and socialist characteristics into international frameworks, creating a hybrid model that prioritises morality alongside skills, whereas the US model takes a pragmatic stance.

Kathryn Anderson-Levitt argues that, even though the United States helped inspire competency movements elsewhere, it has instituted only a partial, silent, and late competency-added reform of its own buried within the Common Core state standards.

Armend Tahirsylaj demonstrates Kosovo's 'loud' borrowing from the European Union, focusing on civic competencies in the context of Kosovo's goal to construct 'young Europeans'.

Finally, Meg Gardinier illustrates how experts, convened by international organisations such as the OECD, constructed new social imaginaries based on competencies in education, including a universalised concept of a 'globally competent student.'

## Lessons from comparing these studies

Taken collectively, these studies offer a range of conceptual and analytic insights that contribute to a deeper understanding of the key inquiries underlying this collection: *Why competencies? Who is promoting competency-based educational reforms? How are they doing it, and to what end?*

### Polysemy

Most of these studies point out the polysemy of the concept of competency. In nearly all of the reforms described in this issue, the meaning of competencies is never spelled out directly, or there is at most some reference to a basic 'generic' definition of the concept. For example, in the OECD DeSeCo project, 'the concept of competence is used in the relatively vague sense of being able to think, act, and learn' (Rychen 2001, 8). It is not so surprising that meanings remain unclear. The task of constructing the notion of competence in general, and key competencies in particular, is a contested and never finished process, as Gardinier (2020) documents in her analysis of experts and policy advisors who act as a kind of 'epistemic community' as they collectively imagine an idealized representation of a 'successful student' that transcends the particularities of different local and national contexts.

Polysemy explains, in part, the popularity of competency-based reforms and policies. It makes possible the surprising alliance of reformers from opposing camps to support competency-based education, as they did in France in 2005, some seeing it as a movement 'back to basics' and others as a door opened to 'relevant' and 'student-centred' instruction (Clément 2020).

The polysemy of competency also makes it easier for administrators to use a competency-based reform as a 'Trojan horse' (as Clément [2020] puts it), operating 'undercover' (as alleged by teachers quoted by Bordoli 2020) to insert neo-liberal managerial and accountability practices into what was ostensibly a curricular reform. Likewise, polysemy makes it possible to modify or even reverse a competency-based reform without much difficulty, as in Sweden's stepping back from transversal competencies in 2011 (Nordin and Sundberg 2020).

While the meaning of competency is flexible, the list of competencies that students ought to learn in school is also fluid. The influential lists and frameworks of regional and international organisations overlap to a degree, but not completely (Nordin and Sundberg 2020); for instance, almost all international lists include communication and digital literacy, but not all include critical thinking or creativity. Indeed, even as the OECD embraced competencies as the conceptual underpinning of the PISA assessment, Andreas Schleicher, Director for Education and Skills at OECD, acknowledged that 'there is no overarching cross-national and cross-cultural agreement on what fundamental competencies 15-year-olds should possess' (2007, 349). For the OECD, the list of competencies is open ended; Schleicher described the OECD's new 2030 Learning Framework as 'really about *developing new ideas* for what PISA should assess' (in an interview quoted by Li and Auld 2020, 10, emphasis theirs).

Once translated into national policies, lists of competencies align even less. Countries do not agree on which competencies matter most, as documented by a Brookings Institute worldwide review of skills or competencies mentioned in countries' curricular or vision statements (Care, Anderson, and Kim 2016). Out of 76 countries that named any 'specific skills beyond literacy and numeracy'[1], the most commonly listed skill, communication, was mentioned by only 30 countries. The next most common skills – creativity, critical thinking and problem solving – were mentioned by only 19–23 countries each (Care, Anderson, and Kim 2016).

In other words, political actors can use the concept of competencies as needed to gain favour both domestically and internationally, but they are not locked into what it means or how it should be implemented. Polysemy matters because it means that a polity can gain legitimacy by rhetorically joining the group of nations said to have adopted competency-based education without adopting the same reform as other countries. Despite the absence of a singular meaning – or perhaps enabled by that polysemy – competencies have become an important concept for policy-makers envisioning and articulating curricular goals, particularly if they draw on results from international assessments such as PISA to help make the case for reform.

## *Hybridity*

The polysemy of competency makes hybridity, the merging of different or even competing ideas, easier to accomplish. Many of the studies in this issue illustrate hybrid variations of competency-based reforms at the national level and thus provide a first look into how the incorporation of competencies can create hybrid discourses within wider national policy initiatives.

Hybridity can result from translating international ideas so that they fit national political, economic, or cultural contexts. Deng and Peng (2020), elegantly demonstrate how P21's competency framework fits US pragmatism while China's competency framework is adapted to its Confucian and socialist context. Other articles describe a different kind of hybrid – a merging of competencies, which are usually described as 'transversal' and 'interdisciplinary', with disciplinary content knowledge and skills. Thus the 2005 French reform (Clément 2020), the 2010 US reform (Anderson-Levitt 2020) and the 2011 Swedish reform (Nordin and Sundberg 2020) each subsumed competencies within disciplinary goals, meshing content-based reform with competency-based reform.

However, hybrids do not necessarily resolve domestic contestation. Bordoli (2020) describes teachers' resistance to the 'bipolar' curriculum reforms in Uruguay that weld a competency-based curricular framework onto a prior content-based curriculum. Indeed, these instances of hybridity can be read as manifestations of contestation in process, particularly when the role and perspective of key actors is highlighted. As the case of Uruguay vividly illustrates, two or more actors vying for the power to define the reform often result in discursive or curricular hybridity. Of course, even if the tensions are temporarily resolved in a synthetic policy document, they may re-emerge at moments

---

[1]http://skills.brookings.edu/

of translation, as when a broad framework must be translated into detailed disciplinary curricula, or the curricula translated into classroom practice (e.g. Clément (2020)).

### Legitimation strategies, silent and loud

The hybridity of Sweden's 2011 reform points to another issue: strategies used in attempts to gain legitimacy for a reform. Nordin and Sundberg show that creative translation of the notion of competencies was an attempt to legitimate the 2011 reform with the Swedish public on the one hand and the OECD on the other.

Scholars have described several strategies to increase the legitimacy of a reform, including 'externalisation' – presenting a domestic idea as if it were borrowed from a prestigious external source (Steiner-Khamsi and Quist 2000; Schriewer 2004) – on the one hand, and 'silent borrowing' – presenting an internationally circulated policy as if it had domestic roots when domestic sources have more cachet – on the other (Waldow 2009). The studies in this issue did not identify any cases of silent borrowing, but Clément (2020) describes reformers in France temporarily externalising by citing the European Commission and the OECD 'to make its conception prevail with the minister and his advisers' at one crucial moment in 2005. At every other moment, France's competency-based reform 'has largely been a national matter' (Tahirsylaj and Sundberg 2020, 12) with 'old national roots that must be recalled in order to understand the recent transformations of the compulsory school curriculum' (Clément 2020).

In contrast to the French case, Tahirsylaj's study of Kosovo' curriculum reform process (2020) describes a different strategy, which he calls 'loud borrowing', referring to cases where (in contrast to case of externalisation) there really is a prestigious external source and borrowers draw attention to this source for purposes that may have little to do with the reform *per se*. In this case, policy makers sought to legitimate the campaign to bring Kosovo fully into the European fold, and hence 'loudly' advertised direct borrowing of key competencies from the European Commission.

The Swedish case points to another aspect of legitimation that is sometimes elided in the comparative education literature. There can be multiple audiences, domestic and external, and different audiences may be swayed by different arguments for legitimacy. This required a delicate balancing act in the Swedish case, where the same reform that emphasised subject-matter knowledge to satisfy the domestic audience nonetheless claimed to incorporate competencies to satisfy the OECD. Here again, the polysemy and 'productive plasticity' of 'competencies' makes the idea particularly useful for politicians, allowing the reform to be described differently to different audiences.

### Actors and contingencies in national and post-national perspectives

Legitimation is one of multiple, complex processes leading to reforms. Several articles in this issue focus on the policy-making process by placing competency reforms in longer historical context (in France, the United States, Sweden, Uruguay) and by tracing in detail the complexity and contingency of the activities through which reform ideas were constructed (e.g. the case of the PISA global competence assessment as well the cases from Russia, France, and the United States). The details make clear in each of these cases that there was no guarantee that a proposed reform would be adopted and implemented. The cases from France and from Uruguay describe outright resistance, while the US case shows that resistance to national standards delayed a competency-related reform for two decades.

In tracing processes, these articles also demonstrate that particular actors mattered; adoption of competencies, resistance to them, or their translation into something different is contingent on the actions of particular individuals and groups, public and private. Individual actors include academic experts (see Aydarova 2020; Gardinier 2020), policy entrepreneurs (in the US case) and politicians (in France, the United States and China). Influential groups included teachers organised in unions and official bodies (in France and Uruguay), competing political parties (again, in France and Uruguay), non-governmental organisations (in the United States), expert networks and epistemic communities (in the cases of OECD DeSeCo and the 2018 PISA Global Competence assessment) and technology corporations (in the United States).

Many of the cases also provide a needed window into how a national 'system' operates. Studies in comparative education do not always portray nations as comprised of complex and heterogeneous actors. Here, particularly in the cases of the United States, France, Russia, and Uruguay, we can see clearly how diverse actors played a role and shaped policy under the umbrella of the national. Thus, our understanding of national systems is enhanced, and we learn not to reduce the state to a unitary actor. Moreover, many of the cases are not, or not just, about traveling policy, as Clément points out (2020). The importance of the national context in its particular historical moments matters strongly in every country case described. The historical perspective also makes visible uneven flows and ebbs over time within countries and through the relationships of key actors. Policies fluctuate as regimes change or the political party in power shifts, as illustrated here in the cases of Uruguay, Sweden and France.

At the same time, there is some fluidity to borders as ideas flow within and beyond the nation-state. In many of the papers, national actors can also be seen in transnational spaces, thus lending support to the claim that we are increasingly in an era of post-national policy-making (Ramirez and Meyer 2012). Experts participating in international symposia and transnational networks serve as conduits for the flow of ideas, as illustrated in Gardinier (2020). In the Russian case, Aydarova (2020) demonstrates the key role of Russian academics who consulted for the World Bank. In the United States, US experts contributed to the OECD's early PISA efforts, while later state governors turned to the OECD for advice on domestic policy-making (Anderson-Levitt 2020). These studies make clear that international organisations have influence; they refer to the role of the European Commission in France and Kosovo, the World Bank in Russia and Kosovo, UNICEF in Kosovo, and the OECD in Sweden, France, Russia, Uruguay and the United States. They also illustrate the global role of international organisations in the construction of new discourses (Nordin and Sundberg 2020) and social imaginaries (Gardinier 2020) that frame what is envisioned as possible in education.

### *Convergence?*

In spite of these uneven flows, the pattern in Table 1 *might* be seen as evidence supporting the claim by world culture theorists that convergence is increasing around shared global scripts (e.g. Ramirez, Meyer, and Lerch 2016) – again with the caveat that the table may miss cases of backtracking. In addition, despite their demonstration of strong motives internal to the nation, some of the studies in this issue also suggest influence by international league tables (e.g. Nordin and Sundberg 2020) and by international trends (Deng and Peng 2020).

However, at the same time, these cases also document divergence due to hybridity and polysemy in competency-based approaches. From the very beginning of the process, experts convened by international organisations to define and select key competencies bring differing perspectives from their home contexts (Gardinier 2020). Then, once a definition gains ascendance, 'as it moves, it morphs' (Cowen 2009). Each nation reinterprets the ideas to suit local cultures, as dramatically illustrated, for example, in the Russian case (Aydarova 2020). Moreover, although the competency-based reforms may be diffusing widely, questions remain. First, are they reaching every country, or will some countries remain unaffected? If the latter, will we see any patterns explaining which countries abstain from the adoption of this reform? Second, will the reform stick? Will this change in curriculum arrive and stay, like compulsory schooling, age-graded instruction, and perhaps mass secondary education (cf. Cohen and Mehta 2017)? Or is this a reform movement that will wash like a wave over different countries at different moments, sometimes having a strong impact but in other cases receding completely? Alternatively, will this movement turn out to be a swing of a pendulum back and forth between a focus on competencies and a focus on subject-matter knowledge, as the recent shifts in England, Sweden, Poland, Japan and Belgium may suggest?

Moreover, if there is indeed convergence, then convergence on precisely what? Or phrased in terms of traveling policies, exactly what is traveling? As noted above, lists of key competencies do not completely overlap, and national policies overlap considerably less so. Where there is agreement, it seems to be on just two principles: that students need to learn a set of (not completely specified) skills, attitudes and knowledge required by work in the global economy, and that schools have a key role in fostering this learning. In other words, there seems to be fairly wide agreement on 'broadening the provision of education beyond traditional disciplines – beyond a focus on literacy and numeracy alone' (Care, Anderson, and Kim 2016, 10), but broadening to what? As a traveling policy, competency-based reforms are vague and open-ended – again, with a polysemy that may make them easy to adopt but difficult to implement and even harder to measure.

## Further questions

As a whole, the research presented in this special issue provides a more nuanced and critical view of competencies than readers find in much of the literature. The issue also raises questions requiring further exploration. As suggested above, more studies are needed of implementation into classroom practice in diverse local and national contexts (as by Mangez 2008). For example, as noted by Deng and Peng (2020), China's shift to a competency-based education will have little effect on practice if its examination system remains unchanged. Indeed, for many of the reforms reported in Table 1, we do not know whether they have even been translated from policy into practicable curricula, let alone implemented in the classroom. Another issue needing further research is how competencies play into assessments at national and international levels. This was briefly explored in the case of the 2018 PISA Global Competence assessment (Gardinier 2020), but much more investigation is needed to establish the link between competency-based approaches to policy and the assessment of competency-based learning outcomes. A third question requiring further investigation, raised by Bordoli (2020) and by Clément (2020), is how competency-based reforms function as 'managerial' reforms enhancing accountability.

Departing from the question of what problems competency-based reforms are meant to solve, another path to understanding the prevalence of competency-based reforms is to investigate who benefits from this global movement (Carson 2001). For instance, will the private sector including transnational corporations benefit by shifting worker preparation further from on-the-job training to schools, which are now charged with preparing students for 'college and career'? Technology companies in particular have often taken the lead in promoting competency-based reforms focused on twenty-first century skills (Morgan 2016; Anderson-Levitt 2020; Deng and Peng 2020); might they benefit from promotion of digital literacy as a key competency? The question of measurability, and the desire to assess and compare student achievement outcomes, is another important facet of competency-based reforms in education, yet the assessment of complex and transversal skills and dispositions is exceedingly difficult. PISA's innovative assessment of collaborativeness required complex computer programs. Will assessment experts as well as technology companies benefit from an expanded demand for competency-based assessments?

Most importantly, will students benefit from these curricular changes as intended? This is a question that will require close scrutiny – and that may yield different answers depending on implementations in many different contexts. Will a competency-infused education enable students to secure better jobs in the global economy? Will the workers that students become benefit as projected – or might the reforms succeed so well that they simply feed an oversupply of highly competent workers, lowering their wages (Brown, Lauder, and Ashton 2010)? Beyond a human capital perspective, will global competency-based reforms lead to students taking more action for collective well-being and sustainable development as the OECD has envisioned? Or alternatively, will policy-makers shy away from global perspectives on competency-based education and, instead, draw on more nationalistic roots in preparing future citizens and workers for the world of 2030?

We invite other comparative education researchers to build on the studies in this special issue and track the multiple meanings of competency-based reforms, their consequences, and their implications as these reforms play out over the next few decades.

## Disclosure statement

No potential conflict of interest was reported by the author(s).

## References

Ananiadou, Katerina, and Magdalena Claro. 2009. *21st Century Skills and Competences for New Millennium Learners in OECD Countries. OECD Education Working Papers*. Paris: OECD.

Anderson-Levitt, Kathryn. 2020. "21st Century Skills in the United States: A Late, Partial and Silent Reform." *Comparative Education* 57 (1). doi:10.1080/03050068.2020.1845059.

Asturia de Barrios, Linda, and Verónica Mérida Arellano. 2007. "The Process of Developing a New Curriculum for Lower Secondary Education in Guatemala." *Prospects* 37 (2): 249–266.

Aydarova, Elena. 2020. "Knowledge for the Elites, Competencies for the Masses: Political Theater of Educational Reforms in the Russian Federation." *Comparative Education*.

Bajaj, Monisha. 2014. "The Productive Plasticity of Rights: Globalization, Education and Human Rights." In *Globalization and Education: Integration and Contestation Across Cultures*, edited by Nellie P. Stromquist, and Karen Monkman, 55–69. Plymouth, UK: R&L Education.

Barrett, Angeline M. 2007. "Beyond the Polarization of Pedagogy: Models of Classroom Practice in Tanzanian Primary Schools." *Comparative Education* 43 (2): 273–294. doi:10.1080/03050060701362623.

Bordoli, Eloísa. 2020. "Curricular Design for Competencies in Basic Education in Uruguay: Positions and Current Debates (2008 -2019)." *Comparative Education*, doi:10.1080/03050068.2020.1845061.

Brown, Phillip, Hugh Lauder, and David Ashton. 2010. *The Global Auction: The Broken Promises of Education, Jobs, and Incomes*. Oxford, UK: Oxford University Press.

Burns, Amy. 2017. "A Cross Canada Inventory: Evidence of 21st Century Educational Reform in Canada." *Interchange* 48 (3): 283–292. doi:10.1007/s10780-017-9301-6.

Care, Esther, Kate Anderson, and Helyn Kim. 2016. *Visualizing the Breadth of Skills Movement Across Education Systems*. Washington, DC: Brookings Institute.

Carson, John. 2001. "Defining and Selecting Competencies: Historical Reflections on the Case of IQ." In *Defining and Selecting Key Competencies*, edited by Dominique Simone Rychen, and Laura Hersh Salganik, 33–44. Bern: Hogrefe & Huber.

Charton, Hélène. 2014. "The Politics of Reform: A Case Study of Bureaucracy at the Ministry of Basic Education in Cameroon." In *States at Work*, edited by Thomas Bierschenk and Jean-Pierre Olivier de Sardan, 249–269. Leiden: Brill.

Clément, Pierre. 2020. "The Introduction of Competence-Based Education Into the Compulsory School Curriculum in France (2002–2017): Hybridity and Polysemy as Conditions for Change." *Comparative Education*, doi:10.1080/03050068.2020.1845062.

Cohen, David K., and Jal D. Mehta. 2017. "Why Reform Sometimes Succeeds." *American Educational Research Journal* 54 (4): 644–690. doi:10.3102/0002831217700078.

Cowen, Robert. 2009. "The Transfer, Translation and Transformation of Educational Processes." *Comparative Education* 45 (3): 315–327. doi:10.1080/03050060903184916.

Delors, Jacques. 1996. *Learning: The Treasure Within*. Paris: UNESCO.

Deng, Li, and Zhengmei Peng. 2020. "A Comparative Analysis of Frameworks for 21st Century Competences in Mainland China and United States: Implications for National Policies." *Comparative Education*, doi:10.1080/03050068.2020.1845063.

Egodawatte, Gunawardena. 2014. "An Analysis of the Competency-Based Secondary Mathematics Curriculum in Sri Lanka." *Educational Research for Policy and Practice* 13 (1): 45–63. doi:10.1007/s10671-013-9145-5.

Engel, Laura C., David Rutkowski, and Greg Thompson. 2019. "Toward an International Measure of Global Competence? A Critical Look at the PISA 2018 Framework." *Globalisation, Societies and Education* 17 (2): 117–131. doi:10.1080/14767724.2019.1642183.

Estonia, Riigi Teataja. 2011a, January 17. *National Curriculum for Upper Secondary Schools*. Tallinn: Government of Estonia. https://www.riigiteataja.ee/en/eli/524092014009/consolide.

Estonia, Riigi Teataja. 2011b, June 1. *National Curriculum for Basic Schools*. Tallinn: Government of Estonia. https://www.riigiteataja.ee/en/eli/524092014014/consolide.

European Commission. Lifelong Learning Programme. 2006. *Key Competences for Lifelong Learning — A European Reference Framework. 2006/962/EC, European Parliament*. Luxembourg: Office for Official Publications of the European Communities.

Gardinier, Meg P. 2020. "Imagining Globally Competent Learners: Experts and Education Policy-Making Beyond the Nation-State." *Comparative Education*, doi:10.1080/03050068.2020.1845064.

Gordon, Jean, Gabor Halasz, Magdalena Krawczyk, Tom Leney, Alain Michel, David Pepper, Elzbieta Putkiewicz, and Jerzy Wisniewski. 2009. *Key Competences in Europe*. Warsaw: Directorate General Education and Culture of the European Commission, CASE-Center for Social and Economic Research.

Grek, Sotiria. 2009. "Governing by Numbers: The PISA 'Effect' in Europe." *Journal of Education Policy* 24 (1): 23–37. doi:10.1080/02680930802412669.

Halász, Gábor, and Alain Michel. 2011. "Key Competences in Europe: Interpretation, Policy Formulation and Implementation." *European Journal of Education* 46 (3): 289–306. doi:10.1111/j.1465-3435.2011.01491.x.

Hartong, Sigrid. 2014. ""Global Policy Convergence Through "Distributed Governance"? The Emergence of "National"." *Education Standards in the US and Germany." Journal of International and Comparative Social Policy* 31 (1): 10–33. doi:10.1080/21699763.2014.977803.

National Research Council (NRC), Hilton, Margaret, Arthur Eisenkraft, William Bonvillian, Marcia C. Linn, Christine Massey, Carlo Parravano, and William Sandoval. 2010. *Exploring the Intersection of Science Education and 21st Century Skills: A Workshop Summary*. Washington, DC: National Academies Press.

Hodgson, Ann, and Ken Spours. 2003. *Beyond A Levels: Curriculum 2000 and the Reform of 14-19 Qualifications*. London: Kogan Page Ltd.

Högberg, Björn, and Joakim Lindgren. forthcoming. "Outcome-Based Accountability Regimes in OECD Countries: A Global Policy Model?" *Comparative Education*.

Houchot, Alain, Florence Robine, Anne Armand, Jean-Pierre Barrue, Jean-Paul Chassaing, Annie Lherete, Pierre Malleus, Jean-Louis Michard, Claudine Ruget, and Alain Sere. 2007 (juin). *Les Livrets de Compétences: Nouveaux Outils Pour L'évaluation des Acquis. Rapport à Monsieur le Ministre de L'Éducation Nationale*. Paris: Inspection générale de l'éducation nationale.

Jules, Tavis D., and Kelly Cebold Sundberg. 2018. "The Internationalization of Creativity as a Learning Competence." *Global Education Review* 5 (1): 35–51.

Kuwait, Ministry of Education. 2015. *Kuwait National Curriculum (KNC): A Guide for Effective Teaching of English Language in Grade One*. Kuwait: Ministry of Education. https://docplayer.net/23399621-Kuwait-national-curriculum-knc-a-guide-for-effective-teaching-of-english-language-in-grade-one-guidelines-for-putting-into-practice.html.

Lauwerier, Thibaut, and Abdeljalil Akkari. 2013. "Quelles Approches pour réformer le curriculum et l'école en Afrique ? Constats et controverses." *Revue Africaine de Recherche en Éducation* 2013 (5): 55–64.

Levin, Henry M. 2012. "More Than Just Test Scores." *Prospects* 42 (3): 269–284. doi:10.1007/s11125-012-9240-z.

Li, Xiaomin, and Euan Auld. 2020. "A Historical Perspective on the OECD's 'Humanitarian Turn': PISA for Development and the Learning Framework 2030." *Comparative Education* 56 (4): 503–521. doi:10.1080/03050068.2020.1781397.

Lightfoot, Michael. 2015. "Education Reform for the Knowledge Economy in the State of Sangon." *Compare* 45 (5): 705–726. doi:10.1080/03057925.2014.916970.

Loobuyck, Patrick. 2020. "The Policy Shift Towards Citizenship Education in Flanders." *Journal of Curriculum Studies*, doi:10.1080/00220272.2020.1820081.

Mangez, Éric. 2008. *Réformer les Contenus D'enseignement.* Paris: Presses Universitaires de France.

Marope, Mmantsetsa, Patrick Griffin, and Carmel Gallagher. 2017. *Future Competences and the Future of Curriculum: A Global Reference for Curricula Transformation.* Geneva: IBE UNESCO.

Martens, Kerstin, and Anja P. Jakobi, eds. 2010. *Mechanisms of OECD Governance: International Incentives for National Policy-Making?* Oxford: Oxford University Press.

Mathou, Cécile. 2018. "Recontextualizing Curriculum Policies: A Comparative Perspective on the Work of Mid-Level Actors in France and Quebec." *Journal of Curriculum Studies* 50 (6): 789–804. doi:10.1080/00220272.2018.1513567.

Mkimbili, Selina, and Septimi Kitta. 2019. "The Rationale of Continuous Assessment for Development of Competencies in Tanzania Secondary Schools." *Advanced Journal of Social Science* 6 (1): 64–70. doi:10.21467/ajss.6.1.64-70.

Møller, Jorunn, and Guri Skedsmo. 2013. "Modernising Education: New Public Management Reform in the Norwegian Education System." *Journal of Educational Administration and History* 45 (4): 336–353. doi:10.1080/00220620.2013.822353.

Morgan, Clara. 2012. "Constructing the OECD Programme for International Student Assessment." In *PISA Under Examination*, edited by Miguel A. Pereyra, Hans-Georg Kotthoff, and Robert Cowen, 47–59. Rotterdam: Sense Publishers.

Morgan, Clara. 2016. "Testing Students Under Cognitive Capitalism: Knowledge Production of Twenty-First Century Skills." *Journal of Education Policy* 31 (6): 805–818. doi:10.1080/02680939. 2016.1190465.

Morgan, Clara, and Riyad A. Shahjahan. 2014. "The Legitimation of OECD's Global Educational Governance: Examining PISA and AHELO Test Production." *Comparative Education* 50 (2): 192–205. doi:10.1080/03050068.2013.834559.

New Zealand. Ministry of Education. 2007. *The New Zealand Curriculum.* Wellington, NZ: Ministry of Education. https://nzcurriculum.tki.org.nz/The-New-Zealand-Curriculum.

Nnang, Edang. 2013. "L'approche par Compétences Dans les Pays en Développement: Effets des Réformes Curriculaires en Afrique Subsaharienne." (PhD diss.). Université de Bourgogne.

Nordin, Andreas, and Daniel Sundberg. 2020. "Transnational Competence Frameworks and National Curriculum-Making: The Case of Sweden." *Comparative Education*, doi:10.1177/1474904116641697.

OECD. 2005. *The Definition and Selection of Key Competencies: Executive Summary.* Paris: OECD.

OECD. 2012. *Lessons from PISA for Japan. Strong Performers and Successful Reformers in Education.* Paris: OECD.

OECD. 2019. *OECD Future of Education and Skills 2030. Conceptual Learning Framework. Concept Note: Transformative Competencies for 2030.* Paris: OECD.

Pagliarello, Marina Cino. 2020. "Aligning Policy Ideas and Power: The Roots of the Competitiveness Frame in European Education Policy." *Comparative Education* 56 (4): 441–458. doi:10.1080/03050068.2020.1769927.

Partnership for 21st Century Learning (P21). 2016. *Framework for 21st Century Learning.* https://www.battelleforkids.org/networks/p21/frameworks-resources.

Pellegrino, James W., and Margaret L. Hilton, 2012. *Education for Life and Work: Developing Transferable Knowledge and Skills in the 21st Century.* Washington, DC: National Academies Press.

Priestley, Mark, and Walter Humes. 2010. "The Development of Scotland's Curriculum for Excellence: Amnesia and Déjà Vu." *Oxford Review of Education* 36 (3): 345–361. doi:10.1080/03054980903518951.

Ramirez, Francisco O., and John W. Meyer. 2012. "Toward Post-National Societies and Global Citizenship." *Multicultural Education Review* 4 (1): 1–28. doi:10.1080/23770031.2009.11102887.

Ramirez, Francisco O., John W. Meyer, and Julia Lerch. 2016. "World Society and the Globalization of Educational Policy." In *Handbook of Global Policy and Policy Making in Education*, edited by Karen Mundy, B. Lingard Andy Green, and Antoni Verger, 43–63. New York: Wiley-Blackwell Press.

Reimers, Fernando. 2020. *Audacious Education Purposes: How Governments Transform the Goals of Education Systems*. Cham, Switzerland: Springer Open.

Robeyns, Ingrid. 2006. "Three Models of Education: Rights, Capabilities and Human Capital." *Theory and Research in Education* 4 (1): 69–84. doi:10.1177/1477878506060683.

Roegiers, Xavier. 2008. *L'approche par Compétences en Afrique Francophone. IBE Working Papers on Curricular Issues*. Genève: BIE-UNESCO.

Rose, Mike. 2004. *The Mind at Work: Valuing the Intelligence of the American Worker*. New York: Penguin.

Rychen, Dominique Simone. 2001. "Introduction." In *Defining and Selecting Key Competencies*, edited by Dominique Simone Rychen, and Laura Hersh Salganik, 1–15. Bern: Hogrefe & Huber.

Sahlberg, Pasi. 2016. "The Global Educational Reform Movement and Its Impact on Schooling." In *Handbook of Global Policy and Policy Making in Education*, edited by Karen Mundy, B. Lingard Andy Green, and Antoni Verger, 128–144. New York: Wiley-Blackwell Press.

Salas-Pilco, Sdenka Z. 2013. "Evolution of the Framework for 21st Century Competencies." *Knowledge Management & E-Learning* 5 (1): 10–24. doi:10.34105/j.kmel.2013.05.002b.

Salganik, Laura Hersh, Dominique Simone Rychen, Urs Moser, and John W. Konstant. 1999. *Projects on Competencies in the OECD Context. Analysis of Theoretical and Conceptual Foundations. Definition and Selection of Competencies*. Neuchâtel: OECD.

Savage, Glenn C., and Kate O'Connor. 2015. "National Agendas in Global Times: Curriculum Reforms in Australia and the USA Since the 1980s." *Journal of Education Policy* 30 (5): 609–630. doi:10.1080/02680939.2014.969321.

Schleicher, Andreas. 2007. "Can Competencies Assessed by PISA Be Considered the Fundamental School Knowledge 15-Year-Olds Should Possess?" *Journal of Educational Change* 8 (4): 349–357. doi:10.1007/s10833-007-9042-x.

Schriewer, Jürgen. 2004. "Multiple Internationalities." In *Transnational Intellectual Networks*, edited by Christophe Charle, Jürgen Schriewer, and Peter Wagner, 473–531. Frankfurt: Campus Verlag.

Schweisfurth, Michele. 2013. *Learner-Centred Education in International Perspective: Whose Pedagogy for Whose Development?* New York: Routledge.

Steiner-Khamsi, Gita, and Hubert O. Quist. 2000. "The Politics of Educational Borrowing." *Comparative Education Review* 44 (3): 272–299.

Sundberg, Daniel, and Ninni Wahlström. 2012. "Standards-Based Curricula in a Denationalised Conception of Education: The Case of Sweden." *European Educational Research Journal* 11 (3): 342–356. doi:10.1080/03050068.2020.1769927.

Tabulawa, Richard. 2009. "Education Reform in Botswana: Reflections on Policy Contradictions and Paradoxes." *Comparative Education* 45 (1): 87–107. doi:10.1080/03050060802661410.

Tabulawa, Richard. 2013. *Teaching and Learning in Context: Why Pedagogical Reforms Fail in Sub-Saharan Africa*. Dakar: CODESRIA.

Tahirsylaj, Armend. 2020. "What Kind of Citizens? Constructing 'Young Europeans' Through Loud Borrowing in Curriculum Policy-Making in Kosovo." *Comparative Education*, doi:10.1080/03050068.2020.1845066.

Tahirsylaj, Armend, and Daniel Sundberg. 2020. "The Unfinished Business of Defining Competences for 21st Century Curricula—A Systematic Research Review." *Curriculum Perspectives* 40 (2): 131–145. doi:10.1007/s41297-020-00112-6.

Takayama, Keita. 2013. "OECD, 'Key Competencies' and the New Challenges of Educational Inequality." *Journal of Curriculum Studies* 45 (1): 67–80.

Thiam, Ousseynou, and Fatima Chnane-Davin. 2017. "L'approche par compétences peut-elle être efficace sur n'importe quel terrain ?" *Cahiers de la Recherche sur L'éducation et les Savoirs* 2017 (16): 117–137.

Trier, Uri Peter. 2003. "Twelve Countries Contributing to DeSeCo: A Summary Report." In *Definition and Selection of Key Competencies. Contributions to the Second DeSeCo Symposium. Geneva, Switzerland, 11-13 February, 2002*, edited by Dominique Simone Rychen, Laura Hersh Salganik, and Mary Elizabeth McLaughlin, 25–34. Neuchâtel: Swiss Federal Statistical Office.

UNESCO. 2014. *Global Monitoring Report 2014. Teaching and Learning: Achieving Quality for All*. Paris: UNESCO.

Verger, Antoni, Lluís Parcerisa, and Clara Fontdevila. 2019. "The Growth and Spread of Large-Scale Assessments and Test-Based Accountabilities: A Political Sociology of Global Education Reforms." *Educational Review* 71 (1): 5–30. doi:10.1080/00131911.2019.1522045.

Waldow, Florian. 2009. "Undeclared Imports: Silent Borrowing in Educational Policy-Making and Research in Sweden." *Comparative Education* 45 (4): 477–494. doi:10.1080/03050060903391628.

Wiśniewski, Jerzy, and Marta Zahorska. 2020. "Reforming Education in Poland." In *Audacious Education Purposes*, edited by Fernando Reimers, 181–208. Cham, Switzerland: Springer Open.

World Bank [International Bank for Reconstruction and Development]. 2018. *"World Bank Development Report. Learning to Realize Education's Promise.".* Washington,, DC: World Bank.

Zhao, Weili. 2019. "Epistemological Flashpoint in China's Classroom Reform: (How) Can a 'Confucian Do-After-Me Pedagogy' Cultivate Critical Thinking?" *Journal of Curriculum Studies* 52 (1): 101–117. doi:10.1080/00220272.2019.1641844.

ⓐ OPEN ACCESS

# Transnational competence frameworks and national curriculum-making: the case of Sweden

Andreas Nordin ⓘ and Daniel Sundberg ⓘ

**ABSTRACT**
Competence-based approaches (CBAs) in education have become an internationally important educational policy concept in recent decades. However, a substantial body of research has suggested that in order to understand and explain the evolution of CBAs, there is a need to analyse curriculum-making as a complex and multi-layered practice. To contribute to this research field, this paper makes use of Vivien Schmidt's concept of discursive-institutionalism (DI), which focuses on ideas and discourse. First, we compare ideas of competences as expressed in four influential CBA frameworks, and second, we exemplify how these ideas, with special reference to the Organisation for Economic Co-operation and Development, have been translated when re-contextualised within Swedish curriculum policy-making. The results show that when re-contextualised within national borders, transnational ideas of competences are reconfigured. In the case of Sweden, this process has led to a national interpretation of CBAs, discussed in this paper as 'hybrid competences.'

## Introduction

In recent years, many countries have experienced a significant institutional and epistemo-logical reframing of their national curriculum policy-making, as powerful organisations such as the United Nations Educational, Scientific and Cultural Organisation (UNESCO), the Organisation for Economic Co-operation and Development (OECD), and the European Union (EU) have started to promote competence-based approaches (CBAs).[1] Although not an entirely global phenomenon, this reframing has affected the way in which curricu-lar knowledge is developed, conceptualised, implemented, and assessed in classrooms in different parts of the world as part of travelling reforms (Anderson-Levitt, Bonnéry, and Fichtner 2017; Hopmann 2008; Morgan and Shahjahan 2014; Takayama 2013; Voogt and Roblin 2012). However, policy transfers seldom involve a linear process of implemen-tation; a dynamic process ensues instead when powerful global discourses meet national cultures and traditions (cf. Anderson-Levitt 2003). National contexts matter for the way(s)

---

This is an Open Access article distributed under the terms of the Creative Commons Attribution-NonCommercial-NoDerivatives License (http://creativecommons.org/licenses/by-nc-nd/4.0/), which permits non-commercial re-use, distribution, and reproduction in any medium, provided the original work is properly cited, and is not altered, transformed, or built upon in any way.

in which global policies take shape within national borders, with attention being placed on processes of recontextualisation, translation, and legitimation (Nordin and Sundberg 2014; Steiner-Khamsi 2012; Schulte 2016; Schriewer 2016; Waldow 2012).

The promotion of CBAs has been analysed and deconstructed as part of transnational discursive agendas, promoting the building of strong knowledge economies (e.g. Labaree 2014; Meyer 2014) and individualised lifelong learning policies (e.g. Takayama 2013). It has also been examined as part of the Programme for International Student Assessment (PISA) discourse and a more general trend towards management by measurement (e.g. Addey et al. 2017). However, although some national case studies have been carried out (e.g. Baek et al. 2018; Nordin and Sundberg 2016), studies on CBAs adopting an analytical lens that lends explanatory power to the national context are still sparse (Anderson-Levitt, Bonnéry, and Fichtner 2017).

The aim of this paper is to contribute to such comparative research on CBAs where the national context is acknowledged as the main site for understanding processes of policy transfer (cf. Steiner-Khamsi 2012). This is done first by examining and comparing influential transnational competence frameworks that, together with others, make up the complex context which national policy-makers and politicians must navigate. Second, the 2011 Swedish curriculum reform is examined as an example of how transnational discourses, with special reference to the OECD, are sometimes translated and reinterpreted in unexpected ways in order to fit domestic policy agendas, thus enabling politicians to maintain public legitimacy. The following questions have guided the analyses: (1) What characterises the conceptualisation of *competence* in four selected influential transnational competence frameworks, and what convergences and/or divergences can be identified? (2) How are transnational ideas on *competence* translated and reconfigured when re-contextualised in the 2011 Swedish curriculum reform? (3) How are competences/ skills defined and positioned in the Swedish context?

The paper consists of three main sections. In the first section, discursive institutionalism (DI) is outlined as a theoretical and methodological point of departure for analysing policy-making within and between different policy levels. The second section directs the analytical focus to the four selected influential transnational competence frameworks making up the transnational context for national policy-making today, and the third and final section focuses on the 2011 curriculum reform in Sweden as an example of how transnational discourses (in the Swedish case, dominated by the OECD) can become subject to translation and reconfiguration when re-contextualised at the national policy level. The paper ends with conclusions and suggestions for further research.

### Policy-making as discourse and ideas

Focusing on policy-making as a process of translation and legitimation directs attention to its discursive aspects and how it is possible to think about and act on policy-making at a certain point in time and space (cf. Broschek 2016; Waldow 2012). To capture these discursive processes, the analytical focus, in turn, has to be directed towards local policy contexts, where aspects such as timing, impact, process, and agency are crucial to the way in which global policies are translated and legitimated (Steiner-Khamsi and Waldow 2012). A focus on translation and legitimation also facilitates an understanding of policy transfer as a multi-directional and multi-purpose process that is not entirely guided by rational and calculable principles (cf. Broschek 2016). As pointed out by Steiner-Khamsi (2012, 7, italics in original), 'local problems are sometimes *created* in line with packaged global solutions, rather than the other way around,' thus highlighting the fact that global policies can be used in their entirety or in a piecemeal manner to legitimate a variety of policy actions at the local level.

In this study, we make use of Vivien Schmidt's discursive institutionalism (DI) (2011, 2015, 2016) as a theoretical approach to analyse these discursive processes of translating and legitimating transnational CBAs, as expressed in some influential transnational competence frameworks and Swedish curriculum policy-making from 2011 onwards. We deliberately use the term 'transnational' rather than 'global' or 'international' when it comes to describing how policy ideas travel, since it emphasises the entanglement of the interaction between multiple levels and actors across binary demarcations of national or global policies. DI grew out of a critique of the older branches of neo-institutionalism, which Schmidt argued placed too much emphasis on institutions as historically path-dependent and populated by rational actors: 'Discursive institutionalism, by contrast, takes a more dynamic view of change (and continuity) by concentrating on the substantive ideas developed and conveyed by "sentient" agents in discursive interaction that inform their policy-oriented actions which in turn serve to alter (or maintain) "institutions"' (Schmidt 2011, 107). Here, the term 'discourse' is used in a generic way, encompassing both the substantive content of ideas and the interactive process where these ideas are conveyed. DI distinguishes between two types of discursive interaction in relation to different policy levels: *coordinative discourse* at the transnational and national levels, where policies are discursively constructed as a set of shared cognitive ideas guiding future policy actions of 'sentient' (thinking, speaking, and acting) agents, and the *communicative discourse* in the political sphere, where politicians interact to maintain public legitimacy. The concept of a coordinative discourse is used herein to capture the coordination of ideas taking place within and between powerful organisations such as the OECD, the EU, and the Swedish government in trying to establish what Haas (1992) has referred to as an 'epistemic community,' emphasising CBAs in national curriculum policy-making, while a communicative discourse refers to the interaction taking place between the Swedish government and the public in order for national politicians to gain and/or maintain public legitimacy.

## Background and foreground ideas

Beyond a distinction between the two types of discursive interaction being made, we will make use of Schmidt's distinction regarding the substantive content of such a discursive interaction in terms of background and foreground ideas.

Background ideas refer to underlying assumptions guiding human action – the lenses through which people interpret and make sense of the world and which sit at the deepest level of the generality of idea: 'Background ideas are core principles that generally stay in the "background" as underlying assumptions, deep philosophies, or taken-for-granted ideas that are rarely questioned or contested except in times of crisis' (Schmidt 2016, 230).

These are the principles that guide the way in which education and schooling are thought of and organised at a fundamental level. As such, background ideas are understood as malleable structures, slowly evolving and being reshaped through their use by actors at different policy levels (Schmidt 2016).

Foreground ideas, on the other hand, are conscious ideas, discussed and debated on a regular basis, which direct attention to the notion of agency and the performativity of ideas. These are the ideas and concepts structuring educational programmes and that are used in political debate. People are not just passive holders of ideas, but are active, as they share their conscious ideas with others in discursive interactions that can lead to collective action (Schmidt 2015). It is these foreground ideas that enable people to argue, deliberate, and communicate in discursive interactions on how to take individual and/or collective action to maintain and/or alter institutions and their structures. Thus, foreground ideas not only enable the questioning of the ideas of others, but also of one's own mental disposition and hidden assumptions. Unlike background ideas, these kinds of ideas change more rapidly as actors use their agency and discursive abilities. A focus on curriculum policy-making as ideas and discourse thus means a focus on the discursive interaction of ideas, as they constitute social institutions and govern human interactions within and between different policy levels (Wahlström and Sundberg 2018).

## Transnational competence frameworks

While competence-based education is a recent worldwide phenomenon, the use of the concept of *competence* related to education policy-making is not new. The concept has old roots in the field of curriculum studies and the so-called competence movement that started in the United States in the 1960s and that later spread internationally with its origins in the mastery learning models in vocational education and training dating back to the 1920s that drew on Burrhus Frederic Skinner's (1904–1990) work on behavioural psychology (Tahirsylaj 2017). When the concept of competence-based education was reintroduced in education policy-making in the 1990s, it was a way to bring about a wider ideational shift from governing by input (educational planning) to governing by learning outcomes. Anderson-Levitt, Bonnéry, and Fichtner (2017) trace the new competence movement to Delors' UNESCO Report, 'Learning: The Treasure Within' (1996) issued by the International Commission on Education for the Twenty-First Century. In the report, UNESCO suggests that future education should be built upon four key pillars: learning to know, learning to do, learning to live together, and learning to be, with the background idea being lifelong learning inside and outside of the formal educational system. The report started a flow of frameworks on how future education should adapt to a fast-paced, late modern knowledge-based economy.

Today, there are many international actors and organisations pushing for CBA reforms and for the integration of competences into national curriculum policies and frameworks. Along with the various notions of competences, such scripts are often accompanied by specifications for types of teaching, learning, and assessment for schools and teachers. Terminology for competences also vary, and are referred to for, example, as 'twenty-first-century skills', 'lifelong learning competences', and 'key competences' (e.g. European Parliament 2007; OECD 2005). These definitions have much in common and all include general elements of collaboration, communication, ICT literacy, and social/cultural skills, often along with skills such as civic participation, creativity, critical thinking, and problem-solving (see also Voogt and Roblin 2012). A systematic research review on competence-based curricula in international literature (Tahirsylaj and Sundberg 2020) shows that one of the most quoted and influential definitions of competences comes from Franz E. Weinert, in which they are viewed as the 'cognitive skills and abilities individuals possess or can learn to solve particular problems, and the associated motivational, volitional and social readiness and abilities to solve problems successfully and responsibly in a variety of situations' (Weinert 2001, 27). This definition was also used in the influential OECD DeSeCo project, which accordingly defines competence as 'the ability to successfully meet complex demands in a particular context' (Rychen, Salganik, and McLaughlin 2003, 2).

## Influential competence frameworks

In comparing policy frameworks for competence-based curricula, one central feature concerns the relationship between the way the target competences/skills are defined and positioned in relation to knowledge as defined by traditional school subjects. These subjects are not simple categories that can be replaced by notions of general competences, but need to be understood as deeply institutionalised patterns which form strong background ideas and premises for national curriculum policy-making (Benavot and Braslavsky 2006). Since there are many different frameworks at play, it is an impossible task to try to grasp the entire picture. Herein, the scope is limited to four frameworks which we have found to be among the more influential ones in transnational policy discourses: *The Assessment and Teaching of Twenty-first Century Skills* (ATC21S; Binkley et al. 2010), *Partnership for Twenty-first Century Skills* (P21 2019a), *the Definition and Selection of Competences* (DeSeCo, OECD 2005) and the *OECD Learning Framework 2030* as part of the OECD's strategy for the Future of Education and Skills 2030 (OECD 2019).

The ATC21S is an international research initiative headquartered at the University of Melbourne and is sponsored by the big international technology companies: Cisco, Intel, and Microsoft. The aim of the programme is to identify and provide learning tools for the necessary skills needed to be successful in the twenty-first-century workplace. As part of the ATC21S international research project, a large group of researchers defined twenty-first-century skills as ways of thinking, ways of working, and tools for working and living in the world (Binkley et al. 2012). P21 was formed in 2002 in the United States and was dissolved in December 2018 when it was absorbed by the organisation Battelle for Kids (P21 2002, 2019a, 2019b, 2015). The organisation's leadership in twenty-first-century education encompassed early learning, learning during school years (K–12), and learning beyond school. Even if the focus was on the American education system, P21's ideas have spread to different parts of the world (Trilling and Fadel 2009). For example, The Asia-Pacific Economic Cooperative, which includes Canada, Australia, China, and Japan among its member countries, has 'enlisted P21's help in formulating strategic plans for the future of education' (Trilling and Fadel 2009, 169). The OECD formulated its own version of twenty-first-century skills and competences through the DeSeCo initiative in 1997, which also underpins PISA (OECD 2005).

In 2016, the OECD launched the Future of Education and Skills 2030 Strategy (OECD 2019). In that strategy, the concept of competency is positioned as a holistic and dynamic concept that implies knowledge, skills, attitudes, and values (OECD 2019). The

OECD Education 2030 project aims to create a common language for curriculum development. It does so by building broad categories of key competences (interacting in socially heterogeneous groups, acting autonomously, and using tools interactively) that were developed in the DeSeCo project. The Education 2030 project has identified three further categories of so-called transformative competences (creating new value, reconciling tensions and dilemmas, and taking responsibility), which address the growing need for young people to be innovative, responsible, and aware (OECD 2018).

In the comparative analysis presented below, these frameworks are treated as empirical examples of the complex and increasingly transnational discursive context in which national governments are embedded, and the analysis is limited to some of the frameworks' ideational characteristics. These characteristics are organised under the following headings and comparative categories: *ways of thinking and organising knowledge, ways of learning and working, tools for working,* and *living in the world,* which previous comparisons have identified as crucial (Voogt and Roblin 2012). Key policy documents defining competences and/or skills were selected for each framework. Searches were undertaken in each document using the following terms: content*, discipline*, subject*, competenc*, and skill*. We also looked into the word frequency in the defining texts using the search terms: competenc*, skills*, literacy*, subject*, content*, discipline* and domain*. The numbers in Table 1 show the relative emphasis (by word frequencies) in each document on the competence-related concepts as compared with school knowledge categories.

### *Comparison of the selected frameworks*

The selected frameworks all emphasise the following characteristics: (a) transversal (i.e. competences are not directly linked to a specific field but are relevant across many fields); (b) multi-dimensional (i.e. they include knowledge, skills, and attitudes); and (c) they are associated with higher-order skills and behaviours that represent the ability to cope with complex problems and unpredictable situations, not only in schools, but also in everyday life (Gordon et al. 2009; Westera 2001). However, the distinction and relationship between knowledge and competences was only addressed in the ATC21S framework.

There are similarities and differences between the four transnational competence frameworks. To start with, there is a strong resemblance between the transnational frameworks in terms of intentions, terminology, and structure. This result is in line with previous reviews, for example, with Voogt and Roblin's (2012) conclusion that the frameworks (ATC21S, P21, and DeSeCo) superficially converge on some shared foreground ideas/intentions and a common set of twenty-first-century competences: collaboration, communication, ICT literacy, and social and/or cultural competences (including citizenship). Most frameworks also mention creativity, critical thinking, productivity, and problem-solving. This is still the case in the newest framework, the Future of Education and Skills 2030 Position Paper (OECD 2018), which also shows a tendency towards using the concept of 'skills' rather than of 'competences.'

The comparison of the frameworks also demonstrates that for the aspect of *organising thinking and knowledge,* subject knowledge is an implicit background idea that is not explicitly addressed in the frameworks. In the ATC21S framework, there is a discussion

## CONTEXTUALIZING GLOBAL FLOWS OF COMPETENCY-BASED EDUCATION

**Table 1.** Comparison of ideational characteristics in four influential competence frameworks.

| The four transnational competence frameworks | | | |
|---|---|---|---|
| Assessment and Teaching for 21st Century Skills (ATC21S) | A Partnership for 21st Century Skills (P21) | Definition and Selection of Competencies (DeSeCo) (OECD) | Future Education and Skills 2030 (OECD) |
| Binkley et al. (2012) (Chapter 2, Defining 21st century skills, Binkley et al. 2012) http://www.atc21s.org | Framework for 21st Century Learning Definitions (2019a, 2019b) http://www.battelleforkids.org | Key Competencies for A Successful Life and a Well-Functioning Society (Rychen, Salganik, and McLaughlin 2003) | OECD: The Future We Want (2018) OECD: Learning Compass 2030: A Series of Concept Notes (2019) |
| *50 pages* | *9 + 2 pages* | *31 pages* | *23 + 146 pages* |
| **Ways of thinking and organising knowledge** | | | |
| Skills | Skill | Competencies | Skills/Transformative Competencies |
| | Interdisciplinary themes (4) | Multi-disciplinary approach (2) | Interdisciplinary (1 + 18) |
| Defined related to 'Core curriculum' (1) home language, mathematics, and science | Undefined related to Key academic subject knowledge in: <ul><li>English, reading, or language arts</li><li>World languages</li><li>Arts</li><li>Mathematics</li><li>Economics</li><li>Science</li><li>Geography</li><li>History</li><li>Government and Civics</li></ul> | Undefined related to School subjects (1) Disciplines (1) Subject-bound curriculum (1) Subject matter areas (1) | Undefined related to Disciplinary knowledge (24) Subjects/disciplines (25) |
| **Ways of learning and working** | | | |
| Skills (202) Competenc* (22) Literacy (42) Creativity and innovation Critical thinking, problem-solving, decision-making Learning to learn, meta-cognition Communication Collaboration (teamwork) Subject (15) Subject domains (7) Traditional subjects (1) Discipline (1) | Skills (56) Competenc* (2) Literacy (7) Communication Collaboration Creativity and innovation Critical thinking and problem-solving Key academic subject knowledge (3) | Skills (25) Competenc* (160 + 74) Literacy (9) Information as a product: Restructuring and modelling of information and developing own ideas (knowledge) Effective communication: Collaboration and virtual interaction School subjects (1) Disciplines (1) Subject-bound curriculum (1) Subject matter areas (1) | Skills (67 + 490) Competenc* (37 + 174) Literacy (7 + 62) Transformative competencies: Creating new value Reconciling tensions and dilemmas Taking responsibility Knowing how to think like a mathematician Subject knowledge (2 + 22) |
| **Tools for working** | | | |
| Web 2.0 technology User-generated content creation and remixing Information literacy ICT literacy | Information literacy, media literacy ICT literacy | Information as a source: Searching, evaluating and organising information Reading literacy Mathematical literacy Scientific literacy | Innovation Implementation in classrooms (18) |
| **Living in the world** | | | |
| Skills related to: Global and local citizenship Life and career | Skills such as: Flexibility and adaptability | Key competencies related to: Ethics and social impact dimensions of | Skills such as: Apply knowledge in unknown circumstances |

| Cultural awareness and social responsibility | Initiative and self-direction<br>Social and cross-cultural skills<br>Productivity and accountability<br>Leadership and responsibility | communication:<br>Social responsibility<br>Social impact | Adaptability, creativity, curiosity and open-mindedness |

Note: Numbers in parentheses indicate word frequencies.

on how some 'core subjects' such as language first spoken, mathematics, and science can provide resources for specified skills (Binkley et al. 2012). However, the issue of alignment between skills and subject knowledge in the curricula is absent in all definitional texts. There is a striking imbalance in how notions of competences/skills dominate over knowledge categories (subjects, disciplines, subject domains etc.). The word frequency for competences/skills and subject knowledge/disciplines has an overall ratio of 837/54 (i.e. 16/1 or 6%).

A common feature of the frameworks when it comes to *ways of learning and working* is the central role of ICT. In all of the frameworks, key competences and skills for the future are closely linked to new emerging technology. Thus, modelling, searching, processing, organising, and evaluating information are crucial components of the prescribed goals and means for learning inside and outside of formal schooling. It is worth noting that the role of new technology is even more prominent in the OECD Future of Education and Skills 2030 framework (OECD 2018). Here, technology is not only seen as a goal and as providing some means for the curricula, but it is framed as the major driver for curriculum change. Comparisons of the frameworks over their chronological timelines may thus indicate that the role of digital technology has emerged not only as the content and means in the frameworks (e.g. digital literacy in DeSeCo), but that it increasingly tends to also be framed as one of the major drivers of change in learning processes (OECD 2005). In the Future of Education and Skills 2030 (OECD 2018), digital technologies are more directly focused on in terms of their role as *learning and working tools* in schools and classrooms, whereas they were only indirectly mentioned in earlier frameworks.

Finally, the comparisons between the frameworks regarding *living in the world* point to an imbalance between promoting skills for the future labour market and/or for citizenship in democracies. All the frameworks consider competences and skills related to 'living in the world,' but only one (ATC21S) explicitly relates to the social aims of schooling (Binkley et al. 2012). There is, however, no alignment with general pedagogical-philosophical ideas about schooling in the definitions, texts, or references. The background ideas behind the four frameworks are different, but the analysis suggests that different influences, especially from learning theories and learner-centred curriculum ideology (in broad terms, behaviourism or constructivism), provide them with their foundational premises for the definitions. Some of the cultural, political, or professional dimensions of educating for the future are addressed in all the frameworks, but it is only in the OECD's framework (OECD 2018) that implications and implementation issues related to the national curricula represent a major theme.

## A complex context for national curriculum-making

The results of the comparison are in line with previous research on transnational competence frameworks (Tahirsylaj and Sundberg 2020; Voogt and Roblin 2012), and they show that organisations adopt different vocabularies, with some speaking of 'competency' and others of 'skills,' and that there are no standardised definitions for the sets of knowledge and skills induced by the twenty-first-century competence-based curricula. Instead, there are different competing ideas on what terms to use, what frameworks to relate to, and how to manage these terms and frameworks discursively within national curriculum-making. National policy-makers thus have to navigate a highly complex discursive context.

In order to develop a more sophisticated analysis of how CBAs are constructed differently within different national and institutional contexts, Voogt and Roblin (2012) have suggested that twenty-first-century competences in relation to national curricula frameworks could be understood in any of the following ways: (a) as more symbolically added to the already existing curriculum as new subjects or as new content within traditional subjects (competence-added curriculum); (b) as integrated *ad hoc* or more systematically as cross-curricular competences that both underpin school subjects and place emphasis on the acquisition of wider key competences (competence-integrated curriculum); or (c) as the main design principles for a new curriculum in which the traditional structure of school subjects is transformed and schools are regarded as learning organisations (competence-transformed curriculum).

In the following section we will make use of these distinctions to analyse how the Swedish government and its National Agency for Education (NAE) navigated the transnational context of CBAs, here dominated by the OECD, when launching the 2011 curriculum reform, with a special focus on how transversal competences are related to school subject knowledge and pre-existing subject structures. The Swedish reform is an interesting national case exemplifying the challenges facing national politicians having to balance external and internal pressures, sometimes ending up with unexpected and unconventional discursive and conceptual compositions.

## Hybrid competences in Swedish curriculum policy-making

During the early 1990s, compulsory schooling in Sweden was decentralised along new managerial principles of public management. The 290 municipalities took over the mandatorship from the state and a new national curriculum for compulsory schools was launched, governed by goals instead of content (as it was previously), and designed in a way that resembled what Voogt and Roblin (2012) described as a competence-transformed curriculum. The focus thus shifted from what was put into education (content) to what came out of it (outcomes), and the responsibility for goal attainment was heavily placed on the teachers. Instead of striving for a strong community and equal conditions for all, individualisation and differentiation were emphasised as drivers of the necessary educational reforms. However, these new ideas were not uncontested. In the light of declining PISA results from 2003 onwards, politicians soon started to advocate for a back-to-basics policy in terms of a reintroduction of content knowledge as the organising principle for curriculum design. The unexpectedly low PISA scores led to a widespread 'scandalisation' (Steiner-Khamsi 2003) of compulsory schooling, not just in the coordinative discourse among the political elite, but also in the wider communicative discourse, where the media came to play an important role in fuelling the national discourse with negative reports from every possible journalistic angle (cf. Nordin 2019). The curriculum, which was organised with a competence rationale, was identified as a problem (Nordin and Sundberg 2016), as it was viewed as not giving enough guidance for teachers. When starting to plan for the new curriculum that was to be launched in 2011, the national discourse advocating for a return to more disciplinary-oriented subject content knowledge had grown to almost hegemonic proportions.

When preparing for the 2011 curriculum reform, the Swedish government thus found itself caught in the midst of a discursive and conceptual crossfire between the OECD and its implicit pressure to conform to the DeSeCo framework underpinning PISA, and the explicit domestic pressure to bring back subject knowledge as the organising principle (Rychen, Salganik, and McLaughlin 2003). The OECD DeSeCo framework (2005), to which there were close collaborative links,[2] provided Swedish policy-makers with a last resort. It could provide legitimation from international experts to back up a 'necessary' curriculum reform, yet it was open enough to allow for core traditional subject knowledge in its construction.

### *Knowledge and competences in the 2011 national Swedish curriculum reform*

In 2011, when the new curriculum for Swedish compulsory schools was launched, subjects and subject knowledge were reintroduced as organising principles for the curriculum design in line with domestic discourse. The official report preceding the curriculum text (Official Government Report 2007) stated that the syllabi for all subjects should describe 'pure subject knowledge' and should not include interdisciplinary content, as was the case in the previous curriculum. However, at the same time, each subject should offer clear guidance on the intended direction of that subject, and it is in this part of the curriculum (subject aims) that the idea of competence can now be found. The Swedish term for talking about competence is 'abilities' (in Swedish, *förmågor*), interpreted as qualities developed over time within specific subjects (NAE 2011). In a comment on the new curriculum reform, the Swedish NAE noted that, although the concept of competences had gained ground internationally within education as promoted by organisations such as the EU and the OECD, it did not occur explicitly as a foreground idea in the Swedish curriculum. However, the NAE emphasised that the concept of knowledge used in the Swedish curriculum 'as a knowledgeable and committed participation and acting, in a specific practice' (NAE 2010, 15; authors' translation) was very similar to that of competences. According to the NAE (2010), the reason for not explicitly introducing the term 'competence' in the Swedish curriculum was that the way knowledge was already established in the curriculum was in line with the meaning of competence, and that the introduction of yet another term would not contribute in any significant way. In doing so, it was possible for the government and the NAE to publicly and politically legitimate a reintroduction of traditional school subjects as organising principles for the design of the new curriculum, while simultaneously connecting to the transnational OECD discourse promoting competences, though in terms of abilities. Put differently, the NAE somewhat paradoxically argued that a shift from a competence-focused curriculum to a knowledge-based curriculum nonetheless, at least to some extent, implied a focus on competences.

### Discursive hybridity on competences

The Swedish use of 'abilities' is defined in the intersection between two different discourses – a neo-conservative discourse, grounded in essentialism and with a strong focus on disciplinary knowledge and school subjects; and a transnational technical-instrumental discourse emphasising learning outcomes (Sundberg and Wahlström 2012).

In analysing the elements of the 2011 Swedish curriculum, one can find both discourses represented in the text. For example, the 'core content' section represents an essentialist subject knowledge discourse following the Piagetian stages of development. There is a direct focus on traditional academic disciplines (such as reading, writing, mathematics, literature, foreign languages, history, art, music and science) and the acquisition of their respective bodies of knowledge, thus striving to ensure a common core curriculum.

In the section on 'goals and aims of the subject,' general 'competence-like' goals for the subject are stated and, in the section entitled 'knowledge requirements,' the kinds of learning outcomes required in order to achieve the different grades are stated. Both sections express a competence-oriented discourse emphasising measurable outcomes for transnational comparison. For example, problem-solving is emphasised, but not as a transversal skill; it is specific to different subject domains.

The Swedish curriculum reform of 2011 can thus be seen as a hybridisation of two radically different discourses.[3] Furthermore, a semantic condensation of knowledge and knowledge requirements, in combination with an intensified interest in national knowledge tests and follow-up of results has meant that the role of instrumental values emphasising the extrinsic values and uses of school knowledge has been increased and the role of subject core content has been strengthened. Looking at the 2011 Swedish curriculum reform thus shows that the competence model has been adapted and translated by incorporating some ideas of transnational policy solutions (as understood by the DI approach) focused on efficiency and a learner-centred approach; this is apparent in the text through the incorporation of 'abilities' subordinated to subject knowledge. However, the programmatic aspects of creating a competence-based curriculum as well as deliberations on the background assumptions of educational philosophies are neglected. Instead, the Swedish curriculum is strongly rooted in institutionalised structures of school subjects, with only limited space for cross-disciplinary themes and competences.

### A competence-added curriculum framework

Returning to Voogt and Roblin (2012) and their distinction of how competences/skills are defined in relation to subject knowledge, subjects, or disciplines in different frameworks, the 2011 Swedish curriculum could be described as a competence-added curriculum. In balancing domestic and international agendas as a legitimation strategy among Swedish policy-makers, the use of competences in the curriculum operates symbolically, adding competence vocabulary in terms of abilities into a curriculum that is otherwise organised along disciplinary subject content lines.

The PISA assessments, and indirectly, the DeSeCo framework, have had an impact on the policy discussion about the Swedish compulsory school system and school outcomes, since Swedish students have performed poorly in these more recent appraisals in relation to how they performed in the international assessment programmes during the 1990s (i.e. PISA, TIMSS, PIRLS etc.). That PISA and other international evaluations have influenced the Swedish curriculum reform of 2011 is clear from an NAE report, which shows that the design of the new syllabuses in Swedish and mathematics took, as their starting point, the results from international studies such as the PISA assessment of 2006 (NAE 2010). The DeSeCo framework thus operated actively in setting the policy agenda and building up reform pressure, but it acted more indirectly on the borderlines of the process of designing the new curriculum in 2011.

The Swedish curriculum can thus be viewed as one version of a transnational curriculum discourse, with its own specific national connotations adding ideational elements from a transnational policy discourse on CBAs, rather than embracing it as a whole. Furthermore, using Sweden as an empirical example shows how transnational policy concepts such as 'competency' and 'skills' become subject to processes of translation when re-contextualised within national borders specific to each country due to their historical, social, and/or cultural premises.

## Conclusions

The competence movement has come to represent a strong coordinative discourse among powerful transnational and in case of P21, national organisations. In this paper, we have looked into four different frameworks of three such powerful organisations. However, using Sweden as an example shows that, irrespective of the competence movements' powerful position in coordinating educational discourses, the national context can play a major role in the ways in which these discourses are communicated and manifested at the national level. As pointed out by Anderson-Levitt (2012, 451), 'meanings are remade not only because local actors inevitably reinterpret ideas in the context of their own framework, but also because they may struggle against the meanings offered or imposed by global actors'.

### *From a competence-integrated to a competence-added curriculum*

Sweden's national 'independence' or 'resistance,' as referred to by Anderson-Levitt (2012), actually led to the opposite development in relation to what was advocated by the competence movement. It also led to a development away from what Voogt and Roblin (2012) talked about as a competence-integrated curriculum launched in the early 1990s, towards a competence-added curriculum launched in 2011 in the wake of declining PISA scores and a public and political demand to reintroduce subject knowledge as the organising principle for curriculum design. In the latest curriculum of 2011 (NAE 2011),[4] the role of competences was thus downgraded and treated more symbolically within a framework that was first and foremost organised around subject knowledge. The Swedish example shows that even in small countries like Sweden, domestic discourses in terms of shared contextual background ideas shaped by history, culture, and domestic politics can play a decisive role in the way in which global policies become part of national agendas.

### *A hybrid competence discourse in Swedish curriculum policy-making*

The act of balancing two powerful discourses, one advocating the introduction of compe-tences at a transnational level, and another advocating the reintroduction of subject content at a national level, led to a kind of hybrid discourse where competences, referred to as abilities, were discursively embedded into a subject content-oriented framework. This was accomplished by understanding skills not as generic, as in the transnational com-petence frameworks described in this paper, but as subject-bound. Abilities are described as developing over time within specific subjects and then as related to the long-term goal of each school subject. In constructing such a hybrid competence discourse, the Swedish government managed to balance the two discourses in a way that enabled them to sim-ultaneously maintain legitimacy at national and transnational levels.

## Notes

1. Due to the lack of uniformity in the use and understanding of 'competence-based education' and/or 'competence-based reforms,' we follow Anderson-Levitt, Bonnéry, and Fichtner (2017) in our use of the broader concept of 'competence-based approaches' (CBAs).
2. For example, prof. Ulf P. Lundgren was the General Director for the National Agency for Edu-cation from 1991–1999 and chaired the Centre for Educational Research and Innovation (*CERI*, OECD) preparing the PISA-tests.
3. For additional examples of hybridisation see Clément, Deng, and Peng, and Bordoli in this special issue.
4. A minor revision of the Swedish national curriculum of 2011 was launched in 2018 with no substantial implications for our analysis or conclusions. In the article we refer to the initial 2011 version. However, in the reference list, the hyperlink is to the revised 2018 version since the 2011 version was removed after the revision was launched in 2018 and no longer possible to retrieve digitally.

## Disclosure statement

No potential conflict of interest was reported by the author(s).

## ORCID

*Andreas Nordin* http://orcid.org/0000-0002-8503-2655
*Daniel Sundberg* http://orcid.org/0000-0003-0644-3489

## References

Addey, Camilla, Sam Sellar, Gita Steiner-Khamsi, Bob Lingard, and Antoni Verger. 2017. "The Rise of International Large-Scale Assessments and Rationales for Participation." *Compare: A Journal of Comparative and International Education* 47 (3): 434–452.

Anderson-Levitt, Kathryn, ed. 2003. *Local Meanings, Global Schooling: Anthropology and World Culture Theory*. New York, NY: Palgrave Macmillan.

Anderson-Levitt, Kathryn. 2012. "Complicating the Concept of Culture." *Comparative Education* 48 (4): 441–454.

Anderson-Levitt, Kathryn, Stéphane Bonnéry, and Sarah Fichtner. 2017. "Introduction to the Dossier: 'Competence-Based' Approaches as 'Traveling' Reforms." *Cahiers de la recherche sur l'éducation et les savoirs* 16: 27–45.

Baek, Chanwoong, Bernadette Hörmann, Berit Karseth, Oren Pizmony-Levy, Kirsten Sivesind, and Gita Steiner-Khamsi. 2018. "Policy Learning in Norwegian School Reform: A Social Network Analysis of the 2020 Incremental Reform." *Nordic Journal of Studies in Educational Policy* 4 (1): 24–37. https://doi.org/10.1080/20020317.2017.1412747.

Benavot, Aaron, and Cecilia Braslavsky. 2006. *School Knowledge in Comparative and Historical Perspective: Changing Curricula in Primary and Secondary Education*. Dordrecht: Springer.

Binkley, Marilyn, Ola Erstad, Joan Herman, Senta Raizen, Martin Ripley, May Miller-Rici, and Mike Rumble. 2012. "Defining Twenty-First Century Skills." Chap. 2 in *Assessment and Teaching of 21st Century Skills*, edited by Patrick Griffin, Barry McGaw, and Esther Care, 17–66. Dordrecht: Springer Netherlands.

Binkley, Marilyn, Ola Erstad, Joan Herman, Senta Raizen, Martin Ripley, and Mike Rumble. 2010. "Defining 21st Century Skills" (Draft White Paper 1, Assessment and Teaching of 21st Century Skills [ATCS], The University of Melbourne, 2010). http://www.ericlondaits.com.ar/oei_ibertic/sites/default/files/biblioteca/24_defining-21st-century-skills.pdf.

Broschek, Jörg. 2016. "The Historical Construction of Social Order: Ideas, Institutions, and Meaning Constellations." *In World Culture Re-Contextualised: Meaning Constellations and Path Dependencies in Comparative and International Education Research*, edited by Jürgen Schriewer, 161–180. New York, NY: Routledge.

Delors, Jacques. 1996. *Learning: The Treasure Within*. Paris: UNESCO. https://unesdoc.unesco.org/ark:/48223/pf0000109590

European Parliament. 2007. *Key Competences for Lifelong Learning: A European Reference Framework. Annex of a Recommendation of the European Parliament and of the Council of 18 December 2006 on Key Competences for Lifelong Learning, Official Journal of the European Union* [30.12.2006/L394]. http://ec.europa.eu/dgs/education_culture/publ/pdf/ll-learning/keycomp_en.pdf

Gordon, Jean, Gabor Halsz, Magdalena Krawczyk, Tom Leney, Alain Michel, David Pepper, Elzbieta Putkiewicz, and Jerzy Wiśniewski. 2009. *Key Competences in Europe: Opening Doors for Lifelong Learners Across the School Curriculum and Teacher Education*. Warsaw: Center for Social and Economic Research on behalf of the CASE Network.

Haas, Peter. 1992. "Introduction: Epistemic Communities and International Policy Coordination." *International Organization* 46 (1): 1–35.

Hopmann, Stefan. 2008. "No Child, No School, No State Left Behind: Schooling in the Age of Accountability." *Journal of Curriculum Studies* 40 (4): 417–456.

Labaree, David F. 2014. "Let's Measure What No One Teaches: PISA, NCLB, and the Shrinking Aims of Education." *Teachers College Record* 116 (9): 1–14.

Meyer, Heinz-Dieter. 2014. "The OECD as Pivot of the Emerging Global Educational Accountability Regime: How Accountable Are the Accountants?" *Teachers College Record* 116: 9.

Morgan, Clara, and Riyad A. Shahjahan. 2014. "The Legitimation of OECD's Global Educational Governance: Examining PISA and AHELO Test Production." *Comparative Education* 50 (2): 192–205.

NAE (Swedish National Agency for Education). 2010. *Skolverkets lägesbedömning 2010*. [National Agency for Education: A Current Assessment, 2010]. Stockholm: Skolverket.

NAE (Swedish National Agency for Education). 2011. *Curriculum for the Compulsory School, Preschool Class and the Leisure-time Centre: Lgr 11*. Stockholm: Swedish National Agency for Education.

https://www.skolverket.se/publikationsserier/styrdokument/2018/curriculum-for-the-compulsory-school-preschool-class-and-school-age-educare-revised-2018

Nordin, Andreas. 2019. "A Data-Driven School Crisis." In *New Practices of Comparison, Quantification and Expertise in Education: Conducting Empirically Based Research*, edited by Christina Elde Mølstad, and Daniel Pettersson, 127–144. London: Routledge.

Nordin, Andreas, and Daniel Sundberg. 2014. *Transnational Policy Flows in European Education*. Oxford: Symposium Books.

Nordin, Andreas, and Daniel Sundberg. 2016. "Travelling Concepts in National Curriculum Policy-Making: The Example of Competencies." *European Educational Research Journal* 15 (3): 314–328.

OECD (Organisation for Economic Co-Operation and Development). 2005. *The Definition and Selection of Key Competencies: Executive Summary*. http://www.oecd.org/dataoecd/47/61/35070367.pdf.

OECD (Organisation for Economic Co-Operation and Development). 2018. *OECD Future of Education and Skills 2030-The Future We Want: Position Paper*. Paris: OECD. http://www.oecd.org/education/2030-project/about/documents/E2030%20Position%20Paper%20(05.04.2018).pdf.

OECD (Organisation for Economic Co-Operation and Development). 2019. *OECD Future of Education and Skills 2030- OECD Learning Compass: A Series of Concept Notes*. Paris: OECD. http://www.oecd.org/education/2030-project/contact/OECD_Learning_Compass_2030_Concept_Note_Series.pdf.

Official Government Report. 2007. *Tydliga mål och kunskapskrav i grundskolan. Förslag till nytt mål- och uppföljningssystem* [Clear Goals and Knowledge Requirements in Compulsory School Education: Proposal for a New System of Goals and Monitoring]. Stockholm: Official Swedish Government Reports.

P21 (Partnership for 21st Century Skills). 2002. *Learning for the 21st Century: A Report and MILE Guide for 21st Century Skills*. Washington: Education Resources Information Centre (Institute of Education Sciences). https://eric.ed.gov/?id=ED480035.

Partnership for 21st Century Skills. 2019a. *Framework for 21st Century Learning*. Columbus: Battele for Kids. http://static.battelleforkids.org/documents/p21/P21_Framework_Brief.pdf.

Partnership for 21st Century Skills. 2019b. *Framework for 21st Century Learning Definitions*. Columbus: Battele for Kids. http://static.battelleforkids.org/documents/p21/P21_Framework_DefinitionsBFK.pdf.

Rychen, Dominique, Laura Salganik, and Mary McLaughlin, eds. 2003. *Definition and Selection of Key Competences: Contributions to the Second DeSeCo Symposium*. Neuchatel: Swiss Federal Statistical Office. http://www.oecd.org/education/skills-beyond-school/41529505.pdf

Schmidt, Vivien A. 2011. "Speaking of Change: Why Discourse is Key to the Dynamics of Policy Transformation." *Critical Policy Studies* 5 (2): 106–126.

Schmidt, Vivien A. 2015. "Discursive Institutionalism: Understanding Policy in Context." In *Handbook of Critical Policy Studies*, edited by Frank Fischer, Douglas Torgerson, Anna Durnová, and Michael Orsini, 170–189. Cheltenham: Edward Elgar.

Schmidt, Vivien A. 2016. "The Roots of Neo-Liberal Resilience: Explaining Continuity and Change in Background Ideas in Europe's Political Economy." *The British Journal of Politics and International Relations* 18 (2): 318–334.

Schriewer, Jürgen. 2016. "Meaning Constellations in the World Society: Revisited." In *World Culture Re-Contextualised: Meaning Constellations and Path Dependencies in Comparative and International Education Research*, edited by Jürgen Schriewer, 1–16. London: Routledge.

Schulte, Barbara. 2016. "World Culture with Chinese Characteristics: When Global Models Go Native." In *World Culture Re-Contextualised: Meaning Constellations and Path Dependencies in Comparative and International Education Research*, edited by Jürgen Schriewer, 67–80. London: Routledge.

Steiner-Khamsi, Gita. 2003. "The Politics of League Tables." *Journal of Social Science Education*. Advance online publication. doi:10.4119/jsse-301.

Steiner-Khamsi, Gita. 2012. "Understanding Policy Borrowing and Lending: Building Comparative Policy Studies." Chap. 1 in *World Yearbook of Education 2012: Policy Borrowing and Lending in Education*, edited by Gita Steiner-Khamsi and Florian Waldow, 3–17. London: Routledge.

Steiner-Khamsi, Gita, and Florian Waldow, eds. 2012. *Policy Borrowing and Lending in Education*. London: Routledge.

Sundberg, Daniel, and Ninni Wahlström. 2012. "Standards-based Curricula in a Denationalized Conception of Education: The Case of Sweden." *European Educational Research Journal* 11 (3): 342–356.

Tahirsylaj, Armend. 2017. "Curriculum Field in the Making: Influences That Led to Social Efficiency as Dominant Curriculum Ideology in Progressive Era in the U.S." *European Journal Of Curriculum Studies* 4 (1): 618–628.

Tahirsylaj, Armend, and Daniel Sundberg. 2020. "The Unfinished Business of Defining Competences for 21st Century Curricula—A Systematic Research Review." *Curriculum Perspectives* 40: 131–145. doi:10.1007/s41297-020-00112-6.

Takayama, Keita. 2013. "OECD, 'Key Competencies' and the New Challenges of Educational Inequality." *Journal of Curriculum Studies* 45 (1): 67–80.

Trilling, Bernie, and Charles Fadel. 2009. *21st Century Skills: Learning for Life in Our Times.* San Francisco: Jossey-Bass.

Voogt, Joke, and Natalie Pereja Roblin. 2012. "A Comparative Analysis of International Frameworks for 21st Century Competences: Implications for National Curriculum Policies." *Journal of Curriculum Studies* 44 (3): 299–321.

Wahlström, Ninni, and Daniel Sundberg. 2018. "Discursive Institutionalism: Towards a Framework for Analysing the Relation Between Policy and Curriculum." *Journal of Education Policy* 33 (1): 163–183.

Waldow, Florian. 2012. "Standardisation and Legitimacy: Two Central Concepts in Research on Educational Borrowing and Lending." In *World Yearbook of Education 2012: Policy Borrowing and Lending in Education*, edited by Gita Steiner-Khamsi, and Florian Waldow, 411–427. New York, NY: Routledge.

Weinert, Franz E. 2001. "Concept of Competence: A Conceptual Clarification." In *Defining and Selecting Key Competencies*, edited by Dominique S. Rychen, and Laura H. Salganik, 45–65. Seattle: Hogrefe and Huber.

Westera, Wim. 2001. "Competences in Education: A Confusion of Tongues." *Journal of Curriculum Studies* 33 (1): 75–88.

# The introduction of competence-based education into the compulsory school curriculum in France (2002–2017): hybridity and polysemy as conditions for change

Pierre Clément

**ABSTRACT**

In France, the notion of competence began to be discussed in the early 1990s and was finally enforced in the Education Act of 23 April 2005. Since its emergence, this notion has been strongly opposed by a certain number of teachers, unions and researchers. To understand how competence-based education finally prevailed, I take into account the fundamentally polysemic nature of this notion. After pointing out its origins, I examine how its different meanings have been synthesised within the Common Core established in 2005. I then study the contradictions to which the implementation of this hybrid object has given rise, before analysing the new compromise that was found in the 2015 reform. To do this, I use the data from numerous archives and a series of interviews with the main actors of curriculum reforms in France since the 1980s.

## Introduction

In France, the notion of competence began to be discussed within the Ministry of National Education in the early 1990s (Ropé and Tanguy 1994; Clément 2013). It was finally enforced in the Education Act of 23 April 2005 which states that public education must at least guarantee any student the means needed to acquire a Common Core consisting of the knowledge and competences (*Socle commun de connaissances et de compétences*) one must master in order to successfully complete schooling, to further one's training, to build one's personal and professional future and to succeed in social life. Since its emergence and more particularly since 2005, the notion of competence has been strongly opposed by a certain number of teachers, unions and researchers who first of all defend a conception of the curriculum which puts the emphasis on knowledge and disciplines. Moreover, they also see competences as the Trojan horse of a utilitarian and neo-liberal conception of school (Clément 2012). The aim of this article is to explain how competence-based education finally prevailed in France despite these strong resistances.

To do this, I use the concept of the field of power developed by Pierre Bourdieu during the 1980s and the 1990s, especially in the lectures on the State at the *Collège de France*

(Bourdieu 2014). As far as public policy is concerned, this concept was used by Bourdieu himself to explain the reform of housing policy in France in the 1970s (Bourdieu 2005). However 'research in public policy analysis remains dominated by approaches that are remote from the concepts and methods of sociology' (Dubois 2015, 199). In order to think about the relationships between the different actors involved in the development of public policies, it relies preferentially on concepts such as policy community, policy networks, concrete action systems or sectors. However, with Vincent Dubois, I argue that 'the approach in terms of field can, more ambitiously, be mobilised to ground a truly sociological analysis of public policy' (Dubois 2015, 204). Thus, to explain the curriculum reforms, I have constructed the concept of 'field of educational power' defined 'as the space of social positions from which power over the education system can be exercised' (Clément 2013, 37).

Using this concept requires holding together a synchronic and a diachronic approach, both from a theoretical and methodological perspective. Theoretically, it requires, on the one hand, to sociologically construct the space of production of curricular reforms by identifying the properties and positions of effective agents; and, on the other hand, to historically retrace the construction and definition of the public problems that these agents are dealing with. Methodologically, this synchronic and diachronic approach requires a combination of the empirical materials usually used by historians and sociologists. Thus, I conducted 48 interviews with the main actors of curriculum reforms in France since the 1980s. I also examined a large number of public archives – notably those of the Ministry of National Education, of the main teachers' unions and of the Socialist Party – and private archives – notably those of P. Bourdieu and of former senior ministry officials. I also systematically consulted numerous printed sources, including official and legal documents, the bulletins of the main teachers' unions and a large corpus of press articles published between 1987 and 1989 and between 2002 and 2006. On the basis of all these sources, I finally set up two prosopographic databases on nearly a hundred key stakeholders in the curriculum reforms of the late 1980s and the first half of the 2000s.[1]

Based on this empirical evidence, I argue that the introduction of the competence-based approach into the compulsory school curriculum in France was made possible by the unlikely alliance between three kinds of actors: pedagogical activists engaged in progressive or lifelong learning education, senior civil servants converted to new public management, and proponents of pedagogical conservatism advocating back to basics. This alliance itself was made possible by the polysemic nature of competences (Ropé and Tanguy 1994; Crahay 2006); as in social and health policies (Jobert 1985; Palier 2008), it is precisely the ambiguous nature of this notion that permitted aggregation of opposite interests and to build a political compromise. Finally, I argue that this alliance between these three groups and this polysemy explain the tensions and the ambiguities surrounding the notion of competences in France since the 1980s. Indeed, this notion appears to be the inconsistent result of a hybridising process (Boyer 1998) between, on the one hand, diverse and even opposing pedagogical and political conceptions and, on the other hand, a national tradition favouring content knowledge and disciplines (Snyders 1965; Durkheim 1977; Houssaye 2014). This hybrid character is even stronger because once the general competences of compulsory schooling have been defined, they must then be translated into the pedagogical language specific to each discipline. As much as the notion of competence conflicts with national tradition, it can also conflict with the pedagogical tradition of each discipline.

In order to develop this argument, I expound firstly the national roots of competences and their introduction in the French education system in the 1990s. Thus, I show that this notion was promoted, on the one hand, by pedagogical activists engaged in progressive education or lifelong learning education and, on the other hand, by managers from the private and public sector. From the 1990s onwards, their joint efforts led to the first definition of French competence-based education, which mixed pedagogical and managerial concerns. Secondly, I show how the Common Core was enshrined in the Education Act of 23 April 2005 thanks to an alliance between educational activists, public managers and proponents of back to basics. Turning my attention to the implementation of the Common Core, I then show that a managerial and utilitarian conception of competences prevailed through tactical borrowing of the European Commission's proposal on Key competences. However, as far as the syllabuses are concerned, this conception of competence was inconsistently translated from one discipline to another. Highly criticised due to its managerial and utilitarian conception, the Common Core was completely rewritten after the arrival of the socialist government in 2012. This government promoted a pedagogical approach to the concept of competence based on transversal competences and soft skills, which permeated all compulsory school curricula, especially the teaching of French.

## A note on compulsory schooling and curricula in France

In France, compulsory schooling takes place between the ages of 3 and 16; it includes nursery school, elementary school and lower secondary school. It consists of both 12 grades (3 in nursery school, 5 in elementary school and 4 in lower secondary school) and 4 cycles. A cycle comprises several grades and constitutes a pedagogical unit. For each cycle, the syllabuses set what has to be taught in each grade and each discipline. These syllabuses are adopted by a ministerial Order and have to be applied throughout the national territory. So officially, syllabuses are identical from one school to another.

First adopted by Parliament in 2005, the Common Core sets, for the first time, the general objectives of compulsory schooling which have from now on legal priority over the syllabuses. For each cycle, grade and discipline, the syllabuses then specify these general objectives as well as the topics to be addressed in order to achieve them.

## The French genealogy of competence-based education

As pointed out by a number of researchers (Takayama 2013; Morgan and Shahjahan 2014; Lightfoot 2015) and activists (Hirtt and de Selys 1998; Laval and Weber 2002), international organisations – such as OECD, UNESCO, the World Bank or the European Union – have played a central role in defining the concept of competences, in its dissemination throughout the world and in its integration into national curricula. However, it would be completely wrong to consider this new pedagogical paradigm as the mere result of a transplant from abroad. Indeed, the notion of competences also has old national roots that must be recalled in order to understand the recent transformations of the compulsory school curriculum in France.

## Competences VS scholasticism: progressive & lifelong learning educators

A crossroads concept par excellence (Tanguy and Ropé 1994), the notion of competence can claim multiple legacies.

In France, from the end of the nineteenth century onwards, it was first and foremost the activists of progressive education who promoted a modern pedagogy that broke with both the model of school organisation inherited from Jesuit secondary schools, in force in state high schools, and the conception of academic excellence that prevailed there. By drawing on the experiments carried out in England, notably by Cecil Reddie with the New School in Abbotsholme (Searby 1989), the French progressive educators invented a complete education aimed at developing character, autonomy and entrepreneurship in students, as illustrated, for example, by the motto of the *École des Roches*: 'well equipped for life' (Duval 2009). For today's education activists influenced by progressive education, competence-based education is a new tool in this ancient struggle that their predecessors began more than 100 years ago. By defending the idea of competence, they aim to fight both the scholastic, formalistic and abstract conception of school knowledge and the traditional pedagogy which has been typical of secondary education and which is seen as the cause of the massive school failure and strong social inequalities of the French education system (Prost 2013, 95).

Alongside progressive education, the pedagogical models and practices which have been invented and tested in the field of lifelong learning are another source from which the notion of competence in France is drawn. Considering the traditional education system as a counter-model, lifelong learning activists set themselves the objective of transforming the school system by importing their own practices (Laot 2000): self-evaluation; involvement and empowerment of learners – who should discover and appropriate knowledge –; ongoing questioning of the usefulness of the knowledge which is transmitted; lightening of curricula; small group work instead of lectures; setting of educational objectives; in-depth transformation of the teacher-student relationship.

## The managerial roots of competences in the private sector ...

As shown by Zarifian (2001), Stroobants (1993) and Tanguy (2001), competence-based education also took root in the business and management world. As early as the 1950s, this notion emerged in the world of executive development. For example, in 1958, Raymond Vatier[2] proposed a definition of training based on the notion of competence:

> Training is all the actions likely to maintain individually and collectively the whole personnel at the level of competence required by the company's activity. This competence refers to the knowledge, skills, willingness to work of each individual and each group. Competence is the happy combination of these three terms: knowledge, skills, good will. (quoted in Tanguy 2001, 38)[3]

The 1980s were to be a second high point in the definition of competence by management professionals. French capitalism then turned its eyes to Japan while Fordism seemed more and more outdated. It is in this context that business consulting firms – notably CEGOS (Cannac 1985) – promoted new models of work organisation no longer based on qualifications, previously defined in collective agreements, but on the individualisation of careers and the mobilisation of the so-called 'third dimension competences' (Dubar 1996), that is to say behavioural and relational skills.

### ... and in the public sector

That being said, it would not be possible to explain how this new pedagogical model has managed to establish itself in general education in France without mentioning the support it has received, within the very core of what Pierre Bourdieu calls the bureaucratic field (Bourdieu 2014), particularly from senior civil servants seeking to reform and modernise the State in the early 1980s (Bezez 2009). With the election of a socialist President of the Republic and the installation of a left-wing government including communist ministers, state intervention in all sectors of the economy and society was set to increase. In these circumstances, the effectiveness of public administration became a major public issue. To deal with this problem, some modernising senior civil servants, public management specialists, consultants and sociologists of organisations (Bezez 2009, 268–290) began to introduce into the State the new principles of work organisation that were then being invented within big companies.

Opposing both the liberals calling for state withdrawal and the defenders of the old Weberian bureaucracy, the public administration reformers promoted a new organisation of public service based on the quality of the service provided, an increased autonomy of local administrative units and an increased accountability of agents, the whole being strictly controlled through the development of performance agreements and evaluation procedures. In 1989, this new organisation was to find a political recognition in the circular on the 'Renewal of the Public Service' published by Socialist Prime Minister Michel Rocard.[4] As a prefiguration of the dissemination of new public management (Hood 1995) in the French public service, this text indicated that the State would initiate 'at its various territorial levels an ambitious policy of developing responsibilities', while stating that 'there can be no autonomy without responsibility, no responsibility without evaluation, and no evaluation without consequences'.[5]

### Competences in the 1990s: between pedagogy and management

It is in this perspective that the 1991–1992 drafting of the *Charte des programmes* (Curriculum Framework) by the Ministry of National Education, 'the first major policy document to incorporate the notion of competences into primary and secondary education' (Anderson-Levitt 2017), should be seen. If, as argued by Anderson-Levitt (2017, 53), this framework expresses 'a shift in pedagogical thinking [...] from content-centered to learner-centered instruction', it can also be seen as a policy instrument that prefigures and makes possible the transformation of the school system's organisation and management.

While national education is presented as a pilot sector of the 'Public Service Renewal' (Chaty 1997, 69), this framework stipulates that official curricula must now explicitly specify the list of the competences to be acquired at the end of a year or cycle and expressly provides for the modalities of their evaluation. It also provides that these required competences constitute the framework within which the autonomy of teachers, pedagogical teams and schools is exercised. This text thus contains the seeds of a decisive change in the nature of school curricula; it is not merely a pedagogical text that sets the formal curriculum but also a management tool that makes it possible to steer by means of objectives and evaluation an educational system that gives more responsibility to local actors.

In the *Charte des programmes*, the link between the writing of curricula in the competence-based form and the new public management was only outlined. Thereafter, it has been constantly emphasised in the 1990s and 2000s. This was the case, for example, in a 1994 report on the lower secondary schools (Bouchez 1994). In a section entitled 'Autonomy: initiative – flexibility – contract', it was indeed stated that the educational policy should now be based on contractual relations. But this requires the setting of 'simple and clear, negotiated and evaluable objectives' (Bouchez 1994, 24). So, the drafting of curricula in the form of a reference framework of competences, sufficiently broken down to make it possible to measure their effective mastery, became the condition to enable 'the State [...] to ensure a "guarantee" for this type of relationship, observe its evolution at all times and above all assess its results' (Bouchez 1994, 24). But this report went further in the managerial use of competences. Breaking with the rule that teachers' salaries mostly depend on seniority, it recommended that the assessment of the competences acquired by pupils should be taken into account when determining the promotion and remuneration of teachers.

That said, it is through the establishment and implementation of the Common Core in 2005–2012 that the link between curricula defined as a set of competences and the new public management was systematically established. In accordance with the 2006 decree stipulating that 'the content requirement of the Common Core is inseparable from an assessment requirement',[6] the implementation of the Common Core went hand in hand with the creation of new mechanisms for the assessment of students' learning: on the one hand, a personal competences booklet,[7] and on the other hand, new standardised national assessments. But, with the implementation of these tools, the meaning of the competence-based education had been profoundly transformed. While the pedagogical legacy of new education tended to disappear in favour of a vision reduced to teaching to the test, competences became a management tool which made it possible to open the black box of the classroom and thus to evaluate the effectiveness of teachers, that of schools and ultimately that of the teaching system as a whole.

## Competence-based education within the Common Core of knowledge and competences (2002–2012): a utilitarian and managerial perspective

As mentioned in the introduction and above, the establishment of the Common Core since 2005 has therefore been a key moment in the process of institutionalising competence-based education in France. I show below that the adoption of this reform is the product of an unlikely alliance between educational militants, reformist unions, senior civil servants and conservative politicians. However, this alliance is also at the root of the uncertainties and contradictions in the Common Core implementation.

### *The adoption of the Common Core of knowledge and competences: an unlikely alliance between progressive pedagogy, new public management and back to basics*

After his re-election in 2002, President Jacques Chirac installed a national commission responsible for preparing and organising a national debate on the school system, which led to the Education Act of 23 April 2005.

At the moment when this major national debate about education took place, the idea of setting up a Common Core for the compulsory education curriculum had already become part of the contemporary climate. Previously a President of the *Conseil national des programmes* (National Council of Curricula) from 1994 to 2002, the new Minister of National Education, Luc Ferry, was the author of the first report advocating the reorganisation of compulsory schooling around a Common Core (Ferry 1995). But for this right-wing minister, both a philosopher and a defender of elitism, the Common Core appeared not as a means of introducing competence-based education in France but first and foremost as a means of going back to the basics, especially language proficiency, in order to halt the decline of the educational level as measured by PISA. By publicly stating that 'placing the student at the centre of the system is demagogic' (*Le Monde*, 17 April 2002), Luc Ferry thus identified himself as a defender of traditional pedagogy and subject content knowledge more than of progressive education.

But at the same time, the idea of a Common Core was also defended by a coalition of teachers, reformist trade unionists, researchers, school heads, parents and activists from associations or pedagogical movements who had in common a vision of themselves as the inheritors of progressive education (George 2002). Even if they agreed on the term 'Common Core', they did not give it the same meaning as the minister. For them, this reform had to be the means, on the one hand, of recognising the pre-eminence of active learning and, on the other hand, of making the pupil's full participation in the life of the community the true purpose of schooling. So, as explained above, competence-based education could thus be presented as a 'democratic promise' to 'transform the "sorting machine" school into a school of emancipation and promotion for all'.[8]

The idea of a Common Core finally found decisive support from Claude Thélot, the president of the commission in charge of organising the national debate and preparing the future law. An *École Polytechnique* and *École nationale de la statistique et de l'administration économique* (ENSAE)[9] graduate, an administrator of the *Institut national de la statistique et des études économiques* (INSEE),[10] a former head of the Evaluation and Forecasting Department (DEP) within the Ministry of National Education and a member of the France's Court of Audit, Claude Thélot can be considered the archetype of the senior official committed to modernising the public sector. During his term as head of the DEP, then as a president of the High Council for School Evaluation (2000–2001), he played a leading role in the institutionalisation of evaluation within the French education system (Pons 2008). Thus, in the footsteps of the proponents of new public management, he saw the Common Core as the means of definitely setting the objectives of compulsory schooling (Thélot 2002). But at the same time, he also strongly supported the setting of these objectives in the form of competences and the inclusion of non-cognitive or behavioural competences.[11] His position thus appeared to be entirely compatible with the one defended by the coalition of educational and reformist activists.

Supported by Minister Luc Ferry, as well as by his successor François Fillon, by some key senior civil servants, by the reformist trade unions and by the majority of educational movements, the Common Core was thus enshrined in law, despite the opposition of SNES, the leading union among secondary school teachers. But the conditions of this victory weighed heavily on the implementation of the reform. The defenders of the Common Core agreed only on a slogan to which they gave different, even opposite, meanings.

However, the application of the law required specifying the content of the five pillars of the Common Core (see Table 1) and a clarification of what a competence is in practice.

### *Setting the content of the Common Core: the tactical borrowing of the European Key competencies*

In order to draw up the decree specifying the content of the Common Core, the new Minister of National Education, Gilles de Robien, designed a scheme to bypass not only the representatives of disciplinary interests (General Inspectors and teachers' associations) and trade union organisations, but also the administration of the Ministry. As he was aware that the logic of the Common Core and competences could be considered irrelevant to the French school tradition, the Minister thus tried to free himself from the procedures usually in force for the drafting of school curricula.[12] So, he entrusted the responsibility for drafting the decree directly to his advisers and to a few experts whose names were kept secret and who worked in complete confidentiality. Their work resulted in a first draft of the Common Core which was a kind of compromise between, on the one hand, the competence-based education and, on the other hand, the traditional logic of knowledge and disciplines.[13]

As required by the Education Act of 23 April 2005, this first draft was then transmitted to the High Council of Education (HCE), an independent advisory board. Yet, influenced by Alain Bouvier and Christian Forestier – two senior officials of the French Ministry of

**Table 1.** Different versions of the common core.

| Education Act of 23 April 2005 | Key competences for lifelong learning. European Commission (10 November 2005) | Recommendations of French High Council of Education (23 March 2006) | Decree of July 11, 2006 | Decree of March 31, 2015 |
|---|---|---|---|---|
| Command of the **French** language | Communication in the **mother tongue** | Command of the **French** language | Command of the **French** language | **Languages** for thinking and communicating |
| Command of the main elements in **mathematics** | **Mathematical** competence **and** basic competences in **science and technology** | Basic competences in **Mathematics and** scientific and technological culture | Main elements in **mathematics and** scientific and technological culture | Methods and tools for learning |
| The **humanistic and** scientific culture needed to exercise citizenship | Cultural expression | **Humanities** | **Humanities** | Forming the person and the citizen |
| Proficiency in a modern **foreign language** | Communication in **foreign languages** | Practice of one **foreign language** | Practice of one **foreign language** | Natural systems and technical systems |
| Command of basic **information** and **communication technologies** | **Digital** competence | Command of basic **information** and **communication technologies** | Command of basic **information** and **communication technologies** | Representations of the world and human activity |
| | Learning to learn Interpersonal, intercultural and **social** competences and **civic** competence | **Social** and **civic** competences | **Social** and **civic** competences | |
| | **Entrepreneurship** | **Autonomy** & **initiative** | **Autonomy** & **initiative** | |

Education known for their support for the cause of modernising the education system and educational reform (Clément 2013, 637–640) –, this council expressed a very negative opinion on the Common Core first draft. As one of its members stated it clearly: 'The text sent to us by the ministry is a piece of shit. It's totally disciplinary. The notion of competence is practically non-existent, there is nothing transversal'.[14] So, in order to free itself from the disciplinary 'lobbies'[15] whose influence was regarded as too strong within the ministry, the HCE undertook to write, not just the advice required by the Education Act, but real specifications of the future decree. In the struggle for power that then took place between the HCE and the ministry's central administration, the works of the European Commission (2005) and of the OECD (Rychen and Salganik 2000) played a decisive role; the HCE used them not only as a pattern to flesh out the notion of competences, but also as a source of legitimacy to make its conception prevail with the minister and his advisers.

The HCE thus proposed to structure the different pillars of the Common Core according to the European Key Competences (Commission of the European Communities 2005). The main competences of the Common Core were therefore defined as the combination of three elements: knowledges, abilities and attitudes (Haut Conseil de l'Éducation 2006). The HCE also added two new pillars exclusively dedicated to transdisciplinary competences – 'social and civic competences', 'autonomy and initiative' – and whose content was very directly inspired by the European project, in which are mentioned 'interpersonal, intercultural and social and civic competences' and 'entrepreneurship' (Commission of the European Communities 2005). Considering that the school system 'has an obligation to produce effective and verifiable results', the HCE finally claimed that 'the requirements in terms of content and assessment are inseparable' and recommended setting learning standards and creating a personal document retracing the evolution of each student's achievements, competence by competence (Haut Conseil de l'Éducation 2006, 3–4). As shown by the comparison between the two texts (Table 1), these HCE recommendations were fully reflected in the final version of the decree.[16]

Indeed, as they had to face both internal and external resistance, the minister and his office saw in the work of the HCE a way to bring to a rapid conclusion a case they feared would 'get stuck in the usual rhythm of the administration's work'.[17] Thus, it was the strategies of national actors involved in domestic political-bureaucratic struggles that explain the introduction in France of the notion of competences as promoted by international organisations, i.e. competences defined not only as the ability to mobilise knowledge, know-how and attitudes in real-life situations, but also as the systematic assessment of this ability.

### *The revision of the syllabuses: the conflicting translation of competences*

As required by the decree of 11 July 2006, the compulsory school syllabuses were then adapted to take the content of the Common Core into account.

The syllabuses in science (mathematics, physics and chemistry, life and earth sciences, technology) for lower secondary schools which were mainly developed in 2007 are undoubtedly the ones that have most integrated the logic of the Common Core and competence-based education. They combine a return to basics and transversal competences. Firstly, in the introduction of these new syllabuses, it is specified that 'at the level of the requirements of the Common Core, any advanced knowledge is excluded: we limit our-selves to simple problems, relating to everyday life'.[18] In mathematics and physics, the syllabuses thus distinguish openly two types of knowledge: on the one hand, the basic knowledge covered by the Common Core, which must, by definition, be acquired by all pupils and, on the other hand, more advanced knowledge only for the best pupils. Secondly, as they put a strong emphasis on interdisciplinary work through a long common introduction to the four disciplines and the six convergence themes, the syllabuses also make it clear how each discipline can serve general training objectives and enable the acquisition of transversal competences. Moreover, the inquiry approach is thus placed at the heart of the syllabuses as part of an approach that 'favours the construction of knowledge by the student'.[19]

Compared to the science syllabuses, those relating to the humanities (in particular French and history-geography) appear to be little affected by the reform: basic knowledge is not distinguished from advanced knowledge, general learning objectives are hardly explained, transversal competences are almost absent, while skills are only developed in a disciplinary mode and soft skills, like curiosity or creativity, are not present.[20]

## The new Common Core of knowledge, competences and culture (2012–2017): back to pedagogy

The Common Core as implemented after 2006 was rejected from the outset by the majority teachers' trade unions (FSU and especially SNES) but also in the end denounced by the educational movements and reformist trade unions that had initially supported it. In fact, for teachers, as well as for pupils and their parents, the implementation of the Common Core mainly resulted in the strengthening of assessment and accountability (Clément 2012). It can be said that a managerial and utilitarian version of the competence-based education finally prevailed. Contrary to what educational activists and reformist trade unions hoped, the introduction of competence-based education led neither to a modernisation of school knowledge nor to a transformation of pedagogical practices. The same people who had supported the principle of the Common Core in 2005 had to recognise that it had become an *'usine à cases'* i.e. 'a technocratic object used to introduce an evaluation of the "performance" of the system and students, centred on simplistic "basic knowledge"'.[21]

While these criticisms against utilitarianism and conservatism were getting sharper, the political changeover in spring 2012 then led to a major shift in the field of educational power. The installation of the new socialist government and the appointment of Vincent Peillon, a progressive philosopher and former teacher educator, to the Ministry of Education resulted in the replacement of many political advisors and high civil servants in charge of education policies. In short, the right-wing proponents of new public management and pedagogical conservatism were replaced by left-wing progressive educators. In such circumstances, the Common Core was rewritten from top to bottom.

### The 2015 new deal: soft skills and transversal competences

First, in order to satisfy the opposition, the new Socialist Minister of National Education, Vincent Peillon, quickly declared that the personal competence booklet would be abandoned and that the national student assessments would become optional. Secondly, while reaffirming the need to organise compulsory schooling around the acquisition of a Common Core, the new Education Act of 8 July 2013 provided that the Common Core would now include culture, which was a way to satisfy the supporters of classical education. Thirdly, the law mandated the new *Conseil supérieur des programmes* (High Council for Curriculum) to draft a new version of the Common Core. Unlike in 2005–2006, the development of this new Common Core took more than a year and a half to complete and was the subject of a long phase of consultation with teachers' representative organisations. Thus, following the publication in June 2014 of a first draft prepared by the High Council for Curriculum, a new decree dated 31 March 2015 provided that the new Common Core of 'knowledge, competences and culture' is now 'composed of five learning fields that constitute the main learning challenges of compulsory schooling'.[22] For each of these five learning fields, 'knowledge and competences objectives'[23] are then specified. The syllabuses in each cycle and in each discipline are now clearly subordinated to the Common Core that is effectively placed at the top of the hierarchy of pedagogical standards. Thus the function of theses syllabuses is to specify these general objectives and to show how to achieve them through the different disciplines.

The comparison with the first version of the Common Core shows that the first main difference is the absence of any explicit or implicit reference to the work of the OECD and the European Union. The openly utilitarian aspects and the mention of economic purposes for education have thus been erased. In accordance with France's republican ideal, 'personal and civic education' appears to be the essential purpose of compulsory education, which should enable pupils 'to develop themselves personally, to develop their sociability, to succeed in the rest of their educational journey, to integrate themselves into the society within which they will live and to participate, as citizens, in its evolution'.[24]

The other difference lies in the diminished prominence of the assessment tools of competences. Contrary to what previously existed, any national assessment tools that were imposed on teachers no longer exist. As it recognises the pedagogical freedom of teachers, the Ministry thus gives them the responsibility to develop, locally and relatively autonomously, the tools to assess the mastery of the objectives of the Common Core.

Whereas competence-based education thus loses its utilitarian and managerial dimension, its pedagogical dimension has, on the contrary, been considerably deepened. First of all, by indicating that each of the five learning fields 'requires the transversal and joint contribution of all disciplines',[25] the new Common Core makes transversal competences – and no longer disciplinary content knowledge –, the very principle of the teaching organisation. Secondly, by defining a competence as 'the ability to mobilise resources (knowledge, skills, attitudes) to accomplish a task or to cope with a complex or unprecedented situation',[26] the new Common Core gives a systematic and much wider place to soft skills, which are now present in all fields of education. For example, the student 'learns control and self-control', 'projects himself in time, anticipates and plans his tasks', 'learns to resolve conflicts without aggression', 'is able to show empathy and kindness', 'knows how to take initiatives, undertakes and implements projects, after having assessed the consequences of his action', 'implements observation, imagination, creativity, sense of aesthetics and quality' or 'takes his place in the group by being attentive to others in order to cooperate or confront each other in a regulated framework'.[27]

From the pedagogical point of view, competence-based education as defined by the 2015 Common Core thus appears to be a break with the pedagogical ideal of classical secondary education based on subject content knowledge. But if we take a closer look at the way it was implemented in the syllabuses of each discipline, this statement has to be qualified.

### The 2015 syllabuses: a consistent but unfinished translation

As in 2006, the compulsory school syllabuses were then rewritten to take into account the provisions of the Common Core. But this time, the syllabuses for the whole of compulsory schooling were rewritten at the same time under the authority of the High Council for Curriculum, were set up by a single decree[28] and were published in a single document. Moreover, the architecture of the syllabuses is common to all cycles and disciplines. In writing the document in this way, the Ministry wanted to ensure that all disciplines would integrate the principles of the new Common Core and ensure the continuity of education throughout compulsory schooling.

In practice, the syllabuses for each cycle are organised into three sections, the numbering of which reflects the new hierarchy of pedagogical standards. Section 1 outlines in two or three pages 'the specificities' of the cycle in question. Section 2 describes the 'essential contributions of the different learning field' to the five areas of the Common Core (it should be noted that the term discipline is not used). Finally, Section 3 describes in detail the content of the various courses. The structure of this third section is also common to all cycles and to all disciplines: after a short introduction, the 'competences' are specified, each of them being related to one of the fields of the Common Core. Then, the end-of-cycle learning objectives are presented, sometimes in the form of standards (for example 'To produce a continuous oral speech of five to ten minutes'[29]). Then, a chart presents the various 'associated knowledge and competences' along with the corresponding 'examples of situations, activities and resources for the student'.[30] Finally, 'benchmarks of progress'[31] are provided. So, as far the layout and the structure of the document is concerned, innovation is important: compared to prior syllabuses, these new ones distinguish themselves by their purpose to ensure coherence and homogenisation from one level or discipline to another.

The pedagogical logic of competences as defined in the previous section is thus much more integrated in all disciplines, but to varying degrees. While its integration is minimal in history and quite substantial in mathematics, sciences and foreign languages – where many academic skills and standards are defined but only a few soft skills or attitudes –, it is the most advanced in French and more specifically in what constitutes the heart of classical culture in France, i.e. the teaching of literature. The 2015 syllabuses indeed definitely break with the very way literary texts are viewed (Clément 2018). Genre- and history-based analytical approaches that structured previous syllabuses were pushed to the background. In fact, literature teaching is now structured into four entries that refer more to attitudes or soft skills than to literary issues: 'seeking oneself, building oneself', 'living in society, participating in society', 'looking at the world, inventing worlds', 'acting on the world'.[32] Thus, in the very logic of the Common Core and competence-based education, personal development seems to become the real purpose of literature teaching.

In the end, there is a now a kind continuum from disciplines that barely integrate competencies to those that are a hybrid of content and competencies to French, organised almost completely around competencies.

## Conclusion

The analysis of the introduction of the competence-based approach into compulsory schooling in France confirms the fundamentally polysemic nature of this notion. As far as France is concerned, this notion draws on different sources: progressive pedagogy and life-long learning on the one hand and, on the other hand, the new management theories which appeared in the 1980s in the private sector and then spread throughout the public sector. First translated into the Common Core, the notion of competence was also defended by those who advocated a return to basics: they saw the identification of basic knowledge and the development of evaluation as a means of combating the decline of pupils' achievements.

Given this polysemic nature, the notion of competence is characterised by its plasticity. Consequently, its reality and the concrete ways in which it is translated into the formal curriculum very strongly depend on the balance of power between the actors involved in the field of educational power. Thus, between 2002 and 2012, under a neo-liberal and conservative right-wing government, a managerial and utilitarian definition prevailed. In contrast, between 2012 and 2017, under a social democratic government, a pedagogical definition prevailed. In short, defining the concept of competences appears as a never-ending and decidedly political process.

My analysis also shows that the implementation of the notion of competence greatly varies from one discipline to another. Each discipline appropriates this notion not only according to the political context but also according to its pedagogical tradition. In that way, this disciplinary variation also underpins some of the hybridity observed in the implementation process.

Finally, I offer a nuanced response to the widely debated question of the influence of the recommendations of international organisations, in this case the European Union and the OECD. As far as France is concerned, some senior officials have made an opportunistic use of these recommendations – tactical borrowing – in order to impose the principle of the competence-based approach. However, once this principle was enshrined in the law, the recommendations of the EU and the OECD ceased to be expressly invoked – and thus were borrowed only silently (Waldow 2009).

## Notes

1. These databases can be accessed upon request.
2. Raymond Vatier (1921–2018) was an engineer in Renault car factories and an activist in Christian trade unions. He was in charge, at the beginning of the 1950s, of recruiting and setting up the training of Renault's young engineers. Appointed to the Ministry of National Education in 1970, he is a central figure of vocational training in France and one of the main intermediaries between this world and the school world.
3. All English translations are mine.
4. Circulaire relative au Renouveau du service public, *Journal officiel de la République française*, 24 February 1989.
5. Ibid.
6. Décret du 11 juillet 2006 relatif au socle commun de connaissances et de compétences
7. Décret du 14 mai 2007 relatif au livret personnel de compétences.
8. https://soclecommun2012.wordpress.com/about/.
9. ENSAE is a prestigious and very selective engineering school that trains its students in mathematics, statistics, economics, finance and, more recently, data sciences.

48     CONTEXTUALIZING GLOBAL FLOWS OF COMPETENCY-BASED EDUCATION

10. INSEE is the main public body responsible for producing statistics on the French economy and society.
11. Interview with Claude Thélot, Paris, 22 January 2007.
12. Interview with Jean-Louis Nembrini (special adviser of the Minister of National Education), Paris, 14 March 2007.
13. 'Le socle commun de connaissances et de compétences. Essai de synthèse', DESCO, 3 October 2005.
14. Interview with a member of the HCE, Paris, 28 March 2007.
15. Alain Bouvier, 'Le socle commun: pourquoi?' 20 September 2006, speech at the CRDP of Orléans-Tours (transcription from the conference recording).
16. Décret du 11 juillet 2006 relatif au socle commun de connaissances et de compétences.
17. Interview with Jean-Louis Nembrini.
18. *Bulletin officiel du ministère de l'Éducation nationale*, hors-série n° 6 (vol. 2), 19 April 2007, 11.
19. Ibid.
20. *Bulletin officiel spécial* n°06, 28 August 2008.
21. Open letter to the Minister of Education, 8 June 2012.
22. Décret du 31 mars 2015 relatif au socle commun de connaissances, de compétences et de culture.
23. Ibid.
24. Ibid.
25. Ibid.
26. Ibid.
27. Ibid.
28. Arrêté du 9 novembre 2015.
29. Ibid.
30. Ibid.
31. Ibid.
32. Ibid.

## Disclosure statement

No potential conflict of interest was reported by the author(s).

## References

Anderson-Levitt, Kathryn. 2017. "Global Flows of Competence-based Approaches in Primary and Secondary Education." *Cahiers de la recherche sur l'éducation et les savoirs* 16: 47–72.

Bezez, Philippe. 2009. *Réinventer l'État: Les réformes de l'administration française (1962–2008)*. Paris: Presses universitaires de France.

Bouchez, Alain, ed. 1994. *Livre blanc des collèges*. Paris: Ministère de l'Éducation nationale.

Bourdieu, Pierre. 2005. *The Social Structures of the Economy*. Cambridge: Polity Press.

Bourdieu, Pierre. 2014. *On the State. Lectures at the Collège de France 1989–1992*. Cambridge: Polity Press.

Boyer, Robert. 1998. "Hybridization and Models of Production: Geography, History, and Theory." In *Between Imitation and Innovation*, edited by Robert Boyer, Elsie Charron, Ulrich Jürgens, and Steven Tolliday, 23–56. Oxford: Oxford University Press.

Cannac, Yves, ed. 1985. *La bataille de la compétence*. Paris: Éditions Hommes et Techniques.

Chaty, Lionel. 1997. *L'administration face au management: Projets de service et centres de responsabilité dans l'administration française*. Paris: L'Harmattan.

Clément, Pierre. 2012. "Le socle commun: 'promesse démocratique' ou cheval de Troie d'une école néolibérale à deux vitesses?" *La pensée* 372: 23–35.

Clément, Pierre. 2013. "Réformer les programmes pour changer l'école? Une sociologie historique du champ du pouvoir scolaire." PhD diss., Université de Picardie.

Clément, Pierre. 2018. "Les programmes de français et l'enseignement de la littérature: ruptures et continuités depuis 1995." *Le français aujourd'hui* 202: 65–80.

Commission of the European Communities. 2005. *Proposal for a Recommendation of the European Parliament and of the Council on Key Competences for Lifelong Learning*. Brussels: Commission of the European Communities.

Crahay, Marcel. 2006. "Dangers, incertitudes et incomplétude de la logique de la compétence en éducation." *Revue française de pédagogie* 154: 97–110.

Dubar, Claude. 1996. "La sociologie du travail face à la qualification et à la compétence." *Sociologie du travail* 38 (2): 179–193.

Dubois, Vicent. 2015. "The Fields of Public Policy." In *Bourdieu's Theory of Social Fields*, edited by Mathieu Hilgers and Eric Mangez, 199–200. Abingdon: Routledge.

Durkheim, Emile. 1977. *The Evolution of Educational Thought*. London: Routledge.

Duval, Nathalie. 2009. *L'école des Roches*. Paris: Belin.

Ferry, Luc. 1995. "Qu'apprendre au collège ?" *Le débat* 87: 128–143.

George, Jacques, ed. 2002. *Manifeste pour un débat public sur l'école*. Paris: La Découverte.

Haut Conseil de l'Éducation. 2006. *Recommandations pour le socle commun*. Paris: Ministère de l'Education nationale.

Hirtt, Nico, and Gérard de Selys. 1998. *Tableau noir*. Bruxelles: EPO.

Hood, Christopher. 1995. "The 'New Public Management' in the 1980s: Variations on a Theme." *Accounting, Organizations and Society* 20 (2–3): 93–109.

Houssaye, Jean. 2014. *La pédagogie traditionnelle*. Paris: Fabert.

Jobert, Bruno. 1985. "Les *politiques sociales* et sanitaires." In *Traité de science politique*, edited by Jean Leca and Madeleine Grawitz, 301–342. Paris: PUF.

Laot, Françoise. 2000. "Le rapport à l'école en formation d'adultes dans les années 60. L'exemple du CUCES-INFA de Nancy." *Recherche et formation* 35: 195–208.

Laval, Christian, and Louis Weber. 2002. *Le nouvel ordre éducatif mondial*. Paris: Syllepse / Nouveaux regards.

Lightfoot, Michael. 2015. "Education Reform for the Knowledge Economy in the State of Sangon." *Compare: A Journal of Comparative and International Education* 45 (5): 705–726.

Morgan, Clara, and Riyad A. Shahjahan. 2014. "The Legitimation of OECD's Global Educational Governance: Examining PISA and AHELO Test Production." *Comparative Education* 50 (2): 192–205.

Palier, Bruno. 2008. "De l'ambiguïté en politique." In *Politiques publiques et démocratie*, edited by Olivier Giraud, 93–107. Paris: La Découverte.

Pons, Xavier. 2008. "L'évaluation des politiques éducatives et ses professionnels. Discours et méthodes (1958–2008)." PhD diss., Sciences-Po Paris.

Prost, Antoine. 2013. *Du changement dans l'école*. Paris: Le Seuil.

Ropé, Françoise, and Lucie Tanguy, eds. 1994. *Savoirs et compétences : De l'usage de ces notions dans l'école et l'entreprise*. Paris: L'Harmattan.

Rychen, Dominique, and Laura Salganik. 2000. "Definition and Selection of Key Competencies." In *Fourth General Assembly of the OECD Education Indicators Programme The INES Compendium Contributions from the INES Networks and Working Groups*, 61–73. Paris: OECD.

Searby, Peter. 1989. "The New School and the New Life: Cecil Reddie (1858-1932) and the Early Years of Abbotsholme School." *History of Education* 18 (1): 1–21.

Snyders, Georges. 1965. *La pédagogie en France aux XVIIe et XVIIIe siècles*. Paris: PUF.

Stroobants, Marcelle. 1993. *Savoir-faire et compétences au travail : Une sociologie de la fabrication des aptitudes*. Bruxelles: Éditions de l'université de Bruxelles.

Takayama, Keita. 2013. "OECD, 'Key Competencies' and the New Challenges of Educational Inequality." *Journal of Curriculum Studies* 45 (1): 67–80.

Tanguy, Lucie. 2001. "Les promoteurs de la formation en entreprise (1945–1971)." *Travail et Emploi* 86: 27–47.

Thélot, Claude. 2002. "Évaluer l'École." *Études* 397: 323–334.

Waldow, Florian. 2009. "Undeclared Imports: Silent Borrowing in Educational Policy-making and Research in Sweden." *Comparative Education* 45: 477–494.

Zarifian, Philippe. 2001. *Le modèle de la compétence: Trajectoire historique, enjeux actuels et propositions*. Paris: Liaisons.

# Knowledge for the elites, competencies for the masses: political theatre of educational reforms in the Russian Federation

Elena Aydarova

**ABSTRACT**
International organisations facilitated the spread of competency-based reforms around the world. Accepting at face value correlations between students' performance on international assessments, such as PISA, and nations' economic development, reformers in different countries began to adopt competency-based standards to improve the quality of education. Hybridising competency discourses circulated by international organisations, Russian reformers introduced new school standards that created a bifurcation of the educational system along the lines of socioeconomic, cultural, and linguistic diversity. This bifurcation is evident in the standards' focus on providing in-depth disciplinary knowledge to students from privileged backgrounds and competencies 'to adapt to the world' to students from underserved groups. The significance of this analysis lies in demonstrating how appropriations and hybridisations of competency discourses in the Russian Federation work to produce elites that govern and workers who accept low positions in social hierarchies of the neoliberal world order.

A global neoliberal imaginary that discursively links educational change with economic development has facilitated the spread of competency-based reforms around the world (Anderson-Levitt 2017; Rizvi and Lingard 2009). Circulating tenets of human capital theory in parallel with their policy advocacy work, international organisations have urged states to adopt competency-based educational approaches to ensure competitiveness of national economies (Spreen 2004; Spring 2015a). As a tool of global neoliberal governance (Grek 2009, 2013), the OECD's international assessment PISA has cemented this focus on competencies by using league tables to compare the performance of students from different countries and by making causal claims about students' competency development and nations' potential for economic advancement (Gorur 2016; Takayama 2008; Spring 2015b). Introduction of competency-based approaches in some cases resulted in curricular convergence (Nordin and Sundberg 2016). In others, it led to the emergence of competing interpretations of what constitutes competencies and how they can be assessed (Pepper 2011). In Spain, the introduction of new models allowed teachers to design integrated curricula (Tiana, Moya, and Luengo 2011), while in Poland competency-based approaches afforded educators opportunities to explore new ways of helping students construct knowledge (Dąbrowski and Wiśniewski 2011).

Yet the pursuit of competency-based education has obscured the processes of bifurcation of educational systems along the lines of privilege and advantage within national and subnational spaces. For example, Takayama (2013) examined how the introduction of competency-based curriculum in Japan facilitated the spread of unequal structures in which students from underserved backgrounds became short-changed by new educational approaches. Drawing on the analysis of vocational education in Australia, Wheelahan (2012) argued that competency-based approaches preclude the development of theoretical knowledge among those whose education becomes focused on job training. According to Wheelahan (2012), this bifurcation leads to divergent outcomes among different social groups because advanced tracks provide access to theoretical knowledge where students not only gain deeper insights into social structures, but also develop tools of critique and action to demand change in those structures.

Drawing on the findings from a multi-sited ethnography of educational reforms in the Russian Federation, I trace how globally-circulated competency discourses entered the space of Russian policy-making and became the foundation for the new school standards. My analysis shows that Russian reformers produced a hybridisation of competencies that justified the creation of a bifurcated system – a significant departure from the equity-oriented system of education inherited from the Soviet past. A knowledge paradigm was made available to students from privileged backgrounds to produce elites to govern, whereas a competency paradigm was offered to the rest of students to obscure socialisation that would turn them into spectators of intensifying social inequality. This move not only justified limited educational provisions for students from lower socioeconomic backgrounds, but also perpetuated the status quo of the unjust neoliberal state.

In what follows, I describe how Marcuse's (1964) and Lyotard's (1984) writing on knowledge in postmodern societies as well as Debord's (1994, 1998) explication of political spectacle shed light on competency-driven transformations in education. Then I present the methodological approaches used in this study as well as analytical strategies applied to the data analysis. The presentation of findings proceeds along three steps. First, I situate the transformations documented in this paper in the global flow of competency-based educational reforms and in the particulars of the Russian educational context. Next, I demonstrate how Russian policy actors appropriated competency-based discourses in the production of new school standards and how those appropriations aligned with a nationally circulated philosophy of a systems-based activity approach developed by Georgiy Shchedrovitsky. Finally, I show how the design of a bifurcated school system emerged from the fusion between competency discourses and Shchedrovitsky's vision for elite rule.

## Theoretical framework

This paper draws on Marcuse's (1964) and Lyotard's (1984) theories of knowledge in postmodern societies and Debord's (1994) theory of spectacle in order to analyse how the dichotomy between knowledge and competencies serves to justify social inequalities and produce acquiescent subjects prepared to accept low positions in unequal systems. Focusing on technological advances in postmodern societies, Marcuse (1964) argued that advanced industrial states engage in producing one-dimensional subjects who accept technocratic social structures and participate in maintaining the existing social order. According to Marcuse (1964), this is accomplished by the use of reduced concepts that foreclose the possibility of attaining understandings of social systems and structures. Basic knowledge that does not attend to the analysis of social processes, relationships, or structures precludes the emergence of critical theoretical understandings (Marcuse 1964). As a result, one-dimensional subjects participate in the reproduction of the existing social order partly because of their limited understanding of historical processes that would allow them to see humans as active agents engaged in transforming the world around them. Instead, through educational systems, entertainment outlets, and depoliticisation of public discourses, these subjects are trained to shun critique in order to adapt to the world as an unchanging structure.

Building on these observations, Lyotard (1984) argued that the commodification of knowledge occurs in parallel with the intensifying struggle to control knowledge as a form of power. In postmodern societies, distinctions emerge in this struggle between those who know for investment and those who know for survival (Lyotard 1984, 6). Redefining social bonds as language games, Lyotard noted how elites obscure this bifurcation and protect their positions in social hierarchies by presenting knowledge as outdated. Lyotard's theory sheds additional light on globally-circulated distinctions between knowledge as an obsolete form insufficient for the ongoing economic transformations and competency as the form that will produce actors able to participate in the global knowledge economy. His writing shows how these distinctions arise concurrently with the rise of a technocratic class that prescribes the parameters of human becoming and eliminates dissent towards its ideas through 'the exercise of terror [which] says: "Adapt your aspirations to our ends – or else"' (Lyotard 1984, 64).

Debord (1994), on the other hand, described new social bonds as a form of spectacle that reproduces itself through distraction, alienation, and isolation. Operating as political theatre (Aydarova 2019), reforms obscure how education becomes reoriented to reproduce inequality. In this context, educational systems are redesigned to produce spectators who are 'supposed to know nothing and deserve nothing. Those who are always watching to see what happens next will never act: such must be the spectator's condition' (Debord 1998, 22). What is important about Debord's observation is that in the end, the shift from the knowledge paradigm to competence-based reforms creates subjects who accept inequality and injustice as a given, thus subjecting themselves to low positions in social hierarchies.

## Methodology

This paper is based on a critical multi-sited ethnography (Marcus 1995; Quantz and O'Connor 1988) conducted in the Russian Federation between May 2011 and December 2015. The study examined a recent wave of neoliberal reforms introduced in the Russian Federation, such as the *New Federal Standards for General School* (Ministry of Education of the Russian Federation 2011, 2012), *Teachers' Professional Standard* (Ministry of Labour of the Russian Federation 2013), and the *Concept of Support for the Development of Pedagogical Education* (Ministry of Education of the Russian Federation 2014). Ethnographic fieldwork incorporated a variety of sites, including a policy-making hub in Lyutvino.[1] Across sites and events, I kept detailed narrative notes of observations, conversations, and experiences (Emerson, Fretz, and Shaw 2011) as I participated in classes, meetings, and presentations. In addition to participant observation, I conducted 80 open-ended semi-structured interviews in Russian with a variety of policy actors: policy-makers, officials from the Ministry of Education (MOE) as well as from international organisations, administrators, teacher educators, and educational researchers in the Russian Federation. In addition to interviews, I assembled reports produced by international organisations, Russian policy texts, academic and mass media publications, as well as videos of interviews and events related to the introduction of reforms. Data was analysed using thematic coding and critical discourse analysis (Fairclough 2003).

Ethnographic engagement with reform processes allowed me to identify a network of reformers and experts who – even though not formally affiliated with the Ministry of Education – played an important role in shaping new waves of Russian educational policies. These policy actors were, for the most part, academics and educational researchers incorporated into global policy networks through their positions as consultants, experts, or analysts for international organisations. They participated in several projects of reforming Russian education – from per-pupil funding to the introduction of the Unified State Exam, from the design of new school and professional teachers' standards to the restructuring of higher education. Through their global connections, reformers introduced competency discourses into national reforms (Figure 1) and garnered resources for reorienting the educational system based on their designs.

## Findings

### *International discourses and national transformations*

Debates about the directions of education reforms in Russia started before the collapse of the Soviet Union in 1991 with the emphasis placed on humanising education and reorienting schools towards serving students' needs, rather than the needs of the state (Dneprov 2006). After 1991, international organisations such as OECD and the World Bank conducted evaluations of the Russian education system and argued that it had to be reformed to make it more market-based and outcome-oriented (Aydarova 2015). This focus on outcomes – rather than inputs and processes traditionally in place –

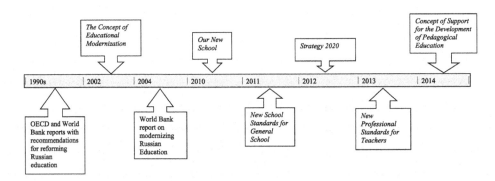

**Figure 1.** Timeline of Russian Educational Reforms.

emphasised the need for the educational system to transition to competencies that students would acquire by going through the P-16 system (OECD 1998, 1999). In 2002, the Government of the Russian Federation laid out a vision for transforming the educational system in a policy paper, *The Concept of Educational Modernization* (Government of the Russian Federation 2010), that redefined the role of the state in educational provision – from provider to overseer – and reoriented the educational system towards a production of neoliberal subjects (Aydarova 2014). This reorientation reflected a hybridisation of the previously utilised approach of 'knowledge, skills, and abilities' (commonly known under the Russian abbreviation 'ZUN') and new competency frameworks:

> General school should form a holistic system of universal knowledge, skills, and abilities as well as students' independent activity and personal responsibility – or the key competencies that determine the quality of modern education. (MOE 2002)

In the report prepared by reformers and experts in their circles, the World Bank (2004) lauded the Russian government's efforts to modernise the educational system, noting the importance of competency-based education for responding to the challenges of 'information societies' and 'knowledge economies'. Using other countries' competency-based standards for K-12 education as a model for the Russian system, the World Bank urged the Ministry of Education to revise general school standards in Russia in order to move education away from knowledge transmission:

> In Russian philosophy of school education, the most important role is played by multidimensional (encyclopaedic) information, whereas most developed countries emphasize the acquisition of skills and the development of applied thinking. This is one of the reasons why Russian students continue to show a high level of theoretical knowledge and a developed ability to solve typical problems, but are often less prepared to apply theoretical knowledge to solve nonstandard problems in real life. (Author's translation, World Bank 2004, 14)

Without explicitly stating it in the text, the authors of the report brought Russian students' performance on international assessments to bear on the decisions about the direction for reform. Russian students performed relatively well in The Trends in International Mathematics and Science Study (TIMSS, referenced in this quote by 'developed ability to solve typical problems'), but at or below OECD average on the Programme for International Student Assessment (PISA, 'less prepared to apply theoretical knowledge'). Debates in reformers' circles and their media appearances emphasised the crisis of the Russian school system that PISA revealed as opposed to a more positive reflection of Russian schools revealed by TIMSS (Aydarova 2019). PISA's alleged ability to test what was needed for the twenty-first century and predict the nation's capacity for economic development based on the quality of its human capital were also used to underscore its value for the Russian context. Reformers and experts in their networks provided translations of the World Bank (2006) reports on the role of competencies in the production of human capital and published analyses of Russian students' performance on international assessments as quality indicators of that human capital (Logos 2004, 2005).

Despite the overall apathy towards international assessments in Russia, reformers and other actors in their networks used Russian students' performance on PISA to reorient the educational system towards 'international standards' (Aydarova 2019, 161). This reorientation towards 'international standards' reflected the pursuit of national economic development laid out in *Strategy 2020*, a set of policy recommendations developed by reformers and experts in their networks that included reforms in financial, social, labour, and educational sectors. Arguing that abandoning the Soviet educational legacy was necessary in order for Russia 'to catch up with the rest of the world' and participate in the global knowledge economy, reformers advocated for a shift in the educational paradigm from knowledge to competency-based approaches (Strategy 2020). With partial funding from the World Bank (Startsev 2012), this shift was introduced through new school standards.

### New school standards: the contents of education

Throughout the 2000s, debates had raged about competencies that should serve as the foundation for school education. Some of the experts in reformers' networks, connected to the World Bank through national agencies that administered the Bank's loans, drew on competency frameworks developed by the Council of Europe, Great Britain, and several Russian regions (VO 2007). Using the World Bank's (2003) reports translated into Russian (World Bank 2006), which in turn replicated the OECD's (2005) *Key Competencies*, these experts called for the use of the key competencies – informational, social, and problem-solving competencies. Reminding their readers that 'educational standards are the model of tomorrow's society' (29), the experts pointed out that competency frameworks proposed in their work did not emerge out of research in education and pedagogy, but were rather a result of 'a clearly articulated demand directed towards the system of education from the outside' (VO 2007, 34). These observations echoed the World Bank report translated into Russian in 2006 that discussed the need to reform education because the corporate sector spends too much money on retraining its workforce.

The group that received the assignment to develop the standards was headed by a close ally of President Putin (Becker and Myers 2014) and the CEO of one of the largest educational publishing houses in Russia *Prosveshchenie* – – Aleksandr Kondakov. Kondakov was also a member of the working group that prepared the World Bank (2004) report that called for the modernisation of Russian education based on the competency paradigm (discussed in the previous section). Echoing the competencies laid out in the OECD DeSeCo (2005) and World Bank (2003) frameworks, the standards were oriented towards problem-solving, information-processing, and social skills. Some competencies discussed in the DeSeCo text found their way into Russian standards in a more or less recognisable form (Table 1). For example, 'the ability to form and conduct life plans' (OECD 2005, 15) appeared in the Russian standards as 'the ability to set goals and create life plans' (MOE 2012, 4). Other skills, however, mutated on the way into the Russian text. The ability 'to assert rights, interests, limits and needs' and 'defend them actively' (OECD 2005, 15) turned into mere 'awareness of rights' and 'respect for law and order' (MOE 2012, 4–5).

Apart from stylistic and semantic transformations, however, there was a difference in how different skills and abilities were grouped together into personal, meta-subject, and subject competencies in the Russian standards (Asmolov 2009; MOE 2011, 2012). Personal competencies incorporated character traits that graduates should display, such as patriotism or 'love for the Motherland' (MOE 2012, 3). Meta-subject competencies represented interdisciplinary skills that could be applied across different contexts, such as the ability to communicate or work in teams. Subject competencies were associated with school disciplines, such as Russian language or math. As one of the standards'

**Table 1.** Competency Framework Used in Russian Federal Standards (MOE 2012, 4).

| Competency Cluster | Competencies |
| --- | --- |
| Personal Competencies | • Readiness and ability for self-development and self-determination<br>• Motivation for learning and goal-oriented learning activity<br>• Systems of relevant social and interpersonal relationships<br>• Systems of value and meaning that reflect personal and civic positions in activity<br>• Awareness of law<br>• Ecological culture<br>• Ability to set goals and create life plans<br>• Ability to acknowledge Russian civic identity in a multicultural society |
| Meta-subject Competencies | • Universal learning activities (regulatory, learning, communicative)<br>• Ability to use universal learning activities in learning and social practices<br>• Independence in planning and carrying out learning activity and organisation of learning collaboration with teachers and peers<br>• Ability to create individual learning plans<br>• Research, project, and social activity skills |
| Subject Competencies | • Skills and abilities specific for different disciplines |

developers explained, this parsing of competencies reflected the advances of the systems activity theory developed by Russian psychologists Vygotsky, Elkonin, and Davydov (Asmolov 2009).

Of these three competency clusters, it was the personal competencies that operated as the core driver of the reform. In a video interview, Kondakov explained that 'the new purposes of school education that are stated in the standard are upbringing, social-pedagogical support, [as well as] the development of a Russian citizen with high morals, responsibility, creativity, and initiative' (Agranovich 2009, n. p.). In the school standards, this emphasis on 'the development of personal qualities' was reflected in the 'portrait of a graduate' that identified the outcomes schools are expected to produce – 'a person who loves his/her Motherland', 'accepts traditional family values', 'follows a healthy lifestyle', and 'is creative', among other abilities (MOE 2012, 3-4; for more see Aydarova 2019). Even among the experts involved in the design of the standards, however, there was shared scepticism about schools' ability to create personal qualities. As one reformer explained to me during an interview, for many years all school children in Russia had been learning about integrity by reading a story about a boy who stole a plum, but 'people around the country continue to steal' (Interview # 56, March 2014).

What was decidedly missing from this portrait of the graduate is any reference to knowledge. During public seminars and policy debates, reformers discussed how overburdened Russian students were by school subjects full of factual knowledge. As one of the standards co-authors explained, 'Today's children do not need concrete knowledge! They have long departed for a different reality, in which each person can use a search engine by him/herself' (VOA 2019). This sentiment echoed what reformers often discussed in their circles – in the information age, knowledge becomes obsolete very quickly, so children do not need knowledge because they can find information online. Instead of receiving knowledge, children should be provided socialisation and learn to solve problems in life (VO 2005).

Yet despite its ubiquitous presence, this focus on socialisation was not applied to all K-12 students in equal measure. Kondakov in his public interviews explained that based on sociological studies conducted in Russia neither families, nor businesses, nor the state cared about subject knowledge (Kondakov 2018). Instead, they wanted to see people with good upbringing or socialisation. In response to these demands, the team that developed the standards proposed to leave only a limited number of mandatory subjects (Russian language, math, physical education, Russia in the world, and safety of life) and introduce the competency-based paradigm of education. At the same time, Kondakov (2012) explained that children who were planning to receive higher education needed to know significantly more to be better equipped for further professional preparation. To meet their needs, the standards incorporated differentiation and advanced tracks (Rus. *profil'noe obrazovanie*), so that students could choose the subjects they could study in-depth (Kondakov 2012).

A more stark explanation of this differentiation emerged from an interview that I conducted with one of the reformers where the shift in educational paradigms was explained in the following way:

> From working with Shchedrovitsky and Davydov, I discovered that the masses do not need to learn how to calculate the derivative of a complex function. But everyone should learn how to think logically. And how to build mathematical models. Some can build simple ones, others more complex ones. So, the focus here is not to study a subject but to use it for development.

When I inquired whether there was consensus on what type of person should emerge as a result of this development, he scoffed in response:

> That would never happen, neither here, nor in the U.S., nor in any country of the world. For a very simple reason – the society is heterogeneous. Different social strata hold different conceptions of how things ought to be. Of course, there will always be parents who will say, 'You have to guarantee that my child can enter a university'. For them, the knowledge paradigm will remain the leading paradigm. But there will also be parents who will say, 'Listen, do whatever you want with my child, just don't bother me. Don't burden me with my child's problems'. There are parents that are beginning to talk about socialisation. Due to internet, due to drugs, due to other asocial patterns of behavior. So, children from a drunk part of town don't need advanced mathematics and the knowledge of algebraic functions. The teacher should use math to develop them as people. (Interview # 55, February 2014)

This explanation showed that the principle of differentiation was based on the family's social background. Well-off parents who seek to maintain their privileged position will demand that their children will receive the knowledge necessary for entering and succeeding in higher education. As the reformer explained, for those parents the knowledge paradigm will remain in place. But for children from less privileged positions, the focus of school education would be competencies or, more specifically, socialisation to minimise the effects of negative social influences.

This differentiation became even more evident in the text of the standard where subject competencies were divided into basic and advanced levels. Basic level competencies would be sufficient for daily functioning in the society, whereas the advanced level competencies were set at the level that allowed students to pursue 'subsequent professional preparation' (MOE 2012, 6), or more specifically, admission to higher education institutions. For example, the basic level for history standards focused on facts and dates, whereas the advanced level was supposed to allow students an opportunity to explore how knowledge is produced in history as a discipline and how various facts can have different interpretations depending on the observer's social position (Figure 2).

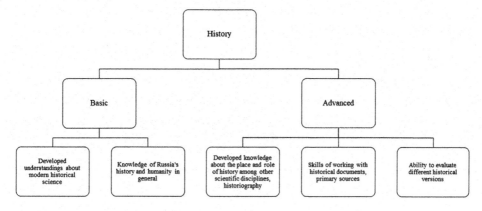

**Figure 2.** Subject Competences – History.

Different tracks, however, afforded students not only different opportunities for their future careers, but also different positioning in the world (Marcuse 1964). Those who receive instruction at the basic level would be presented with the knowledge of history as a completed act and the world around them as a given. Seen through the lens of Debord's (1994) and Marcuse's (1964) theories, this type of knowledge is more likely to produce spectators or docile subjects willing to maintain the status quo. Learning disconnected facts at the basic level teaches students to 'adapt to the world' around them, so that they would accept their position in a social hierarchy. Those who pursue an advanced track could learn about history as a form of struggle with multiple interpretations of processes and events, which would position them as actors who see their own ability to steer social processes and pursue social transformation. Yet because this track would only be accessible to a limited number of school children, only students from more privileged backgrounds would be likely to see themselves as creators of the world.

Even though publicly this differentiation was presented as a matter of individuals' preference for a future professional path, its justification was rooted in a redesign of the social contract between the state, families, and other stakeholders. In a background paper for the standards (Kondakov and Kuznetsov 2008), the authors explained that the new contract emerges from recognising that growing social inequality makes it impossible for the state to provide education of high quality to different social groups. Even though all families might want to receive the maximum from the educational system, they should recognise existing limitations, such as students' motivation levels and 'material and technical, curricular, and staff resources of schools' (11). Therefore, the standards set the framework for a differentiated provision: the minimal provision encapsulated in the basic level of education as the 'agreed-on minimum sufficient for functioning in the society' and the provision of advanced tracks for those who had the means to take advantage of more opportunities ahead. Criticising the Soviet legacy of equality as the underlying principle of educational provision, Kondakov in media interviews explained that education should not be just a public good the way it had been constructed in Russia during the Soviet era, but also a private good. This way 'each family can receive what they want based on their demands, needs, and resources' (Kondakov 2011). This coded language captured the justification for a bifurcated system that delivered different educational goods to students from different socioeconomic backgrounds.

This bifurcation of expectations for different groups of students fit in the overall framework of new designs that reformers and experts pursued. For example, *Our New School* (Government of the Russian Federation 2010), issued as a declaration of reform principles for the educational system encapsulated in the new standards, emphasised the need to have an educational system where students could choose to pursue different educational tracks based on their future plans. *Strategy 2020* that encompassed reform proposals across different sectors followed a similar move in its discussion of what new school education should be like. Reformers who designed that proposal offered two scenarios for the development of the educational system. The restoration scenario consisted of rejecting advanced level as a separate track of education and keeping a 'unified' knowledge base for all school children. Referring to the Soviet model of education that sought to provide equitable access to knowledge and opportunity to all children regardless of their social standing or ethnic background, reformers rejected that model as unsuitable for the twenty-first century. Instead, they emphasised the importance of pursuing the modernisation scenario that moved towards offering different levels of education, with advanced tracks for those who planned to pursue higher education and basic level of education for everyone else. In projections of which scenario would serve the Russian economy best and afford it greater competitiveness in the global economy, reformers emphasised the advantages of modernisation and a bifurcated system offering separate educational tracks to children from different social classes.

### New school standards: educational approaches

The standards' radical departure from the past appeared not only in the shift towards competencies, but also in the introduction of systems activity theory as the main educational approach. As Kondakov explained in his interviews, 'Systems activity approach is a means of producing desired competencies in students, of teaching them how to be successful' (Kondakov 2018). The two approaches on some level were seen as synonymous to each other. As one of the reformers explained to me during an interview:

> Competency-based approaches used to be a fad, precisely just a fad. Technically, there isn't much of a difference [between activity-based and competency-based approaches]. See, Russians don't like to build a model based on common sense. They need to use some weird foreign words and then fight for three years about those three words. So, let it be activity-based, learning through activity. I would add that learning should be oriented towards a result, but then it becomes a competency-based approach, but it had been talked into oblivion and lost its credibility among those who make final decisions about policies. (Interview # 48, February 2014)

As I noted before, systems activity theory was developed by Soviet psychologists, such as Vygotsky, Elkonin, Davydov, and others. Those scholars sought to create a system of learning that would allow students to develop conceptual understandings through the process of discovery (Zuckerman 2014). Based on this approach, a teacher uses dialogue to lead his or her class through a set of tasks that would help students develop their own hypotheses and test them until they reach their own conclusions. While in theory it sounded revolutionary from the perspective of potentially empowering students to take control of their learning, reformers translated this approach into instructions for a teacher to 'know what is developing in your student and support it with the tools of the subject you are teaching' (Interview # 55, February 2014).

This translation was inspired by the work of the Soviet-era philosopher and psychologist Georgiy Shchedrovitsky who had enormous influence on the reformers as many of them and experts in their networks belonged to the circle of Shchedrovitsky's followers. Shchedrovitsky was a strong supporter of radical constructivism, or the ability to change, mould, and design human beings for the needs of state, society, or corporation (Kukulin 2011). In *Logic and Pedagogy* (Shchedrovitsky 1993), which one of the reformers described as a foundational text that shaped reformers' approaches, Shchedrovitsky employed the language of engineering to design formulas for blueprinting human beings of the future with technological precision. He explained that it was necessary to identify the functions different children would perform in the future and use pedagogy as an engineering tool that moulds these children for those functions. Kukulin (2011) discussed Shchedrovitsky's ideas as an 'alternative social blueprinting ... for a transformed human nature' (54). Fundamentally, this meant that students became 'objects' for pedagogical action intended to 'design people' (Shchedrovitsky 1993, n. p.) for social and professional roles, instead of allowing children to pursue their own open-ended becoming. Apart from pursuing a technocratic order, this technological precision was meant to achieve efficiency: since not all children are capable of learning advanced concepts, resources should not be wasted on teaching them those concepts. Instead, the focus should be on basic preparation for life in the society and functioning in the workplace. Thus, calls for teachers to use students' problems as a starting point for instruction was, on the one hand, the acknowledgement of students' varying abilities and, on the other, a step towards determining students' future destinations in the social structure.

Students' future destinations reflected their positions in social hierarchies. Departing from the Soviet pursuit of equality and equity, Shchedrovitsky believed that it was necessary to create an elite class endowed with intellectual resources to govern while the rest of the population would be subjected to the elite rule (e.g. Kakovkin 2004). In a video explanation of the new educational paradigm pursued by the new school standards, Kondakov echoed this position using PISA results:

> We have to understand the risks. PISA shows that Russia falls behind developed nations based on the level of functional literacy and the number of representatives of the elite class who have a high level of preparation ... Unfortunately, we have to acknowledge in Russia, children who belong to this category comprise only 1.4% whereas in European countries – 14%. PISA results show low competitiveness of Russian schools, which means that Russian society and state are also not competitive. (Kondakov, Video Interview, 2011)

In other words, according to Kondakov, PISA revealed that Russia lacked the ability to educate the elite. The standards were designed to address this problem by creating a bifurcated system with deeper disciplinary training for the future elite and socialisation for the rest. Kondakov (2011) went on to explain that this represented 'a model of progressive development based on the best international experience'.

Problems with competency-based education and its fusion with nationally developed systems activity approaches went beyond theoretical underpinnings and agendas of creating a national elite at the expense of the rest of the population. There were also problems with how this approach played out in practice. As reformers and educators shared with me, systems activity approaches presented in the standards were not widespread in Russia. Experts estimated that at the height of their success, schools employing these approaches amounted to only about 7% of all public institutions. At the time of my fieldwork, less than 1% of schools in the country continued to adhere to the principles of developmental education because there were not enough educators who knew how to enact this pedagogy (Interview # 49, February 2014). The activity-based approach also tended to thrive in 'boutique schools' where principals had a strong vision and preparation to implement this approach, but there were challenges in replicating these models in regular public schools. Teachers and schools that implemented activity-based approaches faced opposition from parents who were not familiar with different notation systems or models deployed by this method.

More importantly, however, systems activity theory resulted in the reproduction of inequality. During my interview with a researcher from the Lyutvino Centre for Innovation in Education, I learned that this approach did not serve all children equally well (Interview # 60, March 2014). The research that the centre conducted – despite their overall support for this approach – showed that only children from well-off families were thriving in activity-based classrooms where learning was based on the principles of guided discovery. Children from underserved backgrounds, on the other hand, were only falling further behind. This research, however, was not published for the fear of repercussions from those who held power in policymaking circles.

The Centre's findings did corroborate what was documented (and in some situations censored out) by researchers in other contexts – activity-based approaches can hinder learning for students from working class communities, immigrant families, or racially minoritized groups. This happens, in part, because the process of discovery requires an extensive use of academic language. Students who come from backgrounds where a more restricted code is more common struggle with the elaborated code used in schools and fall behind when the mastery of the latter is required to engage in dialogue and (self)guided discovery (Bernstein 2000; Heath 1983; Theule Lubienski 2000). Thus, the creation of a bifurcated system emerged not only as a project of Shchedrovitsky's followers who sought to create a national elite through educational reforms, but also as an unintended consequence of educational approaches that favoured those students who already brought extensive symbolic resources to school. If widely implemented, the use of activity-based approaches would contribute to the production of elite in ways that re-inscribe existing social hierarchies and reproduce unequal structures, reducing the possibility of social mobility for those who come from underserved backgrounds.

## Conclusion

My analysis of the introduction of competency-based approaches into the Russian system shows that the promise of increased educational quality disguised the attempts to create a two-tiered educational system that would place students from diverse socioeconomic, ethnic, and linguistic backgrounds into separate dead-end tracks. Based on new standards, children from underserved backgrounds were supposed to receive primarily socialisation – or the basic level of competencies that, according to Lyotard (1984), would constitute knowledge for survival. The shift towards developing students' individual qualities rather than providing them with expansive theoretical knowledge similar to the changes in France (Clément, this volume) prevents most students from learning tools of social analysis and critique. For families who wanted and had the means for their children to receive higher education, however, there would always be options to get advanced preparation in key disciplines. These groups from more privileged backgrounds could count on having access to knowledge for investment – investment in one's individual advancement as well as investment into one's ability to become a part of the consolidated power structure.

Ironically, activity-based theory, developed primarily during the Soviet era, became a tool to remove the legacy of Soviet approaches to education. New school standards in conjunction with other reforms that emerged in Russia in the 2010s negated commitments to equity and justice of the Soviet school system that had provided all students with access to intellectually demanding curriculum and had made available pathways to higher education to students from underserved groups (Zajda 2010). This departure from the Soviet legacy, however, fuelled some of the opposition to the reforms, which to this day remain a matter of tremendous controversy and conflict.

The denunciation of the Soviet legacy came hand-in-hand with mobilising activity-based approaches for the purpose of neoliberal social engineering (Anderson 2005). International organisations and policy-entrepreneurs promoted scripts according to which students should develop certain competencies to participate in the global economy (Aydarova 2019; Rizvi and Lingard 2009). Those scripts overlapped with Shchedrovitsky's argument that the society had to blueprint future generations based on the functions they would fulfil in the society. This match between a transnational script and nationally cultivated theories produced traction for reform. As a result, globally circulated competency discourses became appropriated to facilitate Russia's inclusion in the global neoliberal order.

The introduction of new K-12 standards within the context of other policies reformers promoted also reoriented the educational system towards serving businesses and corporations. Reformers and experts often discussed the need for change through the lens of corporate demand for a new type of workforce (Aydarova 2019). The new school envisioned by these changes also became framed as a corporation. In a meeting with representatives of the educational community that addressed proposals put forward in *Strategy 2020*, President Medvedev discussed the culture of educational institutions through the lens of corporate allegiances:

> Any person who enters an educational establishment whether it is a schoolchild even young ones or a university student ... should understand that s/he takes on corporate responsibilities. They should sense their allegiance to the corporation, if you do not live up to the status or title of this corporation, there should be sanctions ... Allegiance to a corporation is a very important thing and that's why behavior code should be accepted by everyone and should be used as a discipline tool. (*Soveshchaniye* 2012)

This statement echoed reformers' perspectives that new standards and educational reforms that accompanied them would become a tool for producing subjects that need competencies and adequate socialisation to become compliant workers desired by international businesses and corporations.

This article raises questions not only about the changes in educational systems but also about the future that is being constructed through these transformations. As Debord (1994, 1998) noted, spectators will never act and are therefore less likely to fight against injustice. Turning educational systems towards the production of compliant workers, spectators, and docile subjects paves the way for the type of social control and social inequality that benefits those already in power in the global neoliberal order. This analysis, however, presents an opportunity for comparative and international education to intervene in the hybridisations of global discourses. More research is needed to support the grassroots struggles against the production of spectators and the normalisation of inequality.

## Note

1. All geographic names used in the paper are pseudonyms. To protect participants' anonymity, I also do not use full citations for the data sources that could reveal their identities and do not include those sources in the reference list.

## Disclosure statement

No potential conflict of interest was reported by the author(s).

## ORCID

*Elena Aydarova* http://orcid.org/0000-0002-0387-2889

## References

Agranovich, Maria. 2009. "Uchitel' Vmesto Urokodatelya: S 1 yanvarya v Rossii Vstupayut Novye Standarty." *Rossiyaskaya Gazeta*, October 8.

Anderson, Gary L. 2005. "Performing School Reform in the Age of the Political Spectacle." In *Performance Theories in Education: Power, Pedagogy, and the Politics of Identity*, edited by Bryant K. Alexander, Gary L. Anderson, and Bernardo P. Gallegos, 199–220. Mahwah: Lawrence Erlbaum Associates.

Anderson-Levitt, Kathryn. 2017. "Global Flows of Competence-Based Approaches in Primary and Secondary Education." *Cahiers de la Recherche sur L'Éducation et les Savoirs* 16: 47–72.

Asmolov, Alexander. 2009. "Sistemno-deyatel'nostnyj Podkhod k Razrabotke Standartov Novogo Pokoleniya." *Pedagogika* 4: 18–28.

Aydarova, Olena. 2014. "Universal Principles Transform National Priorities: Bologna Process and Russian Teacher Education." *Teaching and Teacher Education* 37: 64–75. doi:10.1016/j.tate.2013.10.001.

Aydarova, Olena. 2015. "Glories of the Soviet Past or Dim Visions of the Future: Russian Teacher Education as the Site of Historical Becoming." *Anthropology & Education Quarterly* 46 (2): 147–166. doi:10.1111/aeq.12096.

Aydarova, Elena. 2019. *Teacher Education Reforms as Political Theater: Russian Policy Dramas*. Albany: SUNY Press.

Becker, Jo, and Steven L. Myers. 2014. "Putin's Way: Putin's Friend Profits in Purge of Schoolbooks." *The New York Times*, November 1. https://www.nytimes.com/2014/11/02/world/europe/putins-friend-profits-in-purge-of-schoolbooks.html.

Bernstein, Basil. 2000. *Pedagogy, Symbolic Control, and Identity: Theory, Research, Critique*. Lanham: Rowman & Littlefield.

Dąbrowski, Mirosław, and Jerzy Wiśniewski. 2011. "Translating Key Competences Into the School Curriculum: Lessons from the Polish Experience." *European Journal of Education* 46 (3): 323–334. doi:10.1111/j.1465-3435.2011.01483.x.

Debord, Guy. 1994. *The Society of the Spectacle*. New York: Zone Books.

Debord, Guy. 1998. *Notes on "The Society of the Spectacle."* New York: Verso.

Dneprov, Eduard. 2006. *Obrazovanie i Politika: Noveyshaya Politicheskaya Istoriya Rossiyskogo Obrazovaniya*. Moscow: Geo-Tech.

Emerson, Robert M., Rachel I. Fretz, and Linda L. Shaw. 2011. *Writing Ethnographic Fieldnotes*. 2nd ed. Chicago: University of Chicago Press.

Fairclough, Norman. 2003. *Analysing Discourse: Textual Analysis for Social Research*. London: Routledge.

Gorur, Radhika. 2016. "Seeing Like PISA: A Cautionary Tale About the Performativity of International Assessments." *European Educational Research Journal* 15 (5): 598–616. doi:10.1177/1474904116658299.

Government of the Russian Federation. 2010. *Nasha Novaya Shkola*. http://nasha-novaya-shkola.ru/?q=node/4.

Grek, Sotiria. 2009. "Governing by Numbers: The PISA 'Effect' in Europe." *Journal of Education Policy* 24 (1): 23–37. doi:10.1080/02680930802412669.

Grek, Sotiria. 2013. "Expert Moves: International Comparative Testing and the Rise of Expertocracy." *Journal of Education Policy* 28 (5): 695–709. doi:10.1080/02680939.2012.758825.

Heath, Shirley B. 1983. *Ways with Words: Language, Life and Work in Communities and Classrooms*. Cambridge: Cambridge University Press.

Kakovkin, G. (Director). 2004. *Shchedrovitsky:V Poiskakh Elity*. Moscow: FAS Media.

Kondakov, Alexander. 2011. *Interview for Prosveshcheniye*. https://www.youtube.com/watch?v=_AEGqR4PLxo.

Kondakov, Alexander. 2012. *Interview for Pryamaya Rech'*. https://youtu.be/znH2FceUJiQ.

Kondakov, Alexander. 2018. *Interview for Molokin – Samoye Glavnoe*. https://vk.com/video-132750288_456239032.

Kondakov, Alexander, and Alexander Kuznetsov. 2008. *Kontseptsiya Federal'nykh Obrazovatel'nykh Standartov Obshchego Obrazovaniya*. Moscow: Prosveshcheniye.

Kukulin, Ilia. 2011. "Alternative Social Blueprinting in Soviet Society of the 1960s and the 1970s, or Why Left-Wing Political Practices Have Not Caught on in Contemporary Russia." *Russian Studies in History* 49 (4): 51–92.

Lyotard, Jean-François. 1984. *The Postmodern Condition: A Report on Knowledge*. Minneapolis: University of Minnesota Press.

Marcus, George E. 1995. "Ethnography in/of the World System: The Emergence of Multi-Sited Ethnography." *Annual Review of Anthropology* 24: 95–117.

Marcuse, Herbert. 1964. *One-dimensional Man: Studies in the Ideology of Advanced Industrial Society*. Boston: Beacon Press.

Ministry of Education of the Russian Federation. 2002. *Kontseptsiya Modernizatsii Obrazovaniya do 2010 Goda*. http://www.edu.ru/documents/view/1660/#1.

Ministry of Education of the Russian Federation. 2011. *Standarty Nachal'noy Shkoly*. https://fgos.ru/.

Ministry of Education of the Russian Federation. 2012. *Standarty Sredney Shkoly*. Retrieved from https://fgos.ru/.

Ministry of Education of the Russian Federation. 2014. *Kontseptsiya podderzhki razvitiya pedagogicheskogo obrazovaniya*. https://ac.gov.ru/files/content/1535/04-02-14-opros-project-pdf.pdf.

Ministry of Labor of the Russian Federation. 2013. *Professional'ny Standard Pedagoga*. http://fgosvo.ru/uploadfiles/profstandart/01.001.pdf.

Nordin, Andreas, and Daniel Sundberg. 2016. "Travelling Concepts in National Curriculum Policy-Making: The Example of Competencies." *European Educational Research Journal* 15 (3): 314–328. doi:10.1177/1474904116641697.

OECD. 1998. *Reviews of National Policies for Education: Russian Federation*. Paris: OECD.

OECD. 1999. *Reviews of National Policies for Education: Tertiary Education and Research in the Russian Federation*. Paris: OECD.

OECD. 2005. *The Definition and Selection of Key Competencies*. Paris: OECD.

Olin, I. 2011. *A. Kondakov – Razrabotchik FGOS. Mnenie*. https://proshkolu.ru/user/igorolin/blog/75294.

Pepper, David. 2011. "Assessing Key Competences Across the Curriculum—and Europe." *European Journal of Education* 46 (3): 335–353. doi:10.1111/j.1465-3435.2011.01484.x.

Quantz, Richard A., and Terence W. O'Connor. 1988. "Writing Critical Ethnography: Dialogue, Multivoicedness, and Carnival in Cultural Texts." *Educational Theory* 38 (1): 95–109. doi:10.1111/j.1741-5446.1988.00095.x.

Rizvi, Fazal, and Bob Lingard. 2009. *Globalizing Education Policy*. New York: Routledge.

Shchedrovitsky, Goergiy. 1993. *Logica i Pedagogika*. Moscow: Kastal'.

Sovechchaniye po Vorposam Shkol'nogo Obrazovaniya. 2012. http://kremlin.ru/events/president/news/15073.

Spreen, Carol Anne. 2004. "Appropriating Borrowed Policies: Outcomes-Based Education in South Africa." In *The Global Politics of Educational Borrowing and Lending*, edited by Gita Steiner-Khamsi, 101–113. New York: Teachers College Press.

Spring, Joel. 2015a. *Economization of Education: Human Capital, Global Corporations, Skills-Based Schooling*. New York: Routledge.

Spring, Joel. 2015b. *Globalization and Education: An Introduction*. New York: Routledge.

Startsev, Boris. 2012. *Khroniki Obrazovatel'noy Politiki: 1991-2011*. Moscow: Higher School of Economics.

Takayama, Keita. 2008. "The Politics of International League Tables: PISA in Japan's Achievement Crisis Debate." *Comparative Education* 44 (4): 387–407. doi:10.1080/03050060802481413.

Takayama, Keita. 2013. "OECD, 'Key Competencies' and the New Challenges of Educational Inequality." *Journal of Curriculum Studies* 45 (1): 67–80. doi:10.1080/00220272.2012.755711.

Theule Lubienski, Sarah T. 2000. "Problem Solving as a Means Toward Mathematics for All: An Exploratory Look Through a Class Lens." *Journal for Research in Mathematics Education* 31 (4): 454–482.

Tiana, Alejandro, José Moya, and Florencio Luengo. 2011. "Implementing Key Competences in Basic Education: Reflections on Curriculum Design and Development in Spain." *European Journal of Education* 46 (3): 307–322. doi:10.1111/j.1465-3435.2011.01482.x.

Wheelahan, Leesa. 2012. "The Problem with Competency-Based Training." In *Educating for the Knowledge Economy? Critical Perspectives*, edited by Hugh Lauder, Michael Young, Harry Daniels, Maria Balarin, and John Lowe, 152–166. New York: Routledge.

World Bank. 2003. *Lifelong Learning in the Global Knowledge Economy: Lessons for Developing Countries*. Washington, DC: World Bank.

World Bank. 2006. *Obuchenie na Protyazhenii Zhizni v Usloviyah Novoy Ekonomiki*. Moscow: World Bank.

Zajda, Joseph. 2010. "The Politics of Education Reforms and Policy Shifts in the Russian Federation." In *Globalisation, Ideology and Education Policy Reforms*, edited by Joseph Zajda, 175–191. Dordrecht: Springer.

Zuckerman, Galina. 2014. "Developmental Education." In *The Cambridge Handbook of Cultural Historical Psychology*, edited by Anton Yasnitsky, René van der Veer, and Michel Ferrari, 177–202. Cambridge: Cambridge University Press.

# Curricular design for competencies in basic education in Uruguay: Positions and current debates (2008–2019)

Eloísa Bordoli 

### ABSTRACT
State Basic Education in Uruguay has always been characterised by universal, homogeneous curricular designs, articulated according to subject matter and academic content. Currently, following international trends, a curricular design based on competencies has been encouraged. This article aims to analyse the main features of the new curricular guidelines in elementary (or primary) school, as well as the main debates around them. Criticisms posted by teachers are examined with a post-critical focus on the curricular field, drawing from analysis of documents and interviews with key stakeholders. The main findings reveal three central points of debate: the structuring core of the curricula, assessment methods and the position of the teacher. Also, a hybrid model of curricular policy for basic education has emerged which has generated conflict amongst teaching communities.

## Introduction

State elementary education in Uruguay began during the second third of the nineteenth century, characterised by a progressive extension and coverage throughout the country and based on the central principles of secularism, tuition free access, compulsion and autonomy from all political power. At present, the ANEP[1] (State Education National Administration) is the autonomous entity in charge of pre-school, elementary education, academic high school, technical high school and teacher training; it is independent from the MEC (Ministry of Culture and Education) –hence from political power– in technical, financial and governmental terms. ANEP consists of a Central Board (CODICEN) and four decentralised councils, one for each stage of the educational path: CEIP (nursery and elementary school), CES (academic high school), CETP (technical high school), and CFE (teacher training).[2]

With regards to its technical independence, ANEP's decentralised councils are in charge of the curricular design for all authorised state and public education, which has always been universal, homogenous and articulated according to subjects or fields of knowledge and academic content. Current education authorities, following international guidelines (e.g. OECD 1998; 2011), have encouraged –with difficulty– a curricular design based on competencies, outlined in the MCRN I (Curricular Framework for National Reference I) of 2016. However, the content-based PEIP, the Nursery and Elementary School Curriculum that has also been in force since 2008. Because of this, the teachers operate in a bipolar situation, using two different curriculum guides (2008 and 2016), each based on a different logic. In addition, they must refer to the DBAC (Basic Document for Curricular Analysis), which was released for elementary education in 2016 as a bridge between the content-based curriculum and the new competency-based curricular framework, the MCRN. The present article will focus on elementary education, and besides discussing the MCRN will discuss the PEIP and the DBAC.

In this educational context, this article aims to analyse the main features of the new curricular guidelines in elementary school, as well as the main debates around them. It will focus on the criticism posted by teaching communities, specifically, by the teachers unions and by the Teachers Technical Assemblies (Asambleas Técnico Docente, or ATD), which represent the teaching community to the state and consist of members elected by all teachers. Given the existence of inconsistent policies, the curriculum constitutes a problematic field, holding varied meanings competing for dominance, which is why it is paramount to explore the constructed hegemonic meanings as well as the dissenting or counter-hegemonic ones, formulated and colliding in this specific historical context.

### Conceptual and methodological approach

The research takes hermeneutical and post-critical approaches to the curricular field. In line with the post-critical approach (Laclau and Mouffe 1985), I deconstruct meanings while retaining the perspective of critical resistance (see also Hoy 2005). Two key concepts concern the shape and the treatment given to the issues studied. First, it is necessary to look into the curricular documents or products, as well as their design process. Studying these documents means identifying the technical and political elements at stake, and thus studying the elements to be selected, prioritised, organised and sequenced. In this sense, it is crucial to analyse how foundations, objectives, contents, activities, methodological guidelines and assessment involved in each curricular design interrelate, as well as to examine the political interrelations and power dynamics going on in the given social-historical context. As for the process of curricular design, it is necessary to examine the conditions under which these documents are produced, as well as the stakeholders involved in the design, and the different positions and conflicts originating around it (de Alba 1998). This view entails that the curricular document is not a technical product but rather a particular social-political result involving different education stakeholders. Along these lines, it becomes central to analyse the teaching communities' positions as taken over the course of the process by the ATD and the unions, as they are the key agents in charge of updating and reinterpreting the prescribed curricula during their professional practice (Frigerio 1991).

Secondly, it is important to point out that the curricular texts have two central features: on the one hand, as public documents, they validate and prescribe what has been selected to be taught and learned (Dussel 2006); on the other hand, they consolidate discourses, referring in shorthand to the knowledge validated by a given society (Bordoli 2007), and thus represent an 'open matrix, yet to be (self) written and (self) completed'

(Dussel and Caruso 1996, 80). Accordingly, they are subject to the linguistic game of settling 'some meanings more than others' (Dussel and Caruso 1996, 72), which implies that the curriculum is not free of language opacity and conflict. Also, curricular texts combine conflicting meanings, in constant tension as emerging hybrids in dispute for hegemonising meanings on a symbolic field. This opaque, tense, regulating, normalising, performative, hybrid discourse locates the curriculum at the core of both continuity and change, and also within the arena of political and pedagogical dispute.

Empirically this study has used information from three sources: a) official Documents from ANEP; b) documents from ATD (Teachers Technical Assemblies); c) interviews from teachers that participated in ATD meetings. In the ATD's national meetings, which take place once a year, all the country's representative teachers are reunited. As it is very difficult to hold this meeting more often there is also a Permanent Board that streamlines any process if necessary. ATD provides initiative and counsel on the educational matters concerning its specific field as well as on more general educational matters. The educational authorities are required to get the ATD's advice before passing or modifying study plans and programmes.[3]

The documentary corpus has been made up from a heterogeneous set of 37 documents related to the curricular changes taking place in elementary school in Uruguay during the period of study. These documents have been arranged around three criteria: the document's issuing organisation, chronological order, and characteristics. With this framework, documents were selected from CODICEN and CEIP, both part of ANEP, and from the ATD's National Meetings and Permanent Board (Table 1).

Apart from the documentary sources, twelve interviews were conducted with certified teachers who were ATD members. The purpose of the interviews was to explore in depth the teaching community's positions. Thus, ATD members were interviewed according to three criteria: teaching seniority, ATD membership seniority, and location. The latter factor was considered so that teachers from the capital and from inland areas were equally represented. Four members of the ATD Permanent Board were interviewed and the rest were members of the National Meeting who had taken part in the Curricular Policy Committee.

The empirical material was analysed in terms of what Howarth (2005) calls the 'articulation method', in which theoretical, social and political logics are at stake. The first logic requires the researcher to make concepts explicit across the whole heuristic process (Howarth 2005, 54). Social logics address, in particular, the production conditions of the subject matter in its situational context and in its historically constructed discourse. This implies the need to consider the components of the curricular designs and the

**Table 1.** Documental sources classification criteria.

| Characteristic | ANEP's CODICEN | ANEP's CEIP | Elementary ATD |
|---|---|---|---|
| General strategic guidelines, curricular policies and resolutions. | National Budget and ANEP's guidelines on education policies. MCRN I, II. Memos. | National Budget and CEIP's guidelines on education policies. PEIP, DBAC. Memos. | National ATDs. General guidelines, curricular policies. |
| Technical guidelines. | Reports by Work Committees: MCRN's general, by domain, assessment, etc. | Reports by Work Committees: DBAC, by field of knowledge, assessment, etc. | Reports by Work Committees. |
| Consultations. | Foreign advisers | Local advisers | — |

changes they make to elementary school in Uruguay in terms of the meanings attributed to them in their situational as well as their historical context. The political logics involve understanding of the positions of different stakeholders who take part in the process of the curricular debate (authorities, technicians, teaching communities). This three-party analysis proposed by Howarth provides us with a network allowing for an understanding of curricular discourses' meanings, conflicts and stakeholder positions involved in the curricular design process.

Overall, the curricular designs in force for elementary education were analysed synchronically and with a focus on the diverse positions held and arguments made by the teaching communities as represented by ATD representatives. However, a brief diachronic perspective is required in order to place the current conflicts in the context of the meaning networks built by the ATD during the past decades.

The first section below briefly analyses the two main features of the recent educational debates and, more specifically, the curricular debates in Uruguay. The second section deals with the features of the currently coexisting curricular designs in elementary school and also analyses the arguments of the ATD against the new competencies design, the MCRN Curricular Framework, as well as the DBAC. The DBAC, the Basic Document for Curricular Analysis, served as a hybrid text seeking to articulate school contents with achievement expectations provided in the 2008 programme in the form of graduation profiles, that is, learning requirements for graduation from primary and secondary education. This section includes teachers' arguments, which focus mainly on the political implications of the new competencies design, the way of processing changes and the place of the teacher in the new curricular model. The third and last section summarises and discusses the main findings.

## Contextualisation: main factors in dispute

In the past decades in Uruguay, debates on the educational and, more specifically, curricular field have had two different agendas. On the one hand, authorities have set three guiding orientations: learning and assessment, updating of curricular designs, and teacher training. On the other hand, teaching communities represented by the ATD and the teachers unions have brought the following factors to the symbolic arena of dispute: budget increases and improvement of their working conditions, teachers' participation and autonomy from national political power as well as from international organisations.

This conflicting agenda has made dialogue and negotiation more and more difficult, showing a clear gap between competing priorities and logics when it comes to valuing and planning education. These two perspectives were processed differently during the past decades, as shown below.

### *Neoliberal education reform: focused policies and lack of teachers' participation*

This polarity reached its peak in the 1990s, as neoliberal reforms were implemented in Uruguay, as well as in the neighbouring countries of the region. In 1995 in particular, during our third post-dictatorship government[4], a set of transformations in the national educational system took place in the context of more general changes during the same period. In the 1990s, the State adopted new ways of relating to society and the market. In the previous decades, the welfare state had shown signs of decay, leading to a deep national crisis[5], preparing the general context for a very particular educational reform. Change affected all stages of education: nursery, elementary, academic and technical high school, and teacher training (Rama 2000). Compared to the transformations made to the education systems of the neighbouring countries in the region, these changes could be deemed moderate: ours was catalogued as moderate or neoliberal, as it took place in a peculiar context of institutional persistence, technological innovation and under a conservative government (Bentancur 2008, 228). The main guidelines leading the reform process were: '(…) the consolidation of social equality, raising the status of teachers' training and work, an improvement of education quality and, supporting all these three, a stronger institutional management' (ANEP-CODICEN 1995).

Regarding the curricular design in elementary school, as opposed to middle school[6] and teacher training, no changes were introduced to school programmes. Reforms were designed with no consultation or participation of teaching communities whatsoever, and they roundly opposed the changes introduced by the authorities. The reform had two central features: firstly, the changes introduced were made by educational authorities of ANEP -CODICEN following the advice of OECD's foreign assessors; secondly, impacting the design and implementation of special programmes designed for vulnerable students, there was installation of para-system structures.[7] The latter were funded by international loans, which, among other actions, established compensatory programmes for 'low achieving' schools and 'low achieving' pupils and funded the monitoring and assessment of pupil performance.

The ATD and the teachers unions strongly opposed both the content of the reform and the way it was introduced and implemented. The compensatory and focused nature of the programmes was questioned because it classified schools and pupils, differentiating the 'low achieving' from the others and thus fracturing the universalising principle of one public school for all. The mode of introducing and implementing changes was strongly resisted because of the authorities' vertical, authoritarian management during this period.

### *Education during the progressive period[8]: curricular universalisation and teachers' participation*

In 2005, the national government experienced a meaningful change as a coalition of traditional left-wing and progressive parties, the FA (Frente Amplio [literally *Broad Front*])[9], took office for the first time. This government drove a search for political alternatives to the dominant neoliberal policies which had led, in 2002, to one of the worst economic-financial crises in our history; the FA also prioritised education, as reflected by a budget increase (to 4.5% GNP) and the implementation of consultations which would set the foundations of a new Education Act in 2008. That Act provides for teachers' participation in governing education and reinforces autonomy. The latter, along with participation and integration, together constitute the three ruling principles of our state education national system.[10]

FA's first period in office (2005–2009) was defined as a stage of transition from a neoliberal towards a progressive model, which emphasised education's continuous transformation in order to adapt to society's everyday needs (Yarzábal[11], 2010, 18). ANEP's management was based on four central guidelines, two of which are of relevance to our study: conceiving education from a human rights perspective and promoting teachers' participation (ANEP-CODICEN 2010, 14).

During this period, 2008 was crucial as the year that the General Education Act n° 18.437 was passed and the teacher training programme and the new elementary education programme were approved. The Education Act addressed a historical claim of the teaching community: being represented in the educational administrative entities. This provision illustrates two particular features of the organisation of the state education system in Uruguay, and the historical beliefs of the teaching community about their place in education. Each entity's autonomous organisation is based on the need to place education outside and above structural political disputes amongst parties. The strength of technical, financial and management autonomy is a guarantee when it comes to preserving education and its democratic principles. Also, teachers' direct participation in technical and managerial cases recognises their position in the system.

### Summarising the preceding context

It is possible to claim that the high level of conflict[12] around the State's reforms and, particularly, the educational changes of the 1990s are centred on the value of public policies, the dispute about methods for processing changes, the role of the teaching community in those changes, the development of compensatory focused programmes, the interference of international organisations in educational affairs, and the enforcement of standardised assessment methods. The teaching communities, organised under the ATD and the unions, refused, at a symbolic level, to endorse the reforms and the need for their technical and political participation in the context of their autonomy.

This polarisation led, when FA took office, to its support and promotion of spaces for teachers' involvement, development of education on the basis of human rights, as well as a closer, more complementary relationship between educational and social policies. Although critical of the neoliberal reform of the previous decades, FA introduced, upon taking over, a balanced, gradual set of changes which included, in the domain of education, the changes summarised above, but also ratification and continuation of other policies. In the latter category, national and international standardised assessment models and focused programmes were continued, but not expanded universally. All in all, the new education heads articulated aspects of both conflicting agendas: the one ruling the previous decade, strongly influenced by international entities, and the other vindicating the teaching community.

## Features of curricular documents: positions and debate during the progressive period

Historically, curricula could be seen as having a universal and homogeneous character articulated in terms of educational disciplines and contents. Through past and present centuries, much debate has taken place on whether to have standard programmes designed for all schools in the country or to adapt them to the geographic, social, economic and cultural features of different locations. The progressive period introduced a new debate about keeping the past design of curriculum based on educational disciplines and contents or changing to a new curriculum based on competencies.

This section focuses on the analysis of documents in two dimensions: their elaboration process and their internal logics. As mentioned, the curricular documents for this stage are the PEIP (Nursery and Elementary Programme) of 2008, the MCRN I Curricular Framework of 2016, and the DBAC of 2016, the Basic Document for Curricular Analysis with graduation profiles. Also, different teaching communities' positions about these documents and their elaboration will be outlined.

## Curricular design elaboration process

### 2008 PEIP: collective participation and construction

Discussion and elaboration of the PEIP (the elementary curriculum) took place with broad teacher participation across many opportunities for discussion and through a wide spectrum of consultations. In 2006, the Nursery and Elementary Council began 'a process of pragmatic change along with discussion and proposals from the ATD' (ANEP-CEIP 2008, 9). In this context, ATD sessions were held in every single school in the country, in order to gather information towards construction of the new PEIP. In the following year, a work team was formed, consisting of representatives from the Council, the ATD and the unions. The starting point for this curricular transformation process consisted of three guidelines set by the Inspectors Congress: 'a universal educational policy, the same program for all and a programme based on human rights' (ANEP-CEIP 2008, 9). Following these three guidelines, a central committee and subcommittees for each field of knowledge were formed consisting of elementary and high school teachers, with collaboration from teacher training and the University of the Republic. This process of high participation from teachers in the elaboration of the curriculum was described by the PEIP preface and introduction (ANEP-CEIP 2008).

The teachers' two-year work process on different subject matters and levels of the new programme was unprecedented in the country's curricular history. This participatory model was a milestone, building a feeling of collaborative authorship in teaching, as reflected by interviews with teachers who referred to the programme as 'ours' and 'made by us'. A teacher who used those terms contrasts the elaboration process of the PEIP with the elaboration process of the DBAC.

> The Programme (2008) was a construction by all teachers, made through much participation and discussion. It is open and flexible, allowing the teacher to work autonomously in the classroom on the projects they plan and to establish the sequence of activities; the teacher is the one who selects and prioritises. The DBAC was imposed on us by the authorities and designed by technicians, and never passed through teachers' hands. That is one of the reasons for our rejection. (E.M[13] N° 5).

Teachers supported the PEIP not only because they collectively took part in its design, but also because they claimed it highlighted the national pedagogical and philosophical traditions and was capable of adapting to the reality of education, as opposed to being 'alien ideas brought in by the competency-based curricular models' (E.M. ATD-N N° 11). This claim was reinforced in the resolutions by the ATD National Meetings between 2015 and 2019, as shown below:

The 2008 programme (PEIP) is theoretically and philosophically grounded in an intentionality that guides organisation of the contents, and was planned by Uruguayan teachers, for the Uruguayan reality and for any given school in the country (…). Although prescriptive, an arguable aspect, it allows for teachers' choice on where to start and where to go (ATD 2019, 63).

### *2016 DBAC and 2016 MCRN: process of technical elaboration*

These two documents represent a change in the ANEP's curricular policy, particularly in the sphere of its CEIP (nursery and elementary school), which began with political and technical authorities in education criticising the quality of education and arguing for a need to improve and to adjust education in response to results of learning assessments (ANEP-CEIP 2019, 102–103). In December 2014 the CEIP decided to create a Work Committee to set the graduation profile for year 3 and year 6 elementary schoolchildren (ANEP-CEIP 2014a, 2014b). This work would take place in the context of the FA government's attempt to balance between neoliberal and progressive goals, and would address the need for the teaching communities to connect the forthcoming curricular framework with the curriculum already provided by the PEIP. Two points of this resolution to create a Work Committee are of interest: it specified the need to define 'disciplinary knowledge in teaching', not graduation profiles as in later DBAC-related resolutions, and it summoned the ATD and the unions to take part in the Committee. These two points prove that the authorities now sought the communities' involvement as a way to validate change and that they introduced these changes in the context of the PEIP's disciplinary basis. The resolution's reaffirmation of 'knowledge to intervene in teaching' and its minimisation of terms such as 'competencies' and 'assessment' may be seen in the same way. Also, in previous minutes, the CEIP stated that 'students shall be self-competent as long as they acquire knowledge from content, which build concepts' (ANEP-CEIP 2014c).

These founding arguments of the CEIP and the public release of some PEIP first draft versions (ANEP-CEIP 2015a, 2015b) aimed at articulating the DBAC and the PEIP. They moved the DBAC away from guidelines defined by international organisations such as the OECD[14] (1998, 2010) among others, even though teachers did not feel it moved far enough.

Nevertheless, not only did the ATD decide to reject the DBAC first draft, but also to withdraw from the Committee in charge of the second draft of the curricular analysis (ATD 2015b), demanding that all the teachers who participated in the Committee on behalf of the ATD also remove their names from the first draft (ATD 2015a). This rejection also held for the DBAC second draft and final version, and for the 2016 MCRN (ATD 2017). Teachers did not participate in developing the latter documents; if they had, they probably would not have moved the documents in the direction taken.

One of the interviewed ATD teachers argues:

We are stepping out so the ATD does not get used to legitimation. We went there to take part in the discussion, not to validate something teachers disagree with and were not part of. (EM-ATD-MP[15] N° 3)

The ATD considered that the documents for curricular analysis as well as the MCRN failed to follow or deepen the PEIP 2008, but rather were 'a curricular change undercover' (EM-

ATD-MP N° 3). Interviewees from the ATD Permanent Board and National Meeting strongly agreed on considering these documents an 'undercover', 'sneaky', 'incoherent' curricular shift. Some even went further, stating this change '(...) follows guidelines given by international organisations like OECD and the World Bank' (E.M. ATD-N N° 9).

The controversy over the curricular elaboration process could be seen in the light of curricular policy studies such as Westbury's and colleagues (2016) and Sivesind and Westbury (2016), which address the degree of legitimacy of new designs for plans and programmes. These authors point to the existence of conflicts in the process of change, as well as to the importance of teachers' participation as 'validating authorities'. Other researchers point out that curricular reforms are political, not just technical phenomena, and that the lack of teachers' participation may lead to their failure or at least a deviation of their focus: 'Teachers could respond to reforms by hybridizing them, blending the old and the new by selecting those parts that made their job more efficient or satisfying' (Tyack and Cuban 2001, 25). In Uruguay, foreign consultants hired by the education authorities of ANEP-CODICEN to advise on the process of curricular transformation likewise recommended, regarding our national tradition, that:

(1) Collectives that were traditionally actors in education be included in the definitive stages of the MCRN.
(2) Processes of public consultation should be guaranteed, so that students', families' concerns are voiced (...). (ANEP-CODICEN 2019b, 65).

### *The documents' internal logics: orienting meaning and content of curricular design*

### *2008 PEIP: national pedagogy and teaching contents*
As mentioned before, PEIP's internal logic works along 'fields of knowledge according to their epistemology' and 'teaching contents' (ANEP-CEIP 2008, 10). In this spirit, ANEP claimed: 'The PEIP is an official document containing the selection of knowledge to be taught at school according to the objectives and principles provided by the Education Act' (ANEP-CEIP 2008, 3).

The emphasis put on disciplinary skills and content clearly moved in a different direction from the growing emphasis on competencies and standardised assessment promoted by the OECD (1998, 2010). The programme is structured in eight sections. Its introduction highlights the development process which made it possible, as well as the importance of organisation based on fields of knowledge and on the central role of the teacher and of teaching. The second section presents an extensive 'General Foundation', specifying the guiding principles of education in a human rights perspective: autonomy, secularity, compulsory attendance and tuition free access. Equality, focus on the whole child, freedom and solidarity are presented as key concepts in a citizen's education. In line with critical theory, the programme defines education as a 'liberating practice', and thus as a political action (ANEP-CIEP 2008, 18)'. Paulo Freire (1994) and Henry Giroux (1990), among others, are quoted. Further sections include: the foundations of fields of knowledge, the elaboration of concept networks, contents by field and programmes by year. It may clearly be seen that the disciplines provide the structuring logic behind the programme, and the emphasis is put on teaching.

The foundations and structuring logic behind the PEIP are defended by teachers, and along these lines the ATD claims:

> The PEIP's logic entails a conceptual approach corresponding with an evaluation of processes. Its fundamentals do not involve the acquisition of abilities, skills or competencies, but rather the construction of concepts through the years of schooling. Methodological paths for each field of knowledge are provided in their didactic foundations (ATD 2017, 70).

### 2016 DBAC, 2016 MCRN: graduation profile, competencies and assessment

The DBAC is based on the construction of graduation profiles or learning requirements in School years 3 and 6. Along these lines the need arose to 'agree on and clarify, in the light of the 2008 PEIP, a common horizon leading us all in terms of the basic learning requirements every Uruguayan child is entitled to' (ANEP-CEIP 2016, 14). This document aims to favour an inclusive curriculum based on learning which 'not only guarantees curricular opportunities or justice for all, but also inclusive policies (…) addressing each student's different, unique background, thus destroying educational, social and cultural barriers' (ANEP-CEIP 2016, 14).

MCRN is defined as a 'comprehensive reference to guide all compulsory education' (ANEP-CODICEN 2016, 7), as it includes both elementary and middle school. Its text states that 'the MCRN seeks to boost our students' learning through continuity, sequencing and recurrence of the teaching content' (ANEP-CODICEN 2016, 8). The document affirms it is based on the central position of the student, the learning environment and assessment. It explicitly seeks to avoid the 'technocratic, hegemonic fetishistic conception of competencies' critiqued by Carlos Cullen (1997) (ANEP-CODICEN 2016, 30), and instead aims to define 'culturally dense competencies' in terms of three learning dimensions: 'ethics of citizenship' implying an involvement in democratic life; 'ethics of well-being' implying 'feeling and being in the community'; and 'an ethics of thinking' articulating thought and action in all its complexity (ANEP-CODICEN 2016, 29).

Thus, in the successive documents issued by the education authorities –DBAC, MCRN – there is a progressive shift away from the place given to teaching and the role of the teacher towards the student and the learning of competencies; in this context, national and international standardised assessment becomes central, too. This movement tends to fall in line with international organisations, though only 'slightly' and at times while criticising 'technocratic models'. Also, these changes are not mandatory, but rather are presented as suggestions or trends.

When implemented, these documents result in a dual hybrid curricular policy, because the teacher can follow the PEIP (2008) or follow the DBAC with the MCRN (2016). Moreover, applying this or that design is subject to inspection requirements, and individual inspectors can request teachers to emphasise either one or the other.

The ATDs roundly reject the given curricular policy, not only on the grounds of its elaboration process, as mentioned before, but also regarding its meaning and content. They emphasise the influence of international organisations and assessments that restrict national sovereignty and teachers' autonomy. This criticism of standardised models is based on the foreign nature of the designs, as well as a distortion of the formative purpose that assessment should have (Scott 2014, 2016). It also arises in the context of a globalisation process endured by education with the loss of pedagogic and curricular values, as the global discourse gets 'proselytised' by international organisations (see Rizvi and Lingard 2010).

Interviewed members of the permanent board of the ATD state three arguments against these new curricular guidelines. The competency-based designs being imposed a) lead to 'a reduced, impoverished curriculum' (EM-ATD-MP N°1), b) include standardised assessment and protocols which 'set what to teach and serve the inspectors' purpose of control over us' (EM-ATD-MP N°3) and c) affect the role of the teacher, as 'you lose autonomy (…) they don't just assess learning, they assess you' (EM-ATD-MP N°1). Other interviewees were even more radical, claiming that 'competencies get associated with a commodification of education, as you don't teach them content, but rather make them fit the workforce' (EM-ATD-MP N°3).

National ATDs minutes show a comparative chart of the curricular models in clear conflict, not complementing each other as claimed by the authorities. For teachers there is a clear gap between them: on the one hand the 2008 PEIP, organised around sequenced contents, emphasising process, and on the other hand the new competency-based designs and the graduation profiles implementing labels, emphasising results and pigeonholing students (ATD, 2017).

The ATD minutes argue there are two sets of logics at stake, the authorities', aiming at a curricular reduction, assessment and control, and the teachers', who highlight the working conditions needed for the development of a quality education (ATD 2017). Some of the arguments posed by the teaching community coincide with the criticism made in the academic sphere about the impact that competency-based curricula have on students, such as the watering down effect (Young 2015; Young and Muller 2016; Scott 2016).

## Conclusions

Using Howarth's (2005) articulation method within a postcritical curricular perspective, and drawing on an extensive study of documents and in-depth interviews of teachers, this article investigated the process of curricular shift in Uruguay during the past decade. It made two moves to contextualise the curricular policies. A diachronic move around the processes of educational change over the past decades located networks of meaning and conflict in the medium term. Meanwhile, a synchronic move, aimed at an understanding in political context the changes during the last decade, located the curricular debate and the role of teachers in the processes of change within broader political discursive disputes. The analysis showed that discursive antagonisms around the processes for making curricular change, including the role of teacher communities within that process, has been a locus of conflict during recent decades in Uruguay, notwithstanding the government's progressive political affiliation. Secondly, and especially in the last decade, the role of teachers in establishing education policy has been increasingly recognised, as has the value of their active participation in the consultation processes. However, during the progressive period, two very different moments regarding curricular policy can be identified on an elementary school level. The first one arose in 2008 with the passage of the PEIP. As documents and teachers' testimonies show, this curriculum underwent an extensive and participatory elaboration process, grounded in a national and critical pedagogy with its internal structuring logics articulated around subject contents. These features made teachers feel the PEIP is 'theirs' and regard it as a victory against global tendencies of curricular policies and international assessments. The second moment's milestone in 2016, the passing of the DBAC and the MCRN, was created differently, through central and technical work committees and external consultation. The definition of graduation profiles in terms of competencies as well as the weight of external assessment brought back into the arena of dispute both the concept of what is legitimate to teach and the role of teachers in curricular design and educational change. Such conflict triggered old debates from the past decades, albeit with lower intensity since this time education authorities promoted participation channels, even though they were declined by teaching communities.

From the authorities' point of view, the new set of documents are specifications inspired by the 2008 PEIP. Teaching communities, on the other hand, claim a 'curricular change undercover', elaborated by technicians and without teachers' participation whatsoever. They argue that the concept of competency and the application of standardised assessment aim for to comply with recommendations from international organisations and to commodify education. The authorities, in turn, highlight the need to improve achievement standards. It is in this arena of dispute where both education agendas have been set, seemingly incompatible with one another, and where opposing meanings are built around concepts concerning the learning process, teaching, and the role of teachers. Teachers' autonomy and the influence of international organisations emerge as the opposing poles in dispute. Teachers' know-how for teaching and assessment sits in opposition to models based on competencies and standardised assessment.

As a result of the discursive antagonism pictured herein, one can see the development of a dual curricular policy and hybrid implementation processes. On a local level, these can be understood in the light of the gradualist particularities characterising the FA's government terms in Uruguay. On a global level, the disputes are inscribed—with some local particularities–within the international dynamics around assessment standardisation processes and the successive curricular reforms promoted globally by international organisations over the past decades.

## Notes

1. All entities and organizations are hereinafter referred to as their acronyms.
2. Uruguay, Parliament, General Education Act n° 18.437, 2008: 24.
3. Provided by section 70 of the General Education Act n° 18.437, 2008 (Uruguay, Parliament, General Education Act n° 18.437, 2008: 30).
4. Uruguay was under the most severe civil-military dictatorship in its history from June 27 1976 to March 1 1985.
5. Past decades of reforms led to the recession starting in 1999 and reaching its peak at the 2002 financial crisis and declaration of a banking holiday. This collapse 'made it clearly evident that the *hyperintegrated* society and the *State as the shield of the weak* had (definitely) fallen behind' (Caetano 2005, 320).
6. Equivalent to us (academic or technical) junior high school in the Uruguayan national system.
7. Temporary programs funded by World Bank loans: MECAEP (Elementary School Quality Improvement) and MESyFOD (High School and Teacher Training Quality Improvement).
8. The progressive period went from March 2005 to March 2020 in Uruguay.

# CONTEXTUALIZING GLOBAL FLOWS OF COMPETENCY-BASED EDUCATION 79

9. The arrival of the FA meant a shift of political orientation, as the country had always been led by traditional parties (Colorado and Nacional parties [literally *Red* and *National*]), both on the right of the political spectrum, yet including a range of factions showing notorious shades. Such change took place in a special regional context known as 'the progressive shift' which sought alternatives to neoliberalism (Moreira 2005, 434).
10. Under the provisions of the General Education Act n° 18.437, sections 46, 47 and 48 (Uruguay, Parliament, General Education Act n° 18.437, 2008: 22).
11. President of CODICEN-ANEP during FA's first term (2005-2010).
12. These disputes led on several occasions to 'the use of mechanisms of direct democracy, consisting in resorting to people's approval or disapproval of government acts' (Moreira 2005, 434).
13. EM: Interview with teachers.
14. Organisation for Economic Co-operation and Development
15. EM-ATD-MP: Interview to members of the ATD Permanent Board.

## Disclosure statement

No potential conflict of interest was reported by the author(s).

## ORCID

*Eloísa Bordoli* ⓘ http://orcid.org/0000-0003-0200-9394

## References

Administración Nacional de Educación Pública – Consejo de Educación Inicial y Primaria (ANEP-CEIP). 2008. *Programa de Educación Inicial y Primaria*. Montevideo: Imprenta Rosgal. Accessed July 12 2019. http://www.ceip.edu.uy/documentos/normativa/programaescolar/ProgramaEscolar_14-6.pdf.
Administración Nacional de Educación Pública – Consejo de Educación Inicial y Primaria (ANEP-CEIP). 2014a. "Creación de Comisión de trabajo para definir perfiles de egreso. Resolución N° 1, Acta Ext. N° 127", 3/12/2014. *In Normativas CEIP*. Montevideo: Archivo del CEIP.
Administración Nacional de Educación Pública – Consejo de Educación Inicial y Primaria (ANEP-CEIP). 2014b. "Sobre la Comisión de perfiles de egreso. Resolución N° 1, Acta N° 69", 8/12/2014. *In Normativas CEIP*. Montevideo: Archivo del CEIP.
Administración Nacional de Educación Pública – Consejo de Educación Inicial y Primaria (ANEP-CEIP). 2014c. "Educación Inclusiva. Resolución N° 2, Acta N° 25", 12/5/2014. *In Normativas CEIP*. Montevideo: Archivo del CEIP.
Administración Nacional de Educación Pública – Consejo de Educación Inicial y Primaria (ANEP-CEIP). 2015a. "Resolución N° 3, Acta N° 34, 18/6/15. Difundir los documentos borradores de las especificaciones de Logros de Aprendizaje". *In Normativas CEIP*. Montevideo: Archivo del CEIP.
Administración Nacional de Educación Pública – Consejo de Educación Inicial y Primaria (ANEP-CEIP). 2015b. "Resolución N° 63, Acta Extraordinaria N° 78, 12/8/15 Difundir el segundo Documento Base de Análisis Curricular". *In Normativas CEIP*. Montevideo: Archivo del CEIP.

Administración Nacional de Educación Pública – Consejo de Educación Inicial y Primaria (ANEP-CEIP). 2015c. *Documento Base de Análisis Curricular, primer borrador*. Montevideo: ANEP-CEIP. Accessed August 4 2019. http://www.ceip.edu.uy/documentos/normativa/programaescolar/DocumentoFinalAnalisisCurricular_junio2015.pdf.

Administración Nacional de Educación Pública – Consejo de Educación Inicial y Primaria (ANEP-CEIP). 2015d. *Documento Base de Análisis Curricular, segundo borrador*. Montevideo: ANEP-CEIP. Accessed August 4 2019. http://www.ceip.edu.uy/documentos/normativa/programaescolar/DocumentoFinalAnalisisCurricular_agosto2015.pdf.

Administración Nacional de Educación Pública – Consejo de Educación Inicial y Primaria (ANEP-CEIP). 2016. *Documento Base de Análisis Curricular, Tercera edición*. Montevideo: ANEP-CEIP. Accessed August 4 2019. http://www.ceip.edu.uy/documentos/normativa/programaescolar/DBAC-mayo-2017.pdf.

Administración Nacional de Educación Pública – Consejo de Educación Inicial y Primaria (ANEP-CEIP). 2019. *Memorias del quinquenio 2015–2019*. Montevideo: Impreso en CM IMPRESOS.

Administración Nacional de Educación Pública – Consejo Directivo Central (ANEP-CODICEN). 1995. *Proyecto de Presupuesto, Sueldos, Gastos e Inversiones del CODICEN de la ANEP (Tomos I y II)*. Montevideo: ANEP-CODICEN.

Administración Nacional de Educación Pública – Consejo Directivo Central (ANEP-CODICEN). 2000. *Una visión integral del proceso de "reforma educativa" en Uruguay 1995–1999*. Montevideo: ANEP-CODICEN.

Administración Nacional de Educación Pública – Consejo Directivo Central (ANEP-CODICEN). 2010. *Proyecto de Presupuesto, Sueldos, Gastos e Inversiones del CODICEN de la ANEP (Tomos I)*. Montevideo: ANEP-CODICEN.

Administración Nacional de Educación Pública – Consejo Directivo Central (ANEP-CODICEN). 2016. *Marco Curricular de Referencia Nacional*. Montevideo: ANEP-CODICEN. Accessed August 4 2019. http://www.ceip.edu.uy/documentos/2016/atd/adjuntos/2_Documento_Base_MCRN.pdf.

Administración Nacional de Educación Pública – Consejo Directivo Central (ANEP-CODICEN). 2019a. *Progresiones de Aprendizaje. Documento preliminar*. Montevideo: ANEP-CODICEN.

Administración Nacional de Educación Pública – Consejo Directivo Central (ANEP-CODICEN). 2019b. *Marco Curricular de Referencia Nacional. MCRN. Una construcción colectiva II. Configuraciones Curriculares*. Montevideo: ANEP-CODICEN.

Asamblea Técnico Docente (ATD) de Educación Primaria de Uruguay. 2015a. "Memorando N° 38.15 dirigido al CEIP: 'Participación de delegados de ATD en la elaboración del Segundo Documento Borrador de Análisis Curricular'" (31 de julio de 2015). *In Actas ATD-Primaria*. Montevideo: Archivo de ATD.

Asamblea Técnico Docente (ATD) de Educación Primaria de Uruguay. 2015b. "Memorando N° 37.15 dirigido al CEIP: 'Eliminación de los nombres de los delegados de ATD del Primer -Documento Borrador de Análisis Curricular'" (31 de julio de 2015). *In Actas ATD-Primaria*. Montevideo: Archivo de ATD.

Asamblea Técnico Docente (ATD) de Educación Primaria de Uruguay. 2017. "Marcos Curriculares. Plan Nacional de Educación". In: *XXVII Asamblea Nacional de Delegados: Informes y resoluciones*. Piriápolis, 4 al 8 de Setiembre de 2017, 70–79. Accessed August 4 2019. http://www.ceip.edu.uy/documentos/2017/atd/Documento-final-ATD-nacional-17.pdf.

ATD. 2019. XXX.

Bentancur, Nicolás. 2008. *Las reformas educativas de los años noventa en Argentina, Chile y Uruguay. Racionalidad política, impactos y legados para la agenda actual*. Montevideo: Banda Oriental.

Bordoli, Eloísa. 2007. "La tríada del saber en lo curricular. Apuntes para una teoría de la enseñanza." In *El borde de lo (in)enseñable. Anotaciones sobre una teoría de la enseñanza*, edited by Eloísa Bordoli, and Cecilia Blezio (comps.), 27–52. Montevideo: Facultad de Humanidades y Ciencias de la Educación.

Caetano, Gerardo. 2005. "Introducción general. Marco histórico y cambio político en dos décadas de democracia. De la transición democrática al gobierno de izquierda." In *20 años de democracia. Uruguay 1985–2005: miradas múltiples*, edited by Gerardo Caetano (comp.), 15–74. Montevideo: Taurus.

Cullen, Carlos. 1997. *Entrañas éticas de la identidad docente*. Buenos Aires: La Crujía Ediciones.

de Alba, Alicia. 1998. *Curriculum: crisis, mito y perspectivas*. Buenos Aires: Miño y Dávila.

Dussel, Inés. 2006. "Reformas curriculares en América Latina: Balance y perspectiva". *In II Reunión del Comité Intergubernamental del PRELAC*, Santiago de Chile, 11 al 13 de mayo de 2006, Pp 36.

Dussel, Inés, and Marcelo Caruso. 1996. *De Sarmiento a los Simpsons. Cinco conceptos para pensar la educación contemporánea*. Buenos Aires: Kapelusz.

Freire, Paulo. 1993. *Pedagogía de la esperanza*. México: Siglo XXI.

Freire, Paulo. 1994. *La naturaleza política de la educación*. Buenos Aires: Paidós.

Frigerio, Graciela. 1991. *Curriculum presente. Ciencia ausente. Normas, teorías y críticas. Tomo I*. Buenos Aires: Miño y Dávila.

Giroux, Henry. 1990. *Los profesores como intelectuales. Hacia una Pedagogía Crítica del Aprendizaje*. Barcelona: Paidós. [Henry Giroux. Teachers as Intellectuals: Toward a Critical Pedagogy of Learning. United States: ABC-CLIO, 1988].

Howarth, David. 2005. "Aplicando la teoría del discurso: el método de la articulación", Studia *politicæ*, 5 (Otoño 2005). Córdoba: Facultad de Ciencia Política y Relaciones Internacionales, Universidad Católica de Córdoba, 37–88. Accessed February 2 2019. http://www2.ucc.edu.ar/portalucc/archivos/File/CP_y_RRII/Revista_Studia_Politicae/05/Articulos/Howarth.pdf.

Hoy, David Couzens. 2005. *Critical Resistance: From Poststructuralism to Post-Critique*. Cambridge, Mass.: MIT Press.

Laclau, Ernesto, and Chantal Mouffe. 1985. *Hegemony and Socialist Strategy. Towards a Radical Democratic Politics*. Londres: Verso/NLB.

Mancebo, María Ester, and Pedro Narbondo (coords.). 2010. *Reforma del Estado y políticas públicas de la Administración Vázquez: acumulaciones, conflictos y desafíos*. Montevideo: Fin de Siglo-Clacso-Instituto de Ciencia Política - Universidad de la República.

Moreira, Constanza. 2005. "Final de juego. Del bipartidismo tradicional al triunfo de la izquierda en Uruguay". In: Gerardo Caetano (comp.). *20 años de democracia. Uruguay 1985–2005: miradas múltiples*. Montevideo: Taurus, 431–437.

OECD. 1998. *Making the Curriculum Work*. Paris: OECD. Publications. Accessed August 3 2019. doi:10.1787/9789264163829.

OECD. 2005. *The Definition and Selection of Key Competencies: Executive Summary*. Paris: OECD.

OECD. 2011. "Éducation et compétences," (pp. 54–56), in Des politiques meilleures pour le développement. Recommendations pour la cohérence des politiques. Paris: OECD. https://read.oecd-ilibrary.org/development/des-politiques-meilleures-pour-le-developpement_9789264121140-fr#page56.

OECD. 2017. *PISA 2015 Results (Volume 5): Collaborative Problem Solving*. Paris: OECD. Accessed August 3 2019. http://www.oecd.org/education/pisa-2015-results-volume-v-9789264285521-en.htm.

OECD. 2018. *Learning Framework 2030*. Paris: OECD.

Parlamento de la República Oriental del Uruguay. Ley General de Educación N° 18.437. Publicada el 12 diciembre del 2008. Accessed August 10 2019. http://www.impo.com.uy/bases/leyes/18437-2008.

Rama, Germán. 2000. "Prólogo. Educación y sociedad en Uruguay". In: *Una visión integral del proceso de reforma educativa en Uruguay 1995–1999*. Montevideo: Impresores Asociados-Fotosistemas S.A., 11–15.

Rizvi, Fazal, and Bob Lingard. 2010. *Globalizing Education Policy*. Nueva York: Routledge.

Scott, David. 2014. "Knowledge and the Curriculum." *The Curriculum Journal* 25 (1): 14–28. Accessed September 7 2019. doi:10.1080/09585176.2013.876367.

Scott, David. 2016. "Learning Affordances of Language and Communication National Curricula." *The Curriculum Journal* 27 (1): 46–61. Accessed September 9 2019. doi:10.1080/09585176.2015.1128345.

Sivesind, Kirsten, and Ian Westbury. 2016. ""State-Based Curriculum-Making", Part I." *Journal of Curriculum Studies* 48 (6): 744–756. Accessed August 3 2019. doi:10.1080/00220272.2016.1186737.

Tyack, David, and Larry Cuban. 2001. *En busca de la utopía. Un siglo de reformas de las escuelas públicas*. México: FCE.

Uruguay, Ministerio de Educación y Cultura de la República Oriental del Uruguay. 2018. *Logro y nivel educativo alcanzado por la población (año 2017)*. Montevideo: MEC. Accessed June 14 2019. https://www.mec.gub.uy/innovaportal/file/11078/1/logro-y-nivel-educativo-alcanzado-por-la-poblacion-2017.pdf.

Westbury, Ian, Jessica Aspfors, Anna-Verena Fries, Sven-Erik Hansén, Frank Ohlhaver, Moritz Rosenmund, and Kirsten Sivesind. 2016. "Organizing Curriculum Change: An Introduction." *Journal of Curriculum Studies* 48 (6): 729–743. Accessed September 9 2019. doi:10.1080/00220272.2016.1186736.

Yarzábal, Luis. 2010. "Fundamentos teóricos de las políticas implementadas en el quinquenio". In: Administración Nacional de Educación Pública – Consejo Directivo Central (ANEP-CODICEN). *Una transformación en marcha*. Maldonado: ANEP-UTU, 17–36.

Young, Michael. 2015. "Curriculum Theory and the Question of Knowledge: A Response to six Papers." *Journal of Curriculum Studies* 47 (6): 820–837. Accessed July 4 2019. doi:10.1080/00220272.2015.1101493.

Young, Michael, and Johan Muller. 2016. *Curriculum and the Specialization of Knowledge. Studies in the Sociology of Education*. New York & London: Routledge.

# Moral priority or skill priority: a comparative analysis of key competencies frameworks in China and the United States

Li Deng and Zhengmei Peng

**ABSTRACT**

China and the US have responded to the challenges of a knowledge-based society, technological advancement, and global competition by implementing educational reforms to impart skills or competencies required of 21st century students. This study compares the rationales, content, and curricula design of both countries' key competencies frameworks and explores the possibility of reciprocal learning. Although their frameworks have certain similarities, significant differences have arisen due to cultural factors. The Chinese framework follows the Confucian tradition, emphasising moral education, political inclinations, transferring general competencies to specific-subject ones, and integrating key competencies in the national curriculum. The US framework follows the pragmatic tradition, emphasising generic skills and economic needs. Some US states have attempted to revise curriculum standards or incorporate 21st century skills by identifying their alignment with Common Core State Standards. Both frameworks have deficiencies and face challenges in implementation, and they can learn from each other.

## Introduction

The development of a global knowledge society, the rapid transformation of information technology, and the intensification of economic competition have changed how people live, work, and learn, creating a need to update people's knowledge and skills (Ananiadou and Claro 2009; Anderson 2008; Dede 2010; Halász and Michel 2011; IBE 2012; Voogt and Roblin 2012). Reading, writing, arithmetic (the 3Rs), and subject knowledge are not enough for a 21st-century global knowledge society; the goals of education have shifted to encompass broader skills or competencies (Care, Anderson, and Kim 2016; Tedesco, Opertti, and Amadio 2014) considered crucial for individual success, social prosperity, national economic empowerment, and global competitiveness. The essence of these 'new knowledge economy' skills or competencies (Tan et al. 2017) is applying knowledge to solve problems so as to successfully address real-life needs and challenges (OECD 2005; Silva 2009; Tan, Chua, and Goh 2015).

Various countries, international organisations, and consortia have proposed key competencies, or 21st century skills frameworks, to address these needs and challenges by integrating them in curricula and instruction. In the US, the Brookings Institution considers these combined educational reforms a global movement going beyond traditional academic subjects and finds that this movement has become prominent in education policies and curricula worldwide (Care, Anderson, and Kim 2016). The US and China, the two largest economies in the world, with distinct political systems, also developed their 21st century skills framework and key competencies framework in 2002 (revised in 2007) and 2016, respectively.

In the US, the framework was issued by a non-profit organisation, the Partnership for 21st Century Skills (later changed to the Partnership for 21st Century Learning, or P21, which was absorbed by BattelleforKids in 2018, see also Anderson-Levitt, this issue), leading to the 21st century skills movement, a K-12 education reform that gradually became vital among American education discussions (Sawchuk 2009). This movement has been an important reference for many countries, including China (Lin 2016; Trilling and Fadel 2009). China's framework for key competencies was developed by the Ministry of Education, which defines key competencies as those that have become the major national education policy and national curriculum objectives implemented in Chinese high schools, soon to be implemented in junior high schools, primary schools, and kindergartens (MEPRC 2014).

The literature in English reviews 21st century skills or key competencies frameworks in an international context (Ananiadou and Claro 2009; Chu et al. 2017; Dede 2010; Voogt and Roblin 2012). However, few scholars have reported on China's key competencies reform. In education, China has been significantly influenced by the US since the pragmatist philosopher and educational reformer John Dewey visited in 1919. From the 'quality education' of the 1990s to the New Curriculum Reform initiated in the early 21st century and to the key competencies education reform in 2016, China's education reforms have mainly drawn on the experience of the US, aiming to prevent exam-oriented learning and to cultivate students' all-around development, creativity, and hands-on abilities (Dello-Iacovo 2009; MEPRC 1999; You 2019). The US started to pay attention to Chinese education after students from Shanghai were successful in the Programme for International Student Assessment (PISA) test in 2009, which signalled to the US that it needed to learn from Chinese education in order to maintain its status as the world's educational leader and global superpower (Dillon 2010; Friedman 2013; Tucker 2011). In fact, in the present era of globalisation, China and the US now have frequent educational exchanges and cooperation. With the shift in international policy discourse towards competency-based education reform, it is worth investigating how both countries' key competencies or 21st century skills frameworks have responded and adapted to global education reform and the national needs for 21st-century talents. This comparative analysis aims to help each system become more aware of its strengths, limits, and proclivities, leading to genuine mutual learning (Hardy and Uljens 2018) and further improvements in education policy-making and implementation (Hallak 1991).

This study examines the rationale, contents, and curricula design of the key competencies and 21st century skills frameworks proposed by China and US reformers by analysing their policy documents, curriculum standards, and official websites and by reviewing scholarly literature and newspaper articles. The differences between the frameworks are viewed from a cultural perspective as elaborated below. Curricula design, implementation challenges, as well as possibilities of reciprocal learning are analysed and discussed. For convenience, 'key competencies framework' is sometimes used to refer to both countries' agendas.

## Culture and education policy

Culture is a form of contested meaning-making (Anderson-Levitt 2012) and a set of implicit norms and shared behavioural habits of the actors in a certain system (Muers 2018). Culture plays a vital role in the construction and implementation of education policy (Tan and Chua 2015), as it does in translating and mediating policy from one context to another (Cheng 1998; Phillips 2012; Tan 2013; Tan and Chua 2015). It is appropriate to take a cultural perspective when comparing education policies among nations (Muers 2018).

China and the US have distinct cultural traditions. Although they share an education paradigm, that is, to provide children with specific knowledge and skills, cultural and political differences have led to very different educational processes and patterns of manifestation (Zhao 2018).

Education in China is strongly influenced by Confucian culture, in which individuals belong to the community and should serve it and their family, society, and country. In this culture, morality is the fundamental goal of education, taking precedence over skills. Furthermore, thinking skills are believed to turn morality into calculation and thereby to cultivate egoists (Peng and Deng 2017). After the National Imperial Examination System was established in AD 607, Confucianism gradually developed into the official ideology of China, and Confucian classics became the standard teaching materials for officer-selection examinations. Confucian morality gradually became collectivist and politicised, affecting policy formulation and thus forming an exam-oriented culture, which stresses the cultivation of virtue and competencies through knowledge accumulation and humanistic literacy. Thus, 'education for morality' became 'education for knowledge', that is, education should teach knowledge first, especially solid, systematic knowledge (Peng, Gu, and Meyer 2018).

US education, in contrast, is deeply influenced by pragmatism, which values independent thinking and free exploration, demonstrating a cultural mode based on individualism, with the purpose of serving economic and not communal (including moralistic) ends (Braun 2013). Pragmatism views knowledge from a perspective of independent actors, and knowledge and theories are considered assumptions, their usefulness depending on how much they can be applied to solve problems. This tradition emphasises that truth means what is useful (James 2013). Dewey regarded education as a solution to real problems rather than as the accumulation of knowledge (Dewey 1997). The fundamental task of education, in this view, is to cultivate reflective thinking and problem-solving skills (Dewey 1997). Deweyan pragmatism is the dominant feature of US education, which aims to cultivate citizenship, critical thinking, public practical ability, and career and social skills necessary for adapting to life through inquiry. Deweyan pragmatism is also the main theoretical basis of the 21st century skills education reform in the US (P21 2002).

## Background, motivation, and development

### China's key competencies framework

Commissioned by the Chinese Ministry of Education, the psychologist Chongde Lin, leading 96 educationists and psychologists from five Chinese universities, developed the China Student Development Key Competencies from 2013 to 2016 (Lin 2016). Lin's team referred to 13 frameworks[1] for key competencies in various countries or regions, and international organisations, including the US, and combined them with Chinese traditional culture and China's present needs. The framework proposal was based on the following points.

The initial reason for the framework was to adapt to the trend of global education reform and enhance the competitiveness of Chinese education. Frameworks of key competencies are developed by many countries and regarded as a change in viewpoints in relation to talent (Lin 2016). This change and global education reform on key competencies aroused the interest of China's Ministry of Education. 'To improve national strength and win in the fierce global competition, China needs to formulate a key competencies framework for student development that reflects national conditions and current needs' (Lin 2016, 3).

Second, the framework has the principal goal of achieving the fundamental task of 'establishing morals and cultivating people' (*lide shuren*) (MEPRC 2014). The 'establishing morals' emphasises core socialist values in education, and 'cultivating people' refers to the cultivation of key competencies. In 2012, the Chinese government took *lide shuren* to be the fundamental task of education, and it considered the 'most fundamental' educational question to be 'What kind of person is education going to cultivate?' at the national level (Lin 2016, 1). In response to this question, the Ministry of Education launched a study of key competencies to assess which ones should be promoted to allow students to develop healthily, have happy lives, and successfully fit in to future society (Lin 2016). In 2014, the Ministry of Education announced that the first step of the *lide shuren* project was to create a framework for developing students' key competencies. It added that the framework should be regarded as the basis for studying academic quality standards and revising curriculum schemes and standards, and that it should be used to direct the relevant procedures of curriculum reform (MEPRC 2014). This was the first time that the concept of 'key competencies' was proposed in a Chinese policy document.

Third, the framework proposal was based on promoting the implementation of 'quality education' (Lin 2016, 5). In 2001, China drew on the American educational experience and Dewey's educational philosophy to initiate the New Curriculum Reform and promote quality education. However, almost 20 years later, school education continues to focus on knowledge and not morality, stressing scores and higher education entrance rates and lacking in its ability to cultivate students' social responsibility, creativity, hands-on abilities, physical fitness, social adaptability, and positive emotions (MEPRC 2014; Lin 2016). Therefore, 'the contents of quality education must be enriched, and an assessment system and curriculum system must be established for quality education based on key competencies' (Lin 2016, 5).

## The US 21st century skills framework

The 21st century skills framework in the US was developed by P21, an organisation originally promoted by technology companies but including education experts, other businesses, communities, and political leaders (see also Anderson-Levitt, this issue). It received support from the US Department of Education, Time Warner Foundation, Apple, Cisco, Dell, Microsoft, and the National Education Association and so on (P21 2002). As discussed below, P21 identified three main reasons the 21st century skills framework developed in the US.

First, the business community needs a skilled workforce. Sweeping changes in the social, economic, and digital economy in the US workplace since the late twentieth century have required personnel trained in new skills. However, in light of the 'skills imperative' in the US, the growing shortage of skilled employees threatened the country's economic competitiveness (P21 2010). The workforce no longer met the economic need for high-order skills (P21 2010).

Second, fierce global economic competition since the beginning of the 21st century has threatened the US's competitive edge in the world economy (Kay 2010; Kay and Honey 2006). P21 views 21st-century education as the foundation of US competitiveness and as its economic engine. Therefore, a balanced 21st-century public education system that prepares students, workers, and citizens to win the 'global skills race' would enhance the US's economic competitiveness (P21 2008, 1).

Third, US students' mediocre performance in international tests has made Americans aware of the 'educational crisis' (Dillon 2010). Since the 1990s, US public education has focussed on standardised testing, with teaching subject knowledge and high-order thinking skills sacrificed in favour of teaching test-taking skills (McLachlan 2012; P21 2015). The gap between what schools teach and test and the skills required by students to learn, work, and live in the 21st century is huge (Wagner 2008). Therefore, schools had to change to make 21st century skills the intentional outcome of the US education system, preparing students for rigorous university courses, career challenges, and global competition (Wagner 2008).

## Comparison of Chinese and US motivations

Both China and the US felt that their schools failed to equip their students with 21st century skills such as adaptability and creativity. The frameworks proposed by the two countries were in response to the challenges of the global talent competition, but there are also significant differences between the key actors involved and their motives in developing the frameworks.

The Chinese framework was developed by psychologists and educationists commissioned by the Ministry of Education and is proposed as a clear political commitment to be implemented nationally through a centralised and top-down approach. China's framework lacks broad social participation; the voice of the business community was especially absent during its development process. In contrast, the US framework was mainly proposed by non-governmental actors. As noted by Trilling and Fadel (2009, 171), 'more than thirty-five member organizations, a number of participating departments of education, and hundreds of members of professional education and research organizations' were involved. Scores of educators, business leaders, and policymakers also reviewed the draft framework. It was a decentralised approach that involved broad social participation, integrating the power of three key stakeholder groups: education, business, and government. Of these groups, the business community had a crucial role.

Although international education trends drove the development of China's framework, its main purpose was to implement the national agenda expressed in the *lide shuren* project (MEPRC 2014). The Chinese framework regards key competencies as being part of the 'establishing morals' (*lide*) factor, and it does not directly respond to the needs of domestic enterprises or the social economy. It aims to develop students' well-roundedness rather than workforce skills, and it functions as an educational programme. This places it within the Confucian tradition, in which school education is a form of moral cultivation and is relatively isolated from social life. By contrast, the US framework is largely an economic programme and focuses on cultivating a competitive, adaptive, and productive workforce to meet current and future economic needs and to strengthen global competitiveness (P21 2007). It reflects a pragmatic approach, defined by using education to solve social problems.

## Content of competencies frameworks: what should be learned?

The Chinese and US frameworks have defined what 21st-century students need to learn. The Chinese framework defines the essential moralities and key skills for lifelong learning and social development. The US framework defines the skills students must develop for learning, life, and their career. The competencies or skills of each framework consist of three parts, each with several elements (Table 1).

There are some overlapping elements in the two frameworks. The thinking skills emphasised by the Chinese framework—'rational thinking', 'critical questioning', 'courageous inquiry', 'reflection', and 'problem solving' – correspond to those of the US framework – 'critical thinking and problem solving' and 'creativity and innovation'. In information skills, 'information awareness' in China's framework is consistent with 'information literacy' in the US framework. In personal skills, China's 'self-management' is consistent with 'initiative and self-direction' in the US framework. In cross-cultural competence, the Chinese concept of 'international understanding' is consistent with the US's 'social and cross-cultural skills'. Finally, the Chinese framework's 'social responsibility' shares qualities with the US framework's 'responsibility'.

Both frameworks go beyond the 3Rs and subject knowledge to emphasise skills that are transversal, that is, relating to many fields, including high-order skills and behaviours that enable people to cope with complex problems (OECD 2005; Voogt and Roblin 2012). Most of these skills emphasise high-order thinking, in-depth analysis, transformation of knowledge, and flexible application in problem situations, considered key skills for an uncertain future society.

However, there are also significant differences between the two frameworks. In relation to choice of words, the 'competencies' used in the Chinese framework are a broader concept than the 'skills' used in the US framework. 'Skills' usually refers to the ability to perform tasks and solve problems, while 'competencies' usually refers to applying learning outcomes adequately in certain contexts, involving 'cognitive elements, functional aspects, interpersonal attributes and ethical values' (Ananiadou and Claro 2009, 8;

**Table 1.** Overview of key competencies (China) and 21st century skills (US) frameworks.

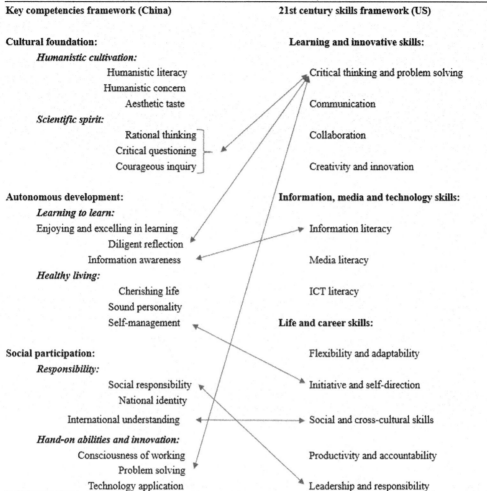

ECDVT 2014, 48), drawing on four aspects: knowledge, skills, attitudes, and values. The Chinese framework contains competencies relating to phrases such as 'humanistic', 'understanding', 'concern', 'aesthetics', 'spirit', and 'awareness', and it considers emotion, attitudes, and values as important elements of the framework. It is a comprehensive competencies framework – concerned with the integrity and completeness of students' capabilities – and it encompasses knowledge, skills, attitudes, and values. The US framework, in contrast, pays more attention to clear, explicit, and transferable skills.

A second significant difference is that the first part of China's framework is the cultural foundation, including the humanistic and scientific knowledge and spirit. The second part is autonomous development, which includes the concepts of learning to learn, cherishing life, and a sound personality. The third part is social participation, including social responsibility, national identity, and hands-on and innovation abilities. The three parts 'emphasize self-cultivation, caring for society and love for family and country'(MEPRC 2014),and their internal logic is that individuals develop competencies based on extensive knowledge and should cultivate collective awareness to serve their community and country.

In contrast, the three main parts of the US framework are 'skills'. The first part, the core of the framework, is the development of learning and innovative skills, including 4C skills (critical thinking and problem solving, communication, collaboration, and creativity and innovation). The second part emphasises individual life and career skills, such as adaptability, productivity, and leadership. The third part relates to developing skills in information technology. The three parts are dominated by individual skill development and pay attention to the people-to-people, people-to-society, and people-to-tools interaction, focusing on learners' effective action and adaptability in social and career life, demonstrating the framework's pragmatic and economic concern with developing problem-solving skills.

China's framework prioritises morality. It specifies essential moralities and key skills and emphasises the former, encouraging cultural-connotation, self-improvement, and thinking skills, with the aim of allowing students to serve society and their country. In 2017, the Chinese government issued its *Opinions on Deepening the Reform of the Educational System and Mechanism*, which further refined the key competencies framework and highlighted moral education, placing it in a more important position (CPGPRC 2017). Yet, at the core of the moral education are the core socialist values, and the moral priority of the Chinese framework is to some extent a political priority. Muju Zhu (2018), an officer of the Ministry of Education of China, stated in an online video interview ($0'26''-1'26''$):

> The most important principle of the Ministry of Education's key competencies-based high school curriculum reform is to adhere to the correct political direction … In the process of teaching, we must incorporate the core socialist values … to cultivate good political and moral qualities in students, guide them to develop a sound personality, and develop the right outlook to life, values, and worldviews.

The US framework emphasises skills, attaching importance to those needed in social and economic life as well as in careers, such as innovation, collaboration, communication, and information and communications technology (ICT) skills. This skill-priority framework focuses on employability to meet the needs of future employers. Terms such as 'competitiveness' and 'global economy' appear frequently in relation to 21st century skills (Kohn 2009a). Renowned critic of recent US reforms based on accountability, Kohn (2009b), believes that the answer to the question 'What do learners need to learn in the 21st century?' in the US framework, is no longer about what supports 'democracy' or what promotes self-improvement and intrinsic good but instead, 'What do companies need?'

## The curricula design of key competencies frameworks in China and the US

The Chinese government has adopted a centralised and top-down approach to implement the key competencies framework. A unified high school national curriculum scheme and standards were formulated based on the framework, and schools across the country then implemented key competencies based on the national curriculum scheme and standards. The curriculum standards (a) clarify the core values and key competencies that students should achieve in each subject, (b) select and reorganise curriculum content, (c) clarify content requirements, (d) establish guidelines for instructional design, and (e) provide suggestions for tests and textbooks to implement the key competencies (MEPRC 2018). In 2017, the Chinese Ministry of Education revised the high school curriculum standards for 20 subjects, with each subject having its own specific competencies embodying those outlined in the framework. The general competencies transferred to subject-specific competencies. For example, the key competencies for the Chinese language include language construction and application, thinking development and promotion, aesthetic appreciation and creation, and cultural inheritance and understanding. For mathematics, key competencies include mathematical abstraction, logical reasoning, mathematical modelling, intuitive imagination, mathematical operations, and data analysis. The aim is to cultivate general competencies through the teaching of each subject and further help students develop rational and balanced personality.

To implement the 21st century skills framework in the US, P21 launched the State Leadership Program and the 21st Century Learning Exemplar Program. States, school districts, and local schools could opt to join these programmes (P21 2012). As of December 2018, 21 US states had joined the State Leadership Program (P21 2018), and some states have revised their content standards based on the framework (WVDE 2008).

There are no uniform national curriculum standards in the US. As most states follow the Common Core State Standards (CCSS), it is impossible to talk about the curriculum integration of 21st century skills in schools bypassing CCSS (Zeitlin 2013). To implement the 21st century skills framework across the US, P21 has tried to show that the framework does not conflict with the CCSS, and it has expressed support for CCSS (CCSSI 2010). According to P21, although many 21st century skills are implicit in the CCSS, it does not contain all the skills necessary for students' success (P21 2011). CCSS encompasses subject-specific skills such as reading, writing, speaking, demonstrating, calculating, and data analysis, whereas 21st century skills are more general. CCSS represents a 'floor' rather than a 'ceiling' of student performance expectations (P21 2011). Therefore, P21 analysed the relationship between CCSS and 21st century skills to develop the P21 Common Core Toolkit, a guide to help stakeholders better understand the relationship between CCSS, curricula, and 21st century skills (P21 2011).

China and the US have different approaches towards curriculum transformation for key competencies. China has adopted an 'integral domination mode' (Guo 2016, 44), with key competencies being 'the DNA of curriculum development' (Zhong 2016, 3) to derive and evolve a curriculum based on full key competencies. The competencies guide the framework and content of each school session, field, and subject through step-by-step specification and layer-by-layer transformation (Guo 2016). However, a formidable challenge is connecting subject-specific competencies at the disciplinary level to general competencies.

In the US, the approach to the curriculum transformation for developing 21st century skills is the 'partial infusion mode' (Guo 2016, 45). The skills are regarded as essential in all educational stages, fields, and subjects, embedded in curriculum objectives and content. The US focuses on infusing 21st century skills in the curriculum, not on how to infer or deduct lower-level curriculum objectives and content, nor on the interface between layers. As the 21st century skills do not dominate, it leaves space for curriculum development at the disciplinary level, which helps to highlight various subjects' features without dissolving the generality and cross-curricula feature of 21st century skills (Guo 2016).

## Conclusion and discussion

Both China and US reformers developed key competencies frameworks in response to the complex challenges of a knowledge-based society and global competition. Their frameworks align in that both select and define the competencies or skills that 21st-century students should master and both attempt to integrate these in curricula. However, the motives and contents of the two frameworks and how they are integrated in curriculum differ greatly. China's framework is government-driving, draws on the frameworks of other countries but mainly responds to local demands, prioritising moral values and containing more comprehensive competencies that emphasise knowledge, skills, attitudes, and values. The US framework is driven by non-governmental actors, emphasises higher-order skills serving economic development and occupational demand. These differences in framework are closely related to the cultural and political context and values of the two countries, which have also affected the implementation of their frameworks.

The Confucian tradition strongly influences the Chinese framework. As Lin (2016, 134) asserts, 'moral values are the core of the key competencies framework'. This 'moral values' can also be interpreted as a form of politically inclined moral education. These all-encompassing moralised and politicised competencies lack focus and fail to respond to Chinese society's – especially the business community's – concerns about global competition.

The US framework reflects the pragmatic skill tradition. Although it seems to be a new idea, skills similar to those now considered 21st century skills have featured in many educational reforms in American history. Ravitch (2009a) regards 21st century skills as 'an old family song' and points out that they are not unique, newly emerging skills. Instead, such skills were taught for more than a century (Sawchuk 2009). Specifically, Dewey is considered the 'father of 21st century learning' (Bennett 2011), and 21st century skills can be considered a contemporary extension of the US educational tradition, with the addition of ICT skills. However, a skill-priority framework 'overemphasizes technical rationality and neglects the importance of moral values and the role of the community in shaping the individual's identity, ethics, and behaviors' (Tan, Chua, and Goh 2015, 307).

Halász and Michel (2011) argue that the conditions for the successful implementation of a competency-based curriculum reform depend on at least two parallel factors: political commitment and implementation capabilities. For implementation capabilities, the easiest part is to change the curriculum goals and standards; it is more difficult to develop new assessment instruments or introduce new evaluation approaches, reform teacher education, school learning environments, and teaching methods.

China has a strong political commitment to implement the framework and has developed the key competencies framework at the national level and integrated it in the national curriculum standards. However, the top-down inculcation and implementation of morality – the core socialist value – may narrow the understanding, cultivation, and application of key competencies and leave little room, at any level, to teach critical thinking and creative thinking skills. Under these circumstances, the space for reform is limited. In addition, most teachers do not have a clear idea of the concept of key competencies, nor are they prepared to teach them. They are accustomed to direct instruction methods rather than to student-centred methods. Furthermore, China's assessment system has not substantially changed: the college entrance examination (*gaokao*) is the Achilles' heel of

21st-century reforms (Cheng, Jackson, and Lee 2017), forcing schooling to concentrate on subject knowledge and academic achievement rather than general competencies (Bulle 2011; Deng and Gopinathan 2016). Although China's framework emphasises general competencies, in practice these are transformed into subject-specific competencies and then into subject knowledge dominated by the assessment system. The concept of competencies dissolves when turned into subject-specific competencies (Willbergh 2015) and becomes counterproductive.

The implementation of the US framework attempts to match the CCSS and adopt a partial infusion model to develop curriculum. In the US, innovation and reform are part of national history and culture, and they are also part of everyday life as opposed to being part of a curriculum guide (Trilling and Fadel 2009). Although US teachers also face the pressures of testing and accountability, they have more autonomy than their Chinese counterparts, and US teachers mainly adopt inquiry-based learning rather than direct instruction, which is better for developing 21st century skills (Deng and Peng 2017). Compared with the uniform high-stakes national paper and pencil test adopted by Chinese universities for enrolment, US higher-education institutions have more freedom in relation to student admission, so there is more freedom in teaching and assessing 21st century skills in K-12 education (Zhao 2018).

Nonetheless, reform in the US is also facing challenges. According to critics of the 21st century skills movement, there has been an overemphasis on skills and a neglect of disciplinary knowledge. Ravitch (2009b) and Hirsch (2009) have noted that skills cannot be acquired without disciplinary knowledge and a broad, well-rounded general education. The group Great Minds (2009) and Ravitch (2009a) criticized education reform based on the argument that 21st century skills undermine the quality of education in the US, and they contend that teaching 21st century skills will marginalise knowledge, hurting the tradition of public education (i.e. liberal education) and risking failure like all previous skills movements in American history (e.g. the life adjustment movement in the 1950s and outcome-based education in the 1980s). Furthermore, the US reform has no unified national policy and national curriculum standards. Lacking strong political commitment, political support, and policy continuity, the reform may not last very long (Halász and Michel 2011).

The challenges faced by the two frameworks may be avoided by their learning from each other. First, it is essential to develop high-order skills in a knowledge-based society in which technology and the nature of work are changing rapidly, together with 'the beliefs, values, and attitudes that shape a person's identity, life goals, relationships with others, and, ultimately, purpose and quality of life' (Tan, Chua, and Goh 2015, 311). Individuals can foster, and care for, a sustainable world in multifaceted and reflective ways only if education includes multiple aspects of knowledge, such as economics, culture, aesthetics, politics, and ethics (Hardy and Uljens 2018). China's framework could learn from the US framework by incorporating more higher-order thinking skills and communication and collaborative skills to meet the needs of economic development, while the US framework could learn from China's by involving moral values and emotional attitudes.

Second, China's reform implementation would be possible in the long term if implementation capacities are developed as they are in the US, for example by giving teachers more autonomy, transforming teaching and evaluation approaches, and further developing students' high-order skills on the basis of moral and knowledge education. Meanwhile, the US can learn from China's tradition of knowledge teaching, especially for students who lack knowledge preparation, while continuing to develop skills. The US reform is also more likely to be implemented in the short term if political support is obtained from local, state, or federal government.

However, changing the cultural factors underlying reform is the greatest obstacle to reform (Halász and Michel 2011). According to Zhao (2018), any attempt to learn from the education policy, educational strategy, or teaching practice of another country is doomed to fail if culture of that country is not borrowed as well. Nevertheless, with the increasing intensity of global exchanges, it is possible to mutually learn from each other in a cultural perspective (Cheng 1998), especially when considering that modern Chinese education has already benefited from American educational concepts such as Dewey's ideas. Future studies should further examine the possibilities of cultural and practical changes in teaching, assessments, teacher education, and learning environments in both Chinese and American schools.

## Notes

1. The 13 key competencies frameworks Lin's team consulted come from various countries, regions and international organisations, including OECD, UNESCO, the US, Japan, Taiwan (China), France, the UK, the EU, Singapore, New Zealand, Finland, Canada, Australian.

## Acknowledgements

We thank Kathryn Anderson-Levitt, Meg Gardinier, Dra. Eloísa Bordoli and Charlene Tan for the helpful comments on an earlier draft.

## Disclosure statement

No potential conflict of interest was reported by the author(s).

## References

Ananiadou, Katerina, and Magdalena Claro. 2009. *21st Century Skills and Competences for New Millennium Learners in OECD Countries*. OECD Education Working Papers, No. 41, OECD Publishing.

Anderson-Levitt, Kathryn M. 2012. "Complicating the Concept of Culture." *Comparative Education* 48 (4): 441–454. doi:10.1080/03050068.2011.634285.

Anderson, Ronald. 2008. "Implications of the Information and Knowledge Society for Education." In *International Handbook of Information Technology in Primary and Secondary Education*, edited by J. Voogt, and G. Knezek, 5–22. New York: Springer.

Bennett, Paul W. 2011. "The Case Against 21st Century Schools." http://www.ourkids.net/school/the-case-against-21st century-schools.

Braun, Jerome. 2013. *Democratic Culture and Moral Character: A Study in Culture and Personality*. Dordrecht, Netherlands: Springer Science + Business Media.

Bulle, Nathalie. 2011. "Comparing OECD Educational Models Through the Prism of PISA." *Comparative Education* 47 (4): 503–521. doi:10.1080/03050068.2011.555117.

Care, Esther, Kate Anderson, and Helyn Kim. 2016. "Visualizing the Breadth of Skills Movement across Education Systems." The Brookings Institution. https://www.brookings.edu/wp-content/uploads/2016/09/global_20160916_breadth_of_skills_movement.pdf.

CCSSI (Common Core State Standards Initiative). 2010. "Statements of Support." http://www.corestandards.org/other-resources/statements-of-support.

Cheng, Kai-ming. 1998. "Can Education Values Be Borrowed? Looking into Cultural Differences." *Peabody Journal of Education* 73 (2): 11–30.

Cheng, Kai-ming, Liz Jackson, and Wing-on Lee. 2017. "Advancing 21st Century Competencies in East Asian Education Systems." Center for Global Education, Asia Society. https://asiasociety.org/files/21st century-competencies-east-asian-education-systems.pdf.

Chu, Samuel Kai Wah, Rebecca B. Reynolds, Nicole J. Tavares, Michele Notari, and Celina Wing Yi Lee. 2017. *21st Century Skills Development Through Inquiry-Based Learning from Theory to Practice*. Singapore: Springer Science.

CPGPRC (Central People's Government of the People's Republic of China). 2017. *Opinions on Deepening the Reform of the Educational System and Mechanism*. The General Office of the Communist Party of China Central Committee and the General Office of the State Council issue. http://www.gov.cn/xinwen/2017-09/24/content_5227267.htm.

Dede, Chris. 2010. "Comparing Frameworks For 21st Century Skills." In *21st Century Skills: Rethinking How Students Learn*, edited by J. Bellanca, and R. Brandt, 51–75. Bloomington, IN: Solution Tree Press.

Dello-Iacovo, Belinda. 2009. "Curriculum Reform and 'Quality Education' in China: An Overview." *International Journal of Educational Development* 29 (3): 241–249. doi:10.1016/j.ijedudev.2008.02.008.

Deng, Zongyi, and S. Gopinathan. 2016. "PISA and High-Performing Education Systems: Explaining Singapore's Education Success." *Comparative Education* 52 (4): 449–472. doi:10.1080/03050068.2016.1219535.

Deng, Li, and Zhengmei Peng. 2017. "How to Implement 21st Century Skills in American Schools: A Study on the 21st Century Learning Exemplar School." [in Chinese] *Studies in Foreign Education* 44 (9): 51–71.

Dewey, John. 1997. *How We Think*. Revised ed. New York: Dover Publications.

Dillon, Sam. 2010. "Top Test Scores from Shanghai Stun Educators." https://www.nytimes.com/2010/12/07/education/07education.html.

ECDVT (European Centre for the Development of Vocational Training). 2014. *Terminology of European Education and Training Policy (Second Edition). A Selection of 130 Key Terms*. Luxembourg: Publications Office of the European Union.

Friedman, Thomas L. 2013. "The Shanghai Secret." https://www.nytimes.com/2013/10/23/opinion/friedman-the-shanghai-secret.html.

Great Minds. 2009. "A Challenge to the Partnership for 21st Century Skills." https://greatminds.org.

Guo, X. M. 2016. "Discussion from Key Competencies to Curriculum Model: A Comparison Based on the Overall Dominance Model and Partial Infiltration Model." [in Chinese] *Journal of the Chinese Society of Education* 11: 44–47.

Halász, Gábor, and Alain Michel. 2011. "Key Competences in Europe: Interpretation, Policy Formulation and Implementation." *European Journal of Education* 46 (3): 289–306. doi:10.1111/j.1465-3435.2011.01491.x.

Hallak, Jacques. 1991. *Educational Policies in a Comparative Perspective: Suggestions for a Research Agenda*. Paris: UNESCO International Institute for Educational Planning.

Hardy, Ian, and Michael Uljens. 2018. "Critiquing Curriculum Policy Reform in Finland and Australia: A Non-Affirmative, and Praxis-Oriented Approach." *Transnational Curriculum Inquiry* 15 (2): 50–82.

Hirsch, E. D., Jr. 2009. "The 21st Century Skills Movement." http://greatminds.net/maps/documents/reports/hirsch.pdf.

IBE (International Bureau of Education). 2012. "Twenty-First Century Skills." United Nations Educational, Scientific, and Cultural Organization. http://www.ibe.unesco.org/en/glossary-curriculum-terminology/t/twenty-first-century-skills.

James, William. 2013. "Pragmatism: A New Name for Some Old Ways of Thinking." http://www.gutenberg.org/files/5116/5116-h/5116-h.htm.

Kay, Ken. 2010. "21st Century Skills: Why They Matter, What They Are, and How We Get There." In *21st Century Skills: Rethinking How Students Learn*, edited by J. Bellanca, and R. Brandt, xiii–xxxi. Bloomington, IN: Solution Tree Press.

Kay, Ken, and Margaret Honey. 2006. "Establishing the R & D Agenda for Twenty-First Century Learning." *New Directions for Youth Development* 110: 63–80. doi:10.1002/yd.168.

Kohn, Alfie. 2009a. "Twenty-First Century Skills? It Depends What You Mean." http://www.alfiekohn.org/blogs/twenty-first-century-skills-depends-mean.

Kohn, Alfie. 2009b. "When 21st Century Schooling Just Isn't Good Enough: A Modest Proposal." *District Administration* 45 (2): 38–39.

Lin, C. D. 2016. *The Study of Key Competencies for 21st Century Students' Development*. [in Chinese] Beijing: Beijing Normal University Publishing Group.

McLachlan, Kurt. 2012. *A Case Study of 21st Century Skills Programs and Practices*. Los Angeles: University of Southern California.

MEPRC (Ministry of Education of the People's Republic of China). 1999. *Central Committee of the Communist Party of China and the State Council's Decision on Deepening Educational Reform and Comprehensively Promoting Quality Education*. http://www.moe.gov.cn/jyb_sjzl/moe_177/tnull_2478.html.

MEPRC (Ministry of Education of the People's Republic of China). 2014. *Opinions on Comprehensively Deepening Curriculum Reform and Implementing the Fundamental Tasks of Establishing Morals and Cultivating People*. http://old.moe.gov.cn//publicfiles/business/htmlfiles/moe/s7054/201404/167226.html.

MEPRC (Ministry of Education of the People's Republic of China). 2018. *Curriculum Scheme for the Senior High School (2017)*. http://www.moe.gov.cn/srcsite/A26/s8001/201801/t20180115_324647.html.

Muers, Stephen. 2018. "Culture, Values and Public Policy." https://www.bath.ac.uk/publications/culture-values-and-public-policy/attachments/culture-values-and-public-policy.pdf.

OECD (Organisation for Economic Cooperation and Development). 2005. *The Definition and Selection of Key Competencies: Executive Summary*. Paris: OECD Publishing.

P21 (Partnership for 21st Century Learning). 2002. "Learning for the 21st Century. A Report and Mile Guide for 21st Century Skills." https://eric.ed.gov/?id=ED480035.

P21 (Partnership for 21st Century Learning). 2007. "Our History." http://www.p21.org/about-us/our-history.

P21 (Partnership for 21st Century Learning). 2008. *21st Century Skills, Education & Competitiveness: A Resource and Policy Guide*. https://files.eric.ed.gov/fulltext/ED519337.pdf.

P21 (Partnership for 21st Century Learning). 2010. *Up to the Challenge: The Role of Career and Technical Education and 21st Century Skills in College and Career Readiness*. http://www.p21.org/storage/documents/CTE_Oct2010.pdf [No longer available. However, the pdf is archived by Internet Archive at https://web.archive.org/web/20170611020155/http://www.p21.org/storage/documents/CTE_Oct2010.pdf].

P21 (Partnership for 21st Century Learning). 2011. *P21 Common Core Toolkit: A Guide to Aligning the Common Core State Standards with the Framework for 21st Century Skills*. https://files.eric.ed.gov/fulltext/ED543030.pdf.

P21 (Partnership for 21st Century Learning). 2012. "Exemplar Program Application." http://www.p21.org/exemplar-program-case-studies/exemplar-program-application [this website is no longer available, but the program can be found at https://www.battelleforkids.org/networks/p21/21st-century-learning-exemplar-program].

P21 (Partnership for 21st Century Learning). 2015. "U.S. Students Need 21st Century Skills to Compete in a Global Economy." http://www.p21.org/news-events/press-releases/369-us-students-need-21st century-skills-to-compete-in-a-global-economy [No longer available, and not archived].

P21 (Partnership for 21st Century Learning). 2018. "Overview of State Leadership Initiative." http://www.p21.org/members-states/partner-states [No longer available on the web; archived here: https://web.archive.org/web/20181222045052/http://www.p21.org/members-states/partner-states].

Peng, Zhengmei, and Li Deng. 2017. "Towards the Core of Educational Reform: Cultivating Critical Thinking Skills as the Core of the 21st Century Skills." [in Chinese] *Research in Educational Development* 24: 21-27.

Peng, Zhengmei, Juan Gu, and Meinert A. Meyer. 2018. "Grundcharakteristiken der Konfuzianischen Allgemeinbildung und Deren Transformation in der Vergangenheit und in der Heutigen Globalisierenden Zeit." *Zeitschrift für Erziehungswissenschaft* 2: 259–278.

Phillips, David. 2012. "The Perils of Policy Borrowing." Centre for Education Research and Policy. https://cerp.aqa.org.uk/perspectives/perls-policy-borrowing.

Ravitch, Diane. 2009a. "21st Century Skills: An Old Family Song." Thomas B. Fordham Institute. https://fordhaminstitute.org/national/commentary/21st century-skills-old-familiar-song.

Ravitch, Diane. 2009b. "Critical Thinking? You Need Knowledge." Boston Globe. http://archive.boston.com/bostonglobe/editorial_opinion/oped/articles/2009/09/15/critical_thinking_you_need_knowledge.

Sawchuk, Stephen. 2009. "Backers of '21st century Skills' Take Flak." http://www.edweek.org/ew/articles/2009/03/04/23pushback_ep.h28.html?_ga=2.262972556.1448258841.1497840310-1451289347.1497840310.

Silva, Elena. 2009. "Measuring Skills for 21st Century Learning." *Phi Delta Kappan* 90 (9): 630–634. doi:10.1177/003172170909000905.

Tan, Charlene.sa. 2013. *Learning from Shanghai: Lessons on Achieving Educational Success.* Dordrecht, Netherlands: Springer.

Tan, Jennifer Pei-Ling, Suzanne S. Choo, Trivina Kang, and Gregory Arief D. Liem. 2017. "Educating for Twenty-First Century Competencies and Future-Ready Learners: Research Perspectives from Singapore." *Asia Pacific Journal of Education* 37: 425–436. doi:10.1080/02188791.2017.1405475.

Tan, Charlene, and Catherine S. K. Chua. 2015. "Education Policy Borrowing in China: Has the West Wind Overpowered the East Wind?" *Compare: A Journal of Comparative and International Education* 45 (5): 686–704. doi:10.1080/03057925.2013.871397.

Tan, Charlene, Catherine S. K. Chua, and Olivia Goh. 2015. "Rethinking the Framework for 21st Century Education: Toward a Communitarian Conception." *The Education Forum* 79 (3): 307–320. doi:10.1080/00131725.2015.1037511.

Tedesco, Juan Carlos, Renato Opertti, and Massimo Amadio. 2014. "The Curriculum Debate: Why It Is Important Today." *Prospects* 44: 527–546. doi:10.1007/s11125-014-9326-x.

Trilling, Bernie, and Charles Fadel. 2009. *21st Century Skills: Learning for Life in Our Times.* New York: John Wiley & Sons.

Tucker, Marc S. 2011. *Surpassing Shanghai: An Agenda for American Education Built on the World's Leading Systems.* Cambridge, MA: Harvard Education Press.

Voogt, Joke, and Natal Pareja Roblin. 2012. "A Comparative Analysis of International Frameworks for 21st Century Competences: Implications for National Curriculum Policies." *Journal of Curriculum Studies* 44 (3): 299–321. doi:10.1080/00220272.2012.668938.

Wagner, Tony. 2008. *The Global Achievement Gap: Why Even Our Best Schools Don't Teach the New Survival Skills Our Children Need—and What We Can Do About It.* New York: Basic Books.

Willbergh, Ilmi. 2015. "The Problem of 'Competence' and Alternatives from the Scandinavian Perspective of Building." *Journal of Curriculum Studies* 47 (3): 334–354. doi:10.1080/00220272. 2014.1002112.

WVDE (West Virginia Department of Education). 2008. *A Chronicle of West Virginia's 21st Century Learning Initiative (2004–2008)*. http://wvde.state.wv.us/tt/2008/21stChronicle082008.pdf.

You, Yun. 2019. "The Seeming 'Round Trip' of Learner-Centred Education: A 'Best Practice' Derived from China's New Curriculum Reform?" *Comparative Education* 55 (1): 97–115. doi:10.1080/03050068.2018.1541662.

Zeitlin, Kenneth S. 2013. "A Study of California Public School District Superintendents and their Implement of 21st Century Skills(dataset)." University of Southern California.

Zhao, Yong. 2018. "Shifting the Education Paradigm: Why International Borrowing Is No Longer Sufficient for Improving Education in China." *ECNU Review of Education* 1 (1): 76–106. doi:10. 30926/ecnuroe2018010105.

Zhong, Q. Q. 2016. "Curriculum Development Based on Core Competencies: Challenges and Issues." [in Chinese] *Global Education* 45: 3–25.

Zhu, M. J. 2018. "20 Questions for the Interpretation of New Curriculum of Senior High School." [in Chinese] Online video interview. http://pckt.xze.cn/resdetail?resid=7956.

# 21st century skills in the United States: a late, partial and silent reform

Kathryn Anderson-Levitt

**ABSTRACT**

This article examines the history of US movements for competencies, often called 'twenty-first century skills', in international context. Ironically, US actors were a source of early ideas about competencies but 'late' adopters of a competency-added reform—a partial and silent policy incorporated within the Common Core State Standards of 2010. The US case might appear to support a realist theory that the country independently invented the same solution to the same problem addressed by other countries' competency-based reforms. However, this article shows that some US actors actually invited international influence, supporting the theory that the common problem was actually a social construction. In addition, soft power exercised by technology corporations partly explains how the solution of a competency-added curriculum was finally adopted by most US states.

In the context of competency-based reforms elsewhere (this theme issue; Anderson-Levitt, Bonnéry, and Fichtner 2017), this article asks what has happened in the United States regarding competencies—often called 'twenty-first century skills' in US parlance. This is an interesting question because scholars cite the United States as a source of ideas about competencies, going back to Taylorism and Bloom's taxonomy (e.g. Ropé 2008). More broadly, globalisation and hence travelling policies in education were long equated with 'Americanisation' (Nederveen Pieterse 2015).

This article will show that, although there has been an explicit movement for twenty-first century skills in the United States, the actual introduction of competencies into policy occurred in the context of a different movement, the campaign for national standards that culminated in the Common Core State Standards in 2010. Seen from an international perspective, the Common Core as a 'competency-added reform' (Voogt and Roblin 2012) is a late, partial and silent policy. This article also shows that some actors in the standards movement invited international influence, offering a rare case of US actors ready to borrow as well as to lend.

After laying out a framework for thinking about US reform in international context, the article sketches the explicit movement for twenty-first century skills. Then, turning to the standards movement, it shows how the Common Core incorporated some twenty-first century skills, and how that silent policy came about. The discussion weighs the evidence for realist, culturalist and critical theories about what led US policy to converge, to some extent, with other nations' competency-based reforms.

## Conceptual framework

### *Competencies, twenty-first century skills, and standards*

In line with typical usage in the United States, I use the term 'competencies' rather than 'competences' and use the term 'twenty-first century skills' interchangeably with 'competencies'. By 'competencies' I mean skills (knowing *how to*) and dispositions (being *ready to*) as opposed to content knowledge (knowing *that*). Advocates generally consider competencies to be transdisciplinary or 'transversal', in contrast with strictly disciplinary skills (Nordin and Sundberg, this issue). Many analysts also associate twenty-first century skills with another notion used in this article, 'higher-order thinking' (e.g. NRC 2012, 1), meaning the more cognitively demanding skills in Bloom's taxonomy, such as applying, analysing, and evaluating knowledge (Anderson et al. 2001).

This article will also refer to 'standards', defined as 'the learning goals for what students should know and be able to do at each grade level'.[1] By that definition, standards might include disciplinary content knowledge, disciplinary skills, and/or competencies.

### *Explaining parallel movements*

To think about the US case in international context, I keep two related questions in mind. First, 'Why competencies?'—that is, what problem is a competency-based reform meant to solve? —and, 'Why now?'—that is, how can we explain why competency-based reforms fall within a particular time frame? Analysis of the US case will identify that time frame as beginning about 1990 and peaking in 2010 with the publication of the Common Core State Standards. The larger transnational framework suggests a similar time frame for other nations' reforms, as illustrated by the table in Anderson-Levitt and Gardinier (this issue).

One theory explaining interest in competencies and its timing is 'realism', an assumption that states act rationally (Meyer et al. 1997, 146). From a realist perspective, economic 'imperatives'—in this case, global competition in a new knowledge economy—prompted countries to develop 'similar responses to common problems' (Inkeles and Siroway 1983, 305). In addition to the new economy, a second 'problem' arising in the 1990s in newly post-socialist societies might have been the need to prepare citizens for democracy (e.g. Tahirsylaj, this issue). Convergence across countries would result because, in response to the common problems, different countries either borrow or independently invent similar solutions—in this case, school curricula teaching students the competencies they will need to be successful workers and/or good citizens.

Theorists raise several challenges to this realist perspective. First, is there really a problem? Since competencies such as problem-solving, communication and collaboration have been crucial to human survival over millennia, and since observational studies document blue-collar workers using higher-order skills on the job (Rose 2004; Scribner 2012.), why assume that human beings lack such skills and dispositions

(Carson 2001)? Second, if there is nonetheless a problem, is it really experienced in common across the globe? The proportion of jobs demanding 'nonroutine cognitive or interpersonal skills' varies, from estimates of less than half the population in higher-income countries to less than one-quarter in lower income countries (World Bank 2016, Fig. 2.17).[2] Finally, why would modifying school curricula be the best solution as opposed to alternatives like increasing job-based training or modifying workplaces to elicit the skills workers are already capable of using?

A second set of theories casts problems and their solutions as social constructions rather than unquestioned realities. World society theory posits a globally shared construction of what a national education system should look like (Schofer et al. 2012), and one could argue that competency-based curricula have become part of that global model. However, world society theory does not specify how a globally shared model comes to be constructed or modified. Alternatively, a 'culturalist' perspective argues that people in different localities construct problems and solutions differently, depending on their particular historical, economic and political circumstances (Anderson-Levitt 2003). However, culturalist theories do not explain larger patterns and simultaneity—how the same problem and solution get identified at the same moment in different parts of the world.

A third set of theories focuses a critical gaze on the exercise of power. Critical theorists ask whether some actor has imposed solutions to problems, real or socially constructed, either through direct coercion or through 'soft power'. Although soft power, 'the ability to get what you want through attraction rather than coercion or payments' (Nye 2004, 256), is a term usually applied to nations and to international organisations (Grek 2010), it also suits the 'framing strategies' used by corporations (Verger, Steiner-Khamsi, and Lubienski 2017, 337). Actions of powerful transnational actors could help explain the simultaneity of reform movements. To identify such actors in this case, one can ask 'Who is gaining and who is losing' by 'casting competency as a significant social problem' (Carson 2001, 35)?

### Research questions

To address whether US actors have in fact pushed for competencies and if so, why and why now, I focus on these research questions:

Has there been a movement or movements for competencies in the United States?
If so, has competency-based reform actually taken place?
If so, how can one explain the interest in competencies and the timing of US movement(s) in domestic context? In international context?

### Methods

I used an eclectic set of research methods to take a historical perspective on these research questions. To identify movements, trace their histories, and determine whether they had actually affected US policy, I began with secondary sources that referenced 'competency-based' or 'twenty-first century skills' promoters within the United States. This led to secondary sources not only on those topics but on the Common Core and the US standards movement as well. To further reconstruct both twenty-first century skills and the US standards movement, I then turned to primary sources such as news reports, organisational reports and websites. I used past versions of websites preserved by Internet Archive.org to look for changes in organisations' messages over time.

To explain how the interest in competencies developed and persisted within the United States, I identified individual as well as institutional actors listed in both secondary and primary sources, including online biographies, and traced their activities over time. One reason to follow actors over time was to assess whether there was continuity in US movements through the decades, since continuity might have supported a realist perspective that the US simply followed its own path without external influence. In addition, following actors helped to avoid 'methodological nationalism' (Dale and Robertson 2008); keeping track of different factions, organisations, and individual actors, including those active both inside and beyond the national context, makes visible that the nation is not a monolith and that its policy borders can be porous.

I used the online biographies to track who had worked with whom, or for which institutions, both within the United States and cross-nationally. I also tracked who cited whom and which organisations cited or co-authored with which other organisations in their reports. Together, the biographical information and citation records served as evidence of possible lines of influence both domestically and cross-nationally. Information from primary and secondary sources on which organisations provided funding for which efforts provided further evidence of lines of influence.

To place the timing of US movements in international perspective, I collected reports in secondary and primary sources of competency-based reforms in other nations. These data are reported in our Introductory Essay (Anderson-Levitt and Gardinier, this issue) because they provide context for all the articles in this issue.

A limitation of this study is that I did not interview individual actors to corroborate or nuance the written information or to discover ideas and actions that had not left a written trace.

## Two movements, one reform

The first finding, as secondary sources soon revealed and as already mentioned, was that competency reform in the United States is a story of two movements. An explicit movement for twenty-first century skills led by the private, non-profit organisation Partnership for 21stCentury Learning (P21)[3] energetically promoted the idea that schools should teach a particular set of twenty-first century skills (P21 2016). However, a different movement, the effort to establish national standards, actually wrote some twenty-first century skills into policy. That is, the standards movement led to the 2010 launch of almost-national Common Core State Standards—and analysts claimed *post hoc* that the Common Core had woven some twenty-first century skills into its disciplinary standards (e.g. NRC 2012).

This article describes both movements with emphasis on the latter, which has had a longer history and more success. As an aid to following the stories and locating them in global context, Table 1 offers a timeline.

### P21's movement for twenty-first century skills

The explicit US movement for twenty-first century skills began in 2002 with the establishment of P21. However, P21 grew out of a prior organisation called the CEO Forum on Education and

# CONTEXTUALIZING GLOBAL FLOWS OF COMPETENCY-BASED EDUCATION   103

**Table 1.** Timeline for the two US movements and international milestones.

| | Twenty-first century skills | US standards movement | Milestones outside the US |
|---|---|---|---|
| 1980s | | *A Nation at Risk*, 1983<br>National Education Goals, 1989 | EC begins focus on education for economic development |
| 1990s | CEO Forum founded 1996 | SCANS report, 1991<br>America 2000, 1991<br>Goals 2000, 1994<br>Goals 2000 dies, 1996<br>Achieve begins, 1996 | OECD begins cross-curricular competencies<br>EC white papers under Delors<br>CONFEMEN report, 1995<br>UNESCO Delors Report, 1996 |
| 2000s | P21 founded 2002 | American Diploma Project template, 2004 | OECD Key Competencies, 2005<br>EU Key Competencies, 2006 |
| 2010s | P21 ends 2018 | Common Core launches, 2010<br>Some states revise or back out<br>Some implementation | |

Technology, founded in 1996. The CEO Forum published several reports on school technology and digital learning, and by 2001 'was regularly using the phrase "twenty-first-century skills"' (Sawchuk 2009, 18). When the CEO Forum ended, P21 began under the same director, Ken Kay, with technology companies like Apple, Cable in the Classroom, Dell, and Microsoft as well as the US Department of Education as founding members.[4] By 2018, P21 listed 22 of the 50 states as 'partners'.[5] Although P21 also recruited four of its 26 'member organisations' from outside the United States[6], the focus of its activities was heavily domestic.

One of P21's activities was to develop and promote lists of twenty-first century skills. Not surprisingly, given the involvement of major technology companies, its first list placed particular emphasis on digital competencies (P21 2003). Its later framework (P21 2016) reduced the emphasis on digital skills and added disciplinary knowledge as well as interdisciplinary themes. P21 also separately promoted four skills from its framework —creativity, critical thinking, communication and collaboration—as the '4 C's'.[7] See Deng and Peng (this issue) for a fuller discussion of P21 and its framework.

The concept of twenty-first century skills never gained the same visibility within the United States as some curricular reforms. Whereas a Google search for 'whole language' literacy instruction or 'Common Core' identifies over two *billion* entries, the term 'twenty-first century learning' elicits 'only' some 400 million entries (one-fifth as many), 'twenty-first century skills' elicits 200 million, and 'competencies in education' 50 million.[8] The movement lost further visibility in 2018 when P21 was absorbed by another organisation, BattelleforKids, and its website disappeared.

However, P21 did attract the attention of one group of critics, prominent scholars and educators including educational historian Diane Ravitch and professor of education and humanities E. D. Hirsch (Cavanagh 2009). These critics claimed that P21's approach to teaching skills 'marginalises knowledge' and that skill was useless 'without prior knowledge of a wide array of subjects' (Cavanagh 2009).[9] Their debate with P21 echoed competency-versus-content tensions in other countries (Clément, this issue; Nordin and Sundberg, this issue).

## *Competencies within the Common Core state standards*

Meanwhile, the US Common Core launched in 2010. The Common Core is not about twenty-first century skills; rather, it resulted from the long effort to establish nationwide educational standards. Traditionally, in the decentralised US system, local school districts had determined curriculum and few states had even state-level standards until the 1990s (Mehta 2013). The Common Core, developed at the state governors' request by a private organisation called 'Achieve', as discussed further below, was written as a model for new state-level standards meant to be similar, if not identical, across the states.

The Common Core contains no transdisciplinary competencies comparable to the key competencies of the OECD (OECD 2005) or the European Union (European Parliament 2007). Rather, it consists of hundreds of discipline-specific learning goals for kindergarten through secondary school in English language arts and mathematics. It also includes thirty-two 'anchor standards' for English language arts and six 'standard mathematical practices', which are goals meant for all grade levels, such as 'Assess how point of view or purpose shapes the content and style of a text' (Common Core 2010a, 10) and 'Make sense of problems and persevere in solving them' (Common Core 2010b, 6–8). However, even the anchor standards and standard practices refer to disciplinary skills.

Nonetheless, after the Common Core launched, some analysts pointed out that its standards incorporated several twenty-first century skills (Table 2). First, P21 identified certain skills from its own framework within some Common Core standards (2011). As an example, P21 suggested that fourth graders would develop the skills of *critical thinking* and *information literacy* in an English lesson that addressed this standard: 'Refer to details and examples in a text when explaining what the text says explicitly and when drawing inferences from the text' (P21 2011, 14). Then, a committee constituted by the National Research Council[10] published a scholarly report on competencies which included an analysis identifying some twenty-first century skills within the Common Core (NRC 2012). A third report, commissioned by the organisation that produced the Common Core, Achieve, identified 'many of the skills most demanded by employers, college

**Table 2.** Twenty-first century skills said to appear in Common Core State Standards.

| Identified by P21 (2011) | Identified by NRC (2012) | Identified by Achieve (2012) |
|---|---|---|
| | Constructing and evaluating evidence-based arguments | |
| | **Non-routine problem solving** | **Problem-solving skills** |
| **Critical Thinking and Problem Solving** | **Critical thinking** | **Reasoning skills** |
| **Communication** | **Complex Communication I: disciplinary discourse** | **Communications skills etc.** |
| | Complex Communication I: Critical reading (ELA only) | |
| | Systems thinking (Math only) | |
| Information literacy (ELA only) | | |
| Information, Media and Technology Skills | | Use of data Research skills (ELA only) |
| | Motivation and persistence (Math only) | |
| | Identity (Math only) | |
| | Attitudes (Math only) | |
| | Self-development (Math only) | |
| Self-Direction (ELA only) | Self-regulation, executive functioning (Math only) | |
| | | Time management skills |
| | Collaboration, team-work (Math only) | Teamwork/collaboration skills |
| Global Awareness (ELA only) | | |

Sources: Drawn from P21 (2011, 6 & 8); Achieve (2012,); NRC (2012, Figure 5–1, Figure 5–2).
'ELA' = Common Core for English, language arts and literacy'; 'Math' = Common Core for mathematics.

professors and society' embedded within the standards (Achieve 2012, 7), and claimed that they had been built in '*explicitly* and *intentionally*' (2012, 8, emphasis in original).

Although the three analyses, which used three different lists of twenty-first century skills as frameworks, did not completely align, they did agree that the Common Core called for problem-solving skills, critical thinking or reasoning, and communication skills. Indeed, it is reasonable to interpret many specific Common Core standards as requiring those skills within the context of disciplinary goals—again, not as transdisciplinary standards. Thus the Common Core might be called, at most, a 'competency-added' reform but would certainly not qualify as a 'competency-integrated' reform or a 'competency-transformed', to use categories that Nordin and Sundberg (this issue) adapted from Voogt and Roblin (2012).

### Late, partial and silent

Seen as a competency-added reform in international perspective, Common Core is 'late' in the sense that over forty polities are reported to have enacted competency-based reforms earlier, as illustrated by the table in Anderson-Levitt and Gardinier (this issue). The US reform happened after competency-based reforms had swept through Europe and had also touched nearly twenty countries in other parts of the world.

Meanwhile, supporters of competencies consider the Common Core to be partial because it incorporates only some, not all, twenty-first century skills on their lists (e.g. NRC 2012). P21 called Common Core the 'floor', not the 'ceiling', for student performance (2011, 3). However, as noted above, advocates do not completely agree on which twenty-first century skills Common Core actually incorporates.

The Common Core is also partial in the sense that it is a patchwork, not a nationwide policy. Only 41 out of 50 states currently subscribe to some version of the standards, and of those, ten states have made 'substantive' modifications in its basic template (Friedberg et al. 2018). The lack of uniformity reflects the US federal structure in which the Constitution gives authority over education to the individual states.

Finally, incorporation of twenty-first century skills within the Common Core represents a silent policy in the sense that standards reformers never advertised the presence of competencies before or during the 2010 launch. For example, when the organisation Achieve was laying groundwork for shared standards, its earliest archived website (2001) described its goals simply as 'high expectations' and 'a challenging curriculum' leading to 'the knowledge and skills essential to succeed in today's increasingly competitive world'.[11] It did not specify those skills. Similarly, the 2009 Common Core website said simply, 'These standards will be … aligned with college and work expectations and include rigorous content and skills', again, without listing particular skills.[12] Only in 2014, three years after the outside reports began identifying twenty-first century skills within the standards, did the Common Core web site begin to specify that 'problem-solving, collaboration, communication, and critical-thinking skills are interwoven into the standards'.[13]

### Why competencies?

### How common core happened

In the US case, then, the question 'Why competencies?' becomes the question 'How did it happen that the Common Core included competencies?' Addressing that question requires as background a skeletal history of the US movement for national standards (see also Table 1):

(1) *Goals 2000.* The first President Bush worked with state governors to craft non-binding National Education Goals, commissioned a study of workplace competencies (SCANS 1991), and proposed legislation called 'America 2000', that would have led to national standards. Congress did not pass America 2000, but did pass a similar law, 'Goals 2000', under President Clinton in 1994. However, two years later, a more conservative Congress killed most of Goals 2000's provisions (Superfine 2005).
(2) *Achieve.* When federal efforts failed in 1996, supporters of national standards shifted to private efforts and eventually proposed privately written standards. State governors, through their private organisation, the National Governors Association, created the non-governmental organisation Achieve (Hartong 2015). Achieve co-authored hypothetical standards for secondary school completion through the American Diploma Project (Achieve et al. 2004), and later, at the governors' request, oversaw drafting of hypothetical 'Common Core State Standards' for each elementary and secondary grade level. Meanwhile, multiple domestic audiences debated standards, from governors concerned with global economic competition to civil rights activists focused on equity within the United States (Mehta 2013).
(3) *Common Core.* In 2009, President Obama linked federal grants[14] to adoption of 'college- and career-ready' state standards, making the brand-new Common Core template attractive to states. Soon, 45 states announced adoption of the Common Core (Gewertz 2019).[15] However, after strong backlash, four states backed out (Ujifusa, Bannerjee, and Tomko 2017) and most states abandoned a plan for common assessments (Gewertz 2019). Nonetheless, research suggests that some teachers are implementing some of the standards (e.g. Schweig, Kaufman, and Opfer 2020).

### How competencies were incorporated

Competencies found a place in the Common Core thanks to a 'progressive' faction within the standards movement. Although there were conservative reformers who expected standards to focus on curricular content ('basics'), other, progressive standards supporters interpreted the goal of 'rigorous content and skills' as demanding higher-order thinking (Mehta 2013). Textbooks had already been increasing in cognitive demandi during the 1970s and 1980s, after an earlier decline in cognitive demand in reading textbooks (Stevens et al. 2015) and peaks and dips in arithmetic textbooks (Baker et al. 2010). In a sense, the progressive standards reformers aimed to establish cognitively demanding goals more firmly and systematically within a curriculum framework shared across the nation.

The progressives had the ear of the first President Bush and of President Clinton, and not surprisingly those presidents' initiatives, America 2000 and Goals 2000, mentioned goals that resembled twenty-first century skills, such as 'to write and communicate effectively', 'to reason', and 'to solve problems' (US Congress 1994). Although the second President Bush favoured pro-basics standards reformers (Mehta 2013), President Obama's administration favoured progressives, and while Obama was president, Achieve tapped progressive experts to write the Common Core.

In arguing for standards promoting higher-order thinking, progressives had used language similar to that of twenty-first century skills advocates. For example, an early, influential essay championed 'hands-on activities', 'cooperative learning', imaginative 'use of computer technology', and 'sustained and imaginative problem-solving' (Smith and O'Day 1991, 239). Later, because the progressive authors of the Common Core aimed for higher-order thinking, they embedded expectations for communication, critical thinking and problem-solving within some disciplinary standards. However, they did not work from a list of skills such as P21's framework, resulting in what P21 considered only a partial reform.

Meanwhile, the authors of the Common Core were silent about twenty-first century skills within the standards because, for them, higher-order thinking, not competencies *per se*, was the goal. Interestingly, the silence of competencies within the Common Core—their complete incorporation within content standards—avoided the content-versus-competencies tension that plagued P21 and that was also present in other cases discussed in this issue (e.g. Clément).

### *Why now?*

In seeking to explain the timing of the United States' competency-added reform, the first question is: Why did the national standards movement, with its vague references to competencies, begin about 1989? Domestic analysts answer this question in domestic terms, seeing the movement as a response to the alarmist 1983 report about US education, *A Nation at Risk* (NCEE 1938; e.g. Mehta 2013; Wixson, Dutro, and Athan 2003).

The second question is: Why did it take another two decades to enact a competency-added standards reform? The simple answer is strong resistance to federal control over education. Congress' fear of federal control defeated Bush's proposal in 1991 and undid Goals 2000 in 1996 (Mehta 2013; Superfine 2005). Much of the backlash after the launch of the Common Core was also a reaction against federal control (McDonnell and Stephen Weatherford 2016). Continuing backlash may also have contributed to silence about competencies within the standards, since supporters would have hesitated to highlight another reason for controversy. As mentioned, avoidance of federal control also explains why Common Core is not a nationwide policy.

In the face of such resistance, one can ask how the Common Core nonetheless took hold. As mentioned, one trigger was the federal funding dangled by the Obama administration. It is also worth noting reformers' persistence. Indeed, some of the same progressive actors promoted the standards movement across decades. For example, Marshall Smith advised the first President Bush on national education goals, helped with Goals 2000 under President Clinton, and served under President Obama when Common Core launched[16]; Susan Pimentel promoted Goals 2000 in the 1990s, helped craft the American Diploma Project in the 2000s, and led the team writing the Common Core English language standards in 2009.[17]

Yet another factor was massive funding from corporations, especially technology corporations, to support development of the Common Core and to campaign for its adoption. Many technology companies were just going public and emerging as rich and powerful players in the late 1980s and 1990s. When federal efforts for standards foundered in 1996, technology corporations—and their foundations which, although charitable organisations, often served corporate policy (Moeller 2020)—stepped in. The Bill and

Melinda Gates Foundation spent over 200 million dollars to fund research legitimising the Common Core, a prime example of 'soft power', and to promote state adoptions and grassroots campaigns (Layton 2014; McDonnell and Weatherford 2013). The William and Flora Hewlett Foundation was another funder, supporting along with Gates such projects as the American Diploma Project (Achieve et al. 2004, 3).

## US competency movements in international perspective

The continuity of ideas and of certain actors across the decades might suggest that US reformers developed and maintained their interests in competencies and standards independent of the rest of the world. However, in fact some US actors engaged with colleagues outside the United States regarding competencies, and there was opportunity for two-way flow of ideas in international spaces. On the one hand, US actors influenced OECD's early work on competencies: in 1984, the United States and France had pressed the OECD to develop easily comparable indicators of achievement (Heyneman 1993), and later, as the OECD took up that work, researchers from the US National Center for Education Statistics contributed ideas about workplace competencies (Martens 2007; Morgan 2007). More recently, one of P21's board members, Charles Fadel, became chair of the education committee of the Business and Industry Advisory Council that officially advises OECD[18], and Andreas Schleicher as OECD Director for Education and Skills cited Fadel's work on curriculum design (Schleicher 2018).

On the other hand, the timing of the US standards movement suggests flow in the other direction, from international sources to the United States. As Table 1 shows, America 2000 and Goals 2000, with their allusions to competencies, coincided with several international pronouncements. Under the leadership of Jacques Delors, the European Commission began to focus on education for 'developing human capital' in 1985 (Pagliarello 2020, 8), issuing white papers on 'fundamental competences' needed by young people (EC 1993, 124) in a 'cognitive society' (EC 1995). The Ministers of Education of Francophone African nations called for competence-based education (CONFEMEN 1995), as did Delors in his much-cited report for UNESCO (Delors 1996). Arguably, US standards reformers may have been responding not only to *A Nation at Risk*, but also to the international discourse that was creating a 'referential web' (Vavrus 2004) of rationales for competency-based reform.

More concretely, some US standards advocates directly invited international influence. In 1996, the governors, meeting with corporate leaders at a National Education Summit, invited a report on education standards in other nations (Achieve 1996), and then tasked Achieve with identifying the best standards from other countries (Hartong 2015). Strikingly, in 2008, the National Governors Association and Achieve invited Schleicher, who was at that time Head of the Indicators and Analysis Division in OECD's Directorate for Education, to participate in an International Benchmarking Advisory Group (Hartong 2015, 218). That group's subsequent report not only advocated for 'a common core of internationally benchmarked standards' (NGA, CCSSO and Achieve 2008, 24), but also argued that students needed 'higher skills' like 'problem-solving' (9), and favourably cited a 'focus on problem solving and the critical evaluation of information' in the OECD's PISA (32). Later, the Common Core website acknowledged 'international benchmarking' as one criterion for good standards.[19]

## Discussion

In summary, there have been two movements relevant to competencies in the United States: the overt movement for twenty-first century skills led by P21 and the movement for national standards. Progressives within the standards movement, aiming to encourage higher-order thinking, turned some twenty-first century skills into policy by weaving them into specific disciplinary standards in the Common Core. But seen as a competency-added reform, the Common Core was a late, partial, and silent policy.

### Global flow ...

From a domestic perspective, the answer to 'Why competencies?' is that they were built into the Common Core merely as a by-product of the authors' interest in higher-order thinking. Domestic events explaining the timing of the competency-added standards movement were a push for rigour in response to *A Nation at Risk*; then decades of resistance to federal control; and ultimately an acceptance of standards prompted by federal funding and a technology-funded campaign. As argued above, the story of twenty-first century skills within the Common Core standards might appear at first to support a realist theory of US reformers responding independently to rising economic competition, while other nations reacted similarly to the same global economy.

However, a realist reading does not take into account the international calls for curriculum reform that coincided with moves by US actors, or the governors' direct engagement with Andreas Schleicher and international benchmarking. Those facts align instead with a world society perspective in which transnational organisations, especially the OECD, constructed the definition of a global problem and its solution.

Granted, the openness of US actors to international influence was not broadcast loudly (in contrast to the case described by Tahirsylaj, this issue). However, neither was it a case of 'silent borrowing' (Waldow 2009), since the governors, Achieve, and the Common Core website acknowledged their use of 'international benchmarking'. Moreover, because there were multiple domestic audiences for standards reforms, no single 'logic of legitimation' (Waldow 2009, 479), whether appeal to international or to domestic authority, would have suited every audience. Whereas the state governors cared about global economic competition, civil rights and equity activists were concerned with equity from one state to another and across ethnic and social class boundaries (Mehta 2013) and would have had little interest in what the OECD said.

The openness of US actors to OECD influence reminds us that global flows should be tracked through time as well as across space. Over time, travelling policies can make a 'round-trip' (You 2019). In this case, ideas that were once 'internal' had in time become 'external'—shared with OECD test developers who were first constructing PISA—and, in much modified form, then became available for later import back into the United States.

### But also domestic contingencies ... and powerful actors

While teaching useful lessons about global flow, this case also demonstrates the importance of domestic politics and historical contingencies, supporting a 'culturalist' interpretation as well. Standards were not bound to happen; the movement was stifled once in

1996, and is still struggling ten years after its launch. Had standards moved forward a few years earlier under the second President Bush, who favoured pro-basics reformers, the standards might well have omitted twenty-first century skills.

Finally, social construction, whether global or domestic, is not the whole story. Examination of the domestic process revealed not only the influence of the OECD, but also the powerful role of technology corporations. Corporate foundations exercised the 'soft power' of funded research and lobbying campaigns to sell the Common Core, just as technology corporations had supported P21. Technology corporations benefit from competency-based reform, as digital literacy appears on most lists of key competencies, promising them well-prepared consumers of digital products. They also benefit because competencies are difficult to assess, thus encouraging test-designers to develop sophisticated testing methods dependent on digital technology, as happened in PISA's recent assessment of collaborativeness (OECD 2017, 22). Moreover, the same corporations push for competencies in transnational settings in alliance with the OECD, as Morgan (2016) has demonstrated. Thus, one of several answers to the question 'Why competencies, and why now?', in the United States and perhaps beyond, is that such reforms serve the interests of technology companies, which have been growing in influence since the 1990s.

This case has offered an unusual illustration of high-powered US reformers like state governors inviting international influence and thereby subtly enhancing the legitimacy of the OECD's educational role. Globalisation of competencies is not, at least not now, a case of Americanisation. Nor is it a movement simply driven by a new global economy; rather, the OECD and other transnational organisations have constructed competencies as a particular solution to an imagined problem (Grek 2010; Steiner-Khamsi 2013), sometimes in partnership with the technology companies that stand to profit from such a solution.

## Notes

1. http://www.corestandards.org/faq/what-are-educational-standards/
2. As pointed out by Silvana Gvirtz in remarks at the 2018 meeting of CIES.
3. Originally called the Partnership for 21st Century Skills.
4. https://web.archive.org/web/20100613154647/http://www.p21.org/index.php?option=com_content&task=view&id=507&Itemid=191
5. https://web.archive.org/web/20181222045052/http://www.p21.org/members-states/partner-states
6. https://web.archive.org/web/20181222071027/http://www.p21.org/members-states/member-organizations
7. https://www.youtube.com/watch?v=QrEEVZa3f98
8. Choice of specific terminology affects the counts, but has little effect on the order of magnitude.
9. At first the critics' group called its website 'Common Core' but changed the name to 'Great Minds' to avoid confusion with the Common Core State Standards when they were proposed.
10. The National Research Council is a program of the US National Academies of Science, a private, non-profit organisation originally established by Congress.
11. https://web.archive.org/web/20011009000237/http://www.achieve.org/
12. From July 4, 2009: https://web.archive.org/web/20090704090533/http://www.corestandards.org/

13. https://web.archive.org/web/20140314163445/http://www.corestandards.org/about-the-standards/frequently-asked-questions/ under 'Content and Quality ...\Do the Common Core Standards incorporate both content and skills?' and Quality of the Standards; see also https://web.archive.org/web/20140313202810/http://www.corestandards.org/what-parents-should-know/
14. In a program called 'Race to the Top,' https://obamawhitehouse.archives.gov/issues/education/k-12/race-to-the-top
15. A 46th state adopted the English language arts but not the mathematics standards.
16. https://learningpolicyinstitute.org/person/marshall-mike-smith; https://www.carnegiefoundation.org/about-us/fellows/mike-smith/; https://en.wikipedia.org/wiki/Marshall_S._Smith
17. https://sites.google.com/site/gefoundation2011a/sue-pimentel
18. http://biac.org/policy_groups/education/.
19. http://www.corestandards.org/assets/Criteria.pdf.

## Acknowledgments

Many thanks to Li Deng and Zhengmei Peng for sharing many sources of information on P21, and to them, Andreas Nordin, Meg Gardinier, and Daniel Sundberg for helpful comments on an earlier version of the manuscript. The analysis presented in this article is my own, and does not necessary reflect the views of others that I have cited.

## Disclosure statement

No potential conflict of interest was reported by the author(s).

## References

Achieve. 2012. *Understanding the Skills in the Common Core State Standards*. Washington, DC: Achieve.

Achieve Inc. 1996. *A Review of the 1996 National Education Summit*. Washington, DC. https://www.achieve.org/files/1996NationalEducationSummit.pdf.

Achieve, Inc., The Education Trust, and Thomas B. Fordham Foundation. 2004. *Ready or Not: Creating a High School Diploma That Counts*. Washington, DC: The American Diploma Project.

Anderson-Levitt, Kathryn M., eds. 2003. *Local Meanings, Global Schooling*. New York: Palgrave Macmillan.

Anderson-Levitt, Kathryn M., Stéphane Bonnéry, and Sarah Fichtner. 2017. "Competence-Based' Approaches as 'Traveling' Reforms." *Cahiers de la Recherche sur L'Éducation et les Savoirs* 16 (27–45), https://journals.openedition.org/cres/3009.

Anderson, Lorin W., David R. Krathwohl, Peter W Airasian, Kathleen A Cruikshank, Richard E Mayer, Paul R Pintrich, James Raths, and Merlin C Wittrock. 2001. *A Taxonomy for Learning, Teaching, and Assessing: A Revision of Bloom's Taxonomy of Educational Objectives*. New York: Longman.

Baker, David, Hilary Knipe, John Collins, Juan Leon, Eric Cummings, Clancy Blair, and David Gamson. 2010. "One Hundred Years of Elementary School Mathematics in the United States." *Journal for Research in Mathematics Education* 41 (4): 383–423.

Blosveren, Kate, and Achieve, Inc. 2012.. . .

Carson, John. 2001. "Defining and Selecting Competencies: Historical Reflections on the Case of IQ." In *Defining and Selecting Key Competencies*, edited by Dominique Simone Rychen, and Laura Hersh Salganik, 33–44. Bern: Hogrefe & Huber.

Cavanagh, Sean. 2009. "'Common Core' Group Takes Aim at Move For 21st-century Skills." *Education Week* 29 (4): 4–4.

Common Core State Standards Initiative. 2010a. *Common Core State Standards for English Language Arts & Literacy in History/Social Studies, Science, and Technical Subjects*. http://www.corestandards.org/ELA-Literacy/.

Common Core State Standards Initiative. 2010b. *Common Core State Standards for Mathematics*. http://www.corestandards.org/Math/.

CONFEMEN (Conférence des ministères de l'éducation des pays ayant le français en partage). 1995. *L'éducation de base: Vers une nouvelle école*. CONFEMEN: Dakar.

Dale, Roger, and Susan Robertson. 2008.Beyond Methodological 'isms' in Comparative Education in an Era of Globalisation. *International Handbook of Comparative Education*. Springer.

Delors, Jacques. 1996. *Learning: The Treasure Within*. Paris: UNESCO.

EC (European Commission). 1993. *Croissance, compétitivité, emploi*. Luxembourg: Office des publications officielles des Communautés européennes.

EC (European Commission). 1995. *Enseigner et apprendre. Vers la société cognitive*. Luxembourg: Office des publications officielles des Communautés européennes.

European Parliament. 2007. *Key Competences for Lifelong Learning: A European Reference Framework*. Annex of a Recommendation of the European Parliament and of the Council of 18 December 2006 on key competences for lifelong learning, Official Journal of the European Union, 30.12.2006/L394.

Friedberg, Solomon, Diane Barone, Juliana Belding, Andrew Chen, Linda Dixon, Francis Fennell, Douglas Fisher, Nancy Frey, Roger Howe, and Tim Shanahan. 2018. *The State of State Standards Post-Common Core*. Washington DC: Thomas B. Fordham Institute.

Gewertz, Catherine. 2019. "Only 16 States Still Share Common-Core Tests, Survey Finds." *Education Week* 38 (23): 6.

Grek, Sotiria. 2010. "International Organisations and the Shared Construction of Policy 'Problems'." *European Educational Research Journal* 9 (3): 396–406. doi:10.2304/eerj.2010.9.3.396.

Hartong, Sigrid. 2015. "New Structures of Power and Regulation Within 'Distributed' Education Policy – the Example of the US Common Core State Standards Initiative." *Journal of Education Policy* 31 (2): 213–225. doi:10.1080/02680939.2015.1103903.

Heyneman, Stephen P. 1993. "Quantity, Quality, and Source." *Comparative Education Review* 37 (4): 372–388.

Inkeles, Alex, and Larry Siroway. 1983. "Convergent and Divergent Trends in National Educational Systems." *Social Forces* 62: 303–333.

Layton, Lyndsey. 2014. "How Bill Gates Pulled Off the Swift Common Core Revolution." *The Washington Post*, June 7.

Martens, Kerstin. 2007. "How to Become an Influential Actor." In *New Arenas in Education Governance*, edited by Kerstin Martens, Alessandra Rusconi, and Kathrin Leuze, 40–54. New York: Palgrave Macmillan.

McDonnell, Lorraine M., and M. Stephen Weatherford. 2016. "Recognizing the Political in Implementation Research." *Educational Researcher* 45 (4): 233–242. doi:10.3102/0013189 (16649945.

McDonnell, Lorraine M., and M. Stephen Weatherford. 2013. "Organized Interests and the Common Core." *Educational Researcher* 42 (9): 488–497. doi:10.3102/0013189(13512676.

Mehta, Jal. 2013. *The Allure of Order*. New York: Oxford University Press.

Meyer, John W., John Boli, George M. Thomas, and Francisco O. Ramirez. 1997. "World Society and the Nation-State." *American Journal of Sociology* 103 (1): 144–181.

Moeller, Kathryn. 2020. "Accounting for the Corporate." *Educational Researcher*, doi:10.3102/0013189(20909831.

Morgan, Clara. 2007. *The OECD Programme for International Student Assessment: Unravelling a Knowledge Network.* PhD dissertation, School of Public Policy and Administration, Carleton University.

Morgan, Clara. 2016. "Testing Students under Cognitive Capitalism." *Journal of Education Policy* 31 (6): 805–818. doi:10.1080/02680939.2016.1190465.

National Commission on Excellence in Education. 1983. *A Nation at Risk.* Washington, DC: Department of Education.

Nederveen Pieterse, Jan. 2015. "History and Hegemony." In *The Routledge International Handbook of Globalization Studies*, edited by Bryan S. Turner, and Robert J. Holton, 111–127. New York: Taylor & Francis.

NGA (National Governors Association), CCSSO (Council of Chief State School Officers), and Achieve Inc. 2008. *Benchmarking for Success.* Washington, DC: National Governors Association.

NRC (National Research Council). 2012. *Education for Life and Work: Developing Transferable Knowledge and Skills in the 21st Century.* Washington, DC: The National Academies Press.

Nye, Joseph S., Jr. 2004. "Soft Power and American Foreign Policy." *Political Science Quarterly* 119 (2): 255–270. doi:10.2307/20202345.

OECD. 2005. *The Definition and Selection of Key Competencies.* Paris: OECD.

OECD. 2017. *PISA 2015 Collaborative Problem-Solving Framework.* https://www.oecd.org/pisa/pisaproducts/Draft%20PISA%202015%20Collaborative%20Problem%20Solving%20Framework%20.pdf.

Pagliarello, Marina Cino. 2020. "Aligning Policy Ideas and Power: The Roots of the Competitiveness Frame in European Education Policy." *Comparative Education*, 1–18. doi:10.1080/03050068.2020.1769927.

Partnership for 21st Century Learning (P21). 2016. *Framework for 21st Century Learning.* https://web.archive.org/web/20160909050313/http://www.p21.org/storage/documents/docs/P21_framework_0816.pdf.

Partnership for 21st Century Skills (P21). 2003. *Learning for the 21st century.* Washington, DC: Partnership for 21st Century Skills. https://web.archive.org/web/20031002142253/http://www.21stcenturyskills.org/downloads/P21_Report.pdf.

Partnership for 21st Century Skills (P21). 2011. *P21 Common Core Toolkit.* https://files.eric.ed.gov/fulltext/ED543030.pdf.

Ropé, Françoise. 2008. "Savoirs et Compétences." In *Dictionnaire de l'éducation*, edited by Agnès van Zanten, 603–608. Paris.

Rose, Mike. 2004. *The Mind at Work.* New York: Penguin.

Sawchuk, Stephen. 2009. "Skills of Business." *Education Week* 29 (14): 18–21.

SCANS (Secretary's Commission on Achieving Necessary Skills), The. 1991. *What Work Requires of Schools: A SCANS Report for America 2000.* Washington, DC: U.S. Department of Labor.

Schleicher, Andreas. 2018. *World Class: How to Build a 21st-century School System.* OECD.

Schofer, Evan, A. Hironaka, D. J. Frank, and W. Longhofer. 2012. "Sociological Institutionalism and World Society." In *The Wiley-Blackwell Companion to Political Sociology*, edited by E. Amenta, K. Nash, and A. Scott. New York: John Wiley.

Schweig, Jonathan D., Julia H. Kaufman, and V. Darleen Opfer. 2020. "Day by Day: Investigating Variation in Elementary Mathematics Instruction That Supports the Common Core." *Educational Researcher* 49 (3): 176–187. doi:10.3102/0013189(20909812.

Smith, Marshall S., and Jennifer A. O'Day. 1991. "Systemic School Reform." In *The Politics of Curriculum and Testing*, edited by S. H. Fuhrman, and B. Malen, 233–267. New York: Falmer.

Steiner-Khamsi, Gita. 2013. "What is Wrong with the 'What-Went-Right' Approach in Educational Policy?" *European Educational Research Journal* 12 (1): 20–33. doi:10.2304/eerj.2013.12.1.20.

Stevens, Robert J., Xiaofei Lu, David P. Baker, Melissa N. Ray, Sarah A. Eckert, and David A. Gamson. 2015. "Assessing the Cognitive Demands of a Century of Reading Curricula." *American Educational Research Journal* 52 (3): 582–617. doi:10.3102/0002831215573531.

Superfine, Benjamin Michael. 2005. "The Politics of Accountability: The Rise and Fall of Goals 2000." *American Journal of Education* 112 (1): 10–43. doi:10.1086/444513.

Ujifusa, Andrew, Sumi Bannerjee, and Gina Tomko. 2017. "Map: Tracking the Common Core State Standards." *Education Week* 36 (11): 16.

United States Congress. 1994. "Goals 2000: Educate America Act." http://www2.ed.gov/legislation/GOALS2000/TheAct/index.html.

Vavrus, Frances. 2004. The Referential web: Externalization Beyond Education in Tanzania. *The Global Politics of Education Borrowing and Lending.* Teachers College Press.

Verger, Antoni, Gita Steiner-Khamsi, and Christopher Lubienski. 2017. "The Emerging Global Education Industry." *Globalisation, Societies and Education* 15 (3): 325–340. doi:10.1080/14767724.2017.1330141.

Voogt, Joke, and Natal Pareja Roblin. 2012. "A Comparative Analysis of International Frameworks for 21st Century Competences." *Journal of Curriculum Studies* 44 (3): 299–321. doi:10.1080/00220272.2012.668938.

Waldow, Florian. 2009. "Undeclared Imports: Silent Borrowing in Educational Policy-Making and Research in Sweden." *Comparative Education* 45 (4): 477–494. doi:10.1080/03050060903391628.

Wixson, Karen K., Elizabeth Dutro, and Ruth G. Athan. 2003. "The Challenge of Developing Content Standards." *Review of Research in Education* 27 (1): 69–107. doi:10.3102/0091732(027001069.

World Bank. 2016. *World Development Report 2016: Digital Dividends.* Washington, DC: World Bank Publications.

You, Yun. 2019. "The Seeming 'Round Trip' of Learner-Centred Education." *Comparative Education* 55 (1): 97–115. doi:10.1080/03050068.2018.1541662.

peace OPEN ACCESS

# What kind of citizens? Constructing 'Young Europeans' through loud borrowing in curriculum policy-making in Kosovo

Armend Tahirsylaj

**ABSTRACT**
Kosovo introduced two major curriculum reforms over the past 20 years – in 2001 and 2011 – each aiming to bring education closer to international trends. Simultaneously, Kosovo underwent major political, social, and cultural changes after the war in 1999, and the declaration of independence in 2008. This article relies on document analysis and uses civic competences definitions in Kosovo and European Commission frameworks to compare conceptions of citizenship for democratic life along three theoretical constructs, namely personally responsible/individualist, participatory/social, and justice-oriented/political. It coins loud borrowing to describe the policy flow into Kosovo education, specifically focusing on the latest 2011 competence-based curriculum reform. The findings show that Kosovo's curriculum alignment with the European Commission key competence approach in 2011 served larger political goals and aspirations to brand Kosovars as 'Young Europeans.' In addition, personally responsible/individualist conception and participatory/social conception of citizenship are dominant in Kosovo, as well as in European Commission frameworks.

## Introduction and purpose

Since the end of war in Kosovo in 1999, two curriculum reforms have attempted to make education more relevant for Kosovo students. While the first wave of curriculum reform in 2001 was an extension of previously content-based curricula, the latest curriculum reform of 2011 is the most ambitious one as it departs from content-based curricula to embrace competence-based education (CBE) approaches to curriculum making (Tahirsylaj 2018). The introduction of the CBE approach in Kosovo followed the transnational policy flows in education over the past 20 years, which has been widespread but not global, and primarily concentrated in Europe (Anderson-Levitt 2017). The 2011 curriculum reform in Kosovo was heavily influenced by the key competences for lifelong learning

---

This is an Open Access article distributed under the terms of the Creative Commons Attribution-NonCommercial-NoDerivatives License (http://creativecommons.org/licenses/by-nc-nd/4.0/), which permits non-commercial re-use, distribution, and reproduction in any medium, provided the original work is properly cited, and is not altered, transformed, or built upon in any way.

recommended by the European Commission (OJEU 2006, 2018). Further, international donor agencies and international consultants shaped the curriculum reform agenda (Tahirsylaj and Wahlström 2019). The 2011 curriculum reform followed Kosovo's independence in 2008 when the political agenda included a campaign to brand Kosovo people as 'Young Europeans' (Hapçiu and Sparks 2012), backed up by the visions for a democratic society in the Kosovo Constitution (Assembly of the Republic of Kosovo 2008).

Against this background, the article has three goals: first, to trace the introduction of competence-based curricula in Kosovo, particularly in relation to key competences promoted at the European Union level that Kosovo aimed to be associated with and eventually be part of. Second, the article then narrows the focus down to civic competences[1], with the associated outcome of 'responsible citizen', as one of the six key competences defined in the new Kosovo Curriculum Framework (KCF) (MEST 2011) to compare the conceptions of civic competences in two directions: externally between the 2011 reform and key civic competences recommended by the European Commission (OJEU 2006), and internally in the curriculum policies in Kosovo between the 2001 and 2011 reforms. Third, lower secondary curricula, and specifically the latest civic education curricula of grades 6 and 7, are examined to identify the opportunities that Kosovo students can expect to have to develop into democratic citizens through the curriculum context in their formal schooling.

To meet its goals, the article borrows from the global education policy flows and policy borrowing scholarship that has defined transnational education policy making as either contributing to convergence or divergence of curricula internationally (Anderson-Levitt 2003; Steiner-Khamsi 2004). Next, focusing on civic competences as one of the key competences in the 2011 KCF, the article relies on empirically based conceptualizations of what it means to be a good citizen in a democratic society by Westheimer and Kahne (2004) who distinguish among three types, namely *personally responsible, participatory*, and *justice-oriented* citizens, and theoretical conceptualizations of civic competences as framed by Biesta (2007). A qualitative approach relying on document analysis and using Kosovo and European Commission policy documents as data sources is applied to meet the objectives of the study.

The article contributes to the ongoing debates on the influence of global education policy flows into national contexts. Kosovo as a convergent case (Tahirsylaj and Wahlström 2019) represents an example of policy transfer as 'loud borrowing'. This characterisation contrasts with the silent borrowing practices identified elsewhere to describe incorporations of global education policy ideas into national contexts without revealing them as such but as a product of within-nation discussion (see Waldow 2009). Loud borrowing is offered to indicate an education policy-making process in which national authorities deliberately pursue and amplify external policies for both educational and political ends. Further, the article makes an original contribution with regard to conceptions of civic competences and democratic citizens in a developing context such as Kosovo where promotion of international policies is favourably viewed by both local policymakers and the general public in efforts to bring Kosovar society closer to standards of developed democracies of (primarily) Western Europe. In this regard, the article highlights the policy *content* by focusing on civic competences that shows Kosovo followed the European framing of key competences, and the policy-making *process* that underlines the uniqueness of the Kosovo context with international organisations and consultants playing a major role in policy-making. This situation of welcoming educational policy solutions from Western-based international organisations and consultants has to be understood within the broader historical journey of Kosovo since the early 1990s when the main call of local politicians was for Western organisations such as the EU and NATO, as well as the US, to intervene to resolve Kosovo's political situation. And the Western nations did end Kosovo's war through NATO's intervention in 1999. As a result, the view of the Western organisations as solution providers extended to many societal domains, such as education and the justice system, for example, after the end of the war in 1999 (Papadimitriou, Petrov, and Greicevci 2007).

In the next sections, first the conceptual and analytical framework is further elaborated, and a literature review related to civic competences is offered, followed by a brief background on Kosovo's context. Next, methodological considerations and data material are provided, then findings and results are presented, ending with discussion, conclusions and avenues for further research.

## Conceptual and analytical framework

The article borrows conceptual tools from two main scholarly strands focusing on civic education – the first is US-based and empirical following the work of Westheimer and Kahne (2004) and the second is European-based and theoretical, following the work of Biesta (2007). There are close overlaps between the two strands, and for the purposes of the article, the two are merged to both frame the study and to create an analytical tool to examine conceptions of civic competences and citizenship dominant in the Kosovo curriculum.

Westheimer and Kahne (2004) studied ten programmes aiming to advance democratic purposes of education through civic education across the US, and empirically forwarded three main conceptions of effective citizenship, including *personally responsible, participatory*, and *justice-oriented*. A *personally responsible citizen* is one that primarily 'Acts responsibly in his/her community' (Westheimer and Kahne 2004, 240). A *participatory citizen*, is an 'Active member of community organizations and/or improvement efforts; Organizes community efforts to care for those in need; [...] Knows strategies for accomplishing collective tasks' (Westheimer and Kahne 2004, 240). And, a *justice-oriented citizen* is the one that 'Critically assesses social, political, and economic structures to see beyond surface causes; Seeks out and addresses areas of injustice; Knows about democratic social movements and how to effect systemic change' (Westheimer and Kahne 2004, 240). This framework maps well with the goals of the present study; however it rests on a larger assumption about education as a 'producer' of certain types of citizens, and by extension, society. This is where Biesta (2007) is helpful as he develops another set of three theoretically-grounded conceptions of citizens for a democratic society.

The three conceptions of democratic subjectivity advanced by Biesta (2007) include the *individualistic*, the *social*, and the *political*. According to Biesta, conceptions of democratic subjectivity need to be built upon a broader definition of what democracy is in the first place. Following John Dewey's social conception of democracy, Biesta (2007) concludes that democracy is about inclusive social and political action, in part, to negate the individualistic and instrumentalist approaches to civic education specifically, and education more broadly construed. Further, Biesta (2007) distinguishes between education *for* democracy and education *through* democracy, where the first approach assumes that democracy can be taught and thus acquired through formal schooling. The second approach counters that democracy cannot be learned if schools themselves are not democratic institutions where students are able to participate in democratic practices.

Turning to the three conceptions, Biesta (2007) defines an *individualistic conception of democratic subjectivity* relying on Immanuel Kant's philosophy (Kant [1784] 1992), itself rooted in the European enlightenment, a period that advanced rational thinking and autonomy as key qualities of individuals. The individualistic conception of democratic subjectivity rests on the understanding that 'The democratic subject is the person who can think for himself, who can make his own judgements without being led by others' (Biesta 2007, 6). Next, Biesta advances the *social conception of democratic subjectivity* following John Dewey's philosophy (Dewey [1916] 1966), which highlights social interaction, participation, and association, and by extension, the idea that being a democratic person involves acting and participating in the social context. Lastly, Biesta (2007) develops a *political conception of democratic subjectivity* building on Hannah Arendt's philosophy (Arendt 1977, 1958) centred around

> [...] an understanding of human beings as *active* beings, as beings whose humanity is not simply defined by their capacity to think and reflect, but where what it means to be human has everything to do with what one *does*. (Biesta 2007, 8, emphasis in the original)

For Biesta (2007), a political conception of democratic subjectivity built on Arendt's philosophy assumes that democracy is exercised in the public sphere where everyone has the possibility to act and be a subject, and at the same time, everyone has the possibility to take up actions and beginnings of others in a diverse and plural world.

To summarise, the two sets of conceptions presented here following Westheimer and Kahne (2004) and Biesta (2007) show clear overlaps. To be personally responsible, one has to be able to think and act based on rational thinking and autonomy; to be a participatory citizen, one has to participate in social contexts; and to be a justice-oriented person, one needs to engage actively and deliberately in the political life. In all conceptualizations, action is crucial for democracy; what varies is the level and degree of action, and there is a rising progression in the level of engagement from being a personally responsible, to a participatory, to a justice-oriented citizen, and correspondingly from an individualistic, to social, to political conceptions of democratic subjectivity. As a result, for the purposes of the present study, the six conceptions are condensed into three by merging *personally responsible* and *individualist*, *participatory* and *social*, and *justice-oriented* and *political*. In turn, these three categories constitute the analytical framework to examine the European Commission and Kosovo curriculum policy documents with the focus on prevailing conceptions related to civic competences.

### *Literature review*

With a few exceptions, research into education reform and recent curriculum reform in particular within the context of Kosovo is limited. For example, Tahirsylaj and Wahlström (2019) have examined the role that education policy context plays in mastery of critical thinking competences. Saqipi (2019) analysed the role that context plays in challenging environments such as Kosovo in adopting far reaching educational reforms such as competence-based curriculum. Zylfiu (2014) surveyed eighth graders across Kosovo regarding their perceptions of participation in democratic life, and found that students felt schools prepared them well for active participation in democratic life; however, about half of the sample reported their membership in political parties was not important. Still, no prior study has examined the conceptions of civic competences in the latest 2011 curriculum policy reform in Kosovo, and therefore, the present article fills a significant gap in the literature.

Internationally, educational research focusing on civic education is abundant, including the International Civic and Citizenship Study (ICCS), a major large-scale assessment administered by the International Association for the Evaluation of Educational Achievement (IEA). The ICCS focuses on how countries prepare students for political participation and citizenship (IEA n.d.). Not surprisingly, considering the role that civic education is routinely ascribed to play, research in the field is dominated by the role that civic education plays in political participation and engagement (see, for example, Torney-Purta, Schwille, and Amadeo 1999; Galston 2004; Biesta 2008). Indeed, after reviewing civic education conceptions in the Scottish curriculum using Westheimer and Kahne's (2004) theoretical framework, Biesta (2008) found that the *personally responsible/individualistic* conception was dominant.

Civic education conceptions gain increased relevance in post-conflict societies such as Kosovo for the purposes of democratising the society (Quaynor 2012). Since 2000, the United Nations Educational, Scientific and Cultural Organization (UNESCO) has promoted democratic citizenship education as an overarching value of education (UNESCO 2008). Studies on civic education in post-conflict societies offer a unique lens into idiosyncrasies of schooling in challenging contexts. A review of literature focusing on citizenship education in post-conflict societies identified the avoidance of controversial issues, the unique role of ethnicity, a lack of trust in political parties and authoritarianism, and to a lesser degree, a movement towards global or regional identities as key findings (Quaynor 2012). More specifically, in a multi-country study that included Kosovo, Weinstein, Freedman, and Hughson (2007) found that segregation of Kosovo's society (and education) along ethnic lines – primarily between an Albanian majority and a Serbian minority – posed challenges for building interethnic social networks that in the long run would overcome historically persisting ethnic divisions. In this regard, the present study contributes to the literature on the opportunities that civic education curricula offer students to master competences to fully participate and engage in democratic life and develop democratic citizenship by identifying dominant conceptions of civic competences in Kosovo curriculum policy.

### Overview of Kosovo context

Constitutionally, Kosovo is defined as a democratic republic, and its constitutional order is based on principles of '[…] freedom, peace, democracy' (Assembly of Republic of Kosovo 2008, 2). The Law on Pre-University Education in Kosovo states that one of the main purposes of pre-university education is, 'to prepare the pupil for a responsible life in the spirit of good understanding, peace, tolerance, gender equality and friendship with members of all communities in the Republic of Kosovo' (Assembly of Republic of Kosovo 2011, 1). The 2011 Kosovo Curriculum Framework notes that one of the main aims of education in Kosovo is to develop knowledge, skills, attitudes and values of pupils required by a democratic society (MEST 2011).

Educationally, a number of reforms have been initiated in the Kosovo context over the past 20 years, including introduction of external assessments at the end of Grades 5, 9, and 12, adoption of a competence-based curriculum, and participation in the Programme for International Student Assessment (PISA) for the first time in 2015 and again in 2018 – where Kosovo was ranked the third from the bottom of all participating countries. These reforms have been heavily supported by the international donor community, including the European Commission, the World Bank, and individual government programmes from Germany, Canada, the US, and the UK to name a few. Schools play a crucial role in new and emerging democracies in establishing a democratic culture (Biesta 2007), and thus it is worth examining Kosovo's curriculum policy while efforts are ongoing to build a democratic society.

### Introduction of competence-based curriculum in Kosovo

Over the past 20 years, the national and international political processes in and about Kosovo have largely determined curriculum reform. First, with the end of the war in 1999, Kosovo became a protectorate under the United Nations, with all sectors, including education, administered by international organisations. Initially, the department of education was run by the United Nations Children's Fund (UNICEF) as a lead agency, coordinating a number of other international donors who provided technical assistance and other resources for the education sector. Introduction of a new Kosovo Curriculum Framework in 2001 was one of the first major curriculum reforms that attempted to modernise curricula and bring the education sector closer to international trends.

The declaration of independence in 2008 created a new momentum in Kosovo's society, and another phase of establishing stronger institutions run and managed by local authorities was initiated. This brought curriculum reform to the forefront of policy initiatives. The process was initiated in 2009 with a revision of the prior curriculum framework. It ended in 2011 with adoption of a new curriculum framework based on competence-based education approaches in line with the 2006 EU recommendations for key competences (Tahirsylaj 2018). Again, international organisations played a crucial role in the new curriculum reform since; as in 2001, UNICEF was the lead agency in providing technical assistance. They mainly brought in the same international educational consultants who had written the 2001 curriculum framework as noted in the list of contributors in DES (2001) and MEST (2011).

Two phases – as a policy and as a practice – are observed when we refer to introduction of competence-based curricula (CBC) in Kosovo's education system. The policy phase pertains to the formal adoption of the Kosovo curriculum framework (KCF) by the Kosovo Government and Assembly in 2011. Because the decision coincided with the changes in Kosovo's political status as well as with change in the leadership of the education sector in Kosovo, the KCF document as such has been labelled as a 'political statement' (Tahirsylaj 2018, 45) in efforts to demonstrate to the international community Kosovo's aspirations to eventually join the EU. Harmonising educational goals with those of the EU was the first step to show Kosovo's pro-reform and pro-European orientation (Tahirsylaj 2018). The practice phase related to the slow introduction of CBC into classroom practice. The implementation of CBC was initially piloted in a small number of schools across

## CONTEXTUALIZING GLOBAL FLOWS OF COMPETENCY-BASED EDUCATION

the country, while full implementation only started in 2017 when the new CBC was rolled out in Grades 1, 6 and 10 to correspond with the first grades of elementary, lower-secondary, and upper-secondary respectively. In the meantime, the 2011 KCF was slightly revised in 2016; however its core focus on key competences was maintained.

## Methodological approach

Methodologically, the article uses document analysis as a qualitative research method to meet its aims (Bowen 2009). 'Primary documents' (Cohen, Manion, and Morrison 2011) produced by respective authorities in Kosovo and the European Commission are reviewed in the analysis, which are in the public domain and accessible online. For the purposes of the study, the focus is on two documents published by the European Commission on key competences (OJEU 2006, 2018), primarily on the 2006 document since it was the basis for Kosovo competences adopted in the 2011 curriculum framework. The two Kosovo curriculum frameworks of 2001 and 2011 are first reviewed, and in addition, the focus is also on Core Curricula for Lower Secondary Education (MEST 2012) and civic education subject curriculum as defined by MEST in lower secondary education (Grades 6–9). Specifically, civic education curricula for grades 6 and 7 are examined, as these two are the only yet developed following the latest competence-based curriculum in place in Kosovo.

As noted above, the conceptions of citizenship and subjectivity as developed by Westheimer and Kahne (2004) and Biesta (2007) serve as analytical tools for the document and policy analysis. Therefore, a deductive approach through direct content analysis of the curriculum documents[2] under scrutiny is applied (Hsieh and Shannon 2005).

## Key results and findings

### Civic competences in Kosovo curriculum frameworks and EC documents

Considering the chronology of competence-based education (CBE) since the 1990s, three key projects and developments stand out as critical to understanding the spread of CBE internationally. The first is the OECD's Definition and Selection of Key Competences (DeSeCo) in the second part of 1990s; second, the introduction of OECD's PISA in 2000; and third, the adoption of European Commission recommendations on key competences in 2006 (Tahirsylaj and Sundberg 2020). Despite a number of definitions available, competences have been defined as a combination of knowledge, skills and attitudes appropriate to the context, and key competences, specifically, are those that all individuals need for personal fulfilment and development, active citizenship, social inclusion and employment (OJEU 2006). The 2011 KCF listed six key competences, mostly an adaptation of the eight listed in the 2006 European Commission Reference Framework (ECRF) (see Tahirsylaj 2018 for details).

Since the focus of the article is on civic competences, Table 1 presents definitions and goals of civic/citizenship education and/or competences as outlined in Kosovo's 2001 Curriculum Framework (DES 2001), the 2006 EC Reference Framework (OJEU 2006), the 2011 KCF (MEST 2011), and the 2018 ECRF.

In the light of the personally responsible/individualist, participatory/social, and justice/oriented/political framework adopted in the study, an analysis of the definitions and goals

# 122    CONTEXTUALIZING GLOBAL FLOWS OF COMPETENCY-BASED EDUCATION

**Table 1.** Definitions and conceptions of civic education/competences in Kosovo and EC documents.

| 2001 KCF | 2006 ECRF | 2011 KCF | 2018 ECRF |
|---|---|---|---|
| **Education for democratic citizenship and for human rights** *(as a cross-curricular objective)* | **Social and civic competences** *(as a key competence)* | **Civic competences – 'Responsible citizen'** *(as a key competence)* | **Citizenship competence** *(as a key competence)* |
| Goals for democratic citizenship & human rights: • the nature of citizenship in a democratic society: what are the **rights, responsibilities and duties of a citizen within a society** based on a democratic constitution; • what does **participatory citizenship** mean and how can citizens be **involved constructively** in public affairs; • how can citizens control the Government and **influence public decisions**; • what does it mean to respect the law, and **how can citizens participate in the process of improving existing laws**; • how can citizens **participate in civil society**; • how can citizens ensure that human rights are observed and respected in daily life situations. (DES 2001, 44–45) | Civic competence equips individuals to **fully participate in civic life**, based on knowledge of social and political concepts and structures and a commitment to **active and democratic participation**.<br><br>Civic competence is based on knowledge of the concepts of **democracy, justice, equality, citizenship, and civil rights** [...]. [...] Skills for civic competence relate to the **ability to engage effectively with others in the public domain**, and to **display solidarity** [...]. This involves critical and creative reflection and **constructive participation in community** or neighbourhood activities as well as **decision-making** at all levels, from local to national and European level, in **particular through voting**. (OJEU 2006, 16–17) | Competences and outcomes related to civic competences: • competences for **interpersonal, cultural, and social relationships**; • understanding and respecting **diversity** among people; • exercising **tolerance and respect** for others; • assuming accountability for issues of general public interest, responsibility and **civic participation**; • **tolerating and undertaking useful changes** in one's private life, for an entire society and for the environment. (MEST 2011, 16) | Citizenship competence is the ability **to act as responsible citizens and to fully participate in civic and social life**, based on understanding of social, economic, legal and political concepts and structures, as well as global developments and sustainability.<br><br>Essential knowledge, skills and attitudes related to this competence *(text not shown since almost identical to ECRF 2006)* (OJEU 2018, 10–11) |

Notes: Adapted from DES (2001), MEST (2011), and OJEU (2006, 2018). Words in **bold** indicate relevant concepts related to conceptions of citizenship.

of civic/citizenship education/competences reveals a number of relevant issues. First, the comparison of Kosovo curriculum frameworks of 2001 and 2011 shows that the status of civic competence became central in the 2011 framework as a *key* competence since in 2001 it was only elaborated on as a cross-curricular objective. Also, the definition and goals of civic education in 2001 are contextualised for the Kosovo context as a post-war society, with a focus on personal freedom and personal responsibility, in line with a personal responsible/individualist conception of citizenship within the democratic society. The 2001 KCF also calls for participation in civic life and respect for human rights and highlights the role of education for democratic citizenship. In the 2011 KCF, the outcome of civic education/competences is clearly defined as 'a responsible citizen'. However, the conception of civic competences and associated outcomes point to a personally responsible/individualist, and to a lesser degree, to participatory/social conception of citizenship.

Next, the comparison of 2006 ECRF and 2011 KCF definitions and goals of civic competences shows both similarities and differences. In both documents, there is a clear focus on the role of civic education for democracy, in that mastery of civic competences needs to lead to responsible participation in civic life. However, the 2006 ECRF places more emphasis on the participation function of civic competences, particularly participation in the democratic process of voting. The 2011 KCF is less specific in defining goals related to civic competences than the 2001 KCF and 2006 ECRF documents; however, the civic competence concepts used in the 2011 KCF align better with the 2006 ECRF, especially in terms of having the central role as a *key* competence.

### Civic competences in the latest grades 6 and 7 civic education curricula in Kosovo

The 2011 KCF is an umbrella document that outlines the vision and goals of education in Kosovo, which is further defined and detailed in other curriculum documents for primary, lower-secondary and upper-secondary levels (MEST 2011). The 2011 KCF introduced the concept of curriculum stages, which represent '[...] the reference point for the progress of learning, organizing learning activities, and the approach and assessment criteria for mastering the competences of KCF' (MEST 2012, 18). For example, lower secondary education included curriculum stage 3, labelled 'Further development and orientation' covering Grades 6–7, and stage 4, labelled 'Reinforcement and orientation' covering Grades 8–9 (MEST 2011). Accordingly, civic competences are defined first at curriculum stage 3, and then within civic education curriculum in Grades 6 and 7. Table 2 summarises the definitions and conceptions of civic education in the lower secondary core curriculum (stage 3) and civic education curricula in Grades 6 and 7.

As shown in Table 2, the curriculum stage 3 lists eight broad learning outcomes to be mastered by students in relation to civic competences for the stage. These learning outcomes are further detailed in the civic education curricula for grades 6 and 7. The columns on grades 6 and 7 curricula in Table 2 only show the broader purposes and visions for civic education. Further specific learning outcomes for each of the grades are not given here, but they build on the same purposes. The analysis of the core concepts highlighted in Table 2 reveals the focus on personally responsible/individualist conceptions of citizenship, and to some extent on participatory/social conceptions as overall the focus is placed on teaching students to become active and responsible citizens for navigating the world through an understanding of how institutions work, and how to relate to the social context. An underlying assumption of these conceptions seems to be related to the age of students at curriculum stage 3, mostly at 12–13 years old, who are yet to become eligible voters at 18. Thus, curriculum stage 3 highlights the preparation for what is yet to come in students' life, or in Biesta's (2007) terms, more education *for* (eventual) democratic participation, and less education *through* democracy.

However, the learning outcome that expects students to 'Identify prejudices that might exist in school and in the surrounding area and suggests concrete actions to fight them' (MEST 2012, 23) hints towards the conceptions of justice-oriented/political citizenship in line with Westheimer and Kahne (2004), who argue that a justice-oriented citizen seeks to address areas of injustice. Additionally, *responsible decision-making* could potentially have a justice-oriented/political application if such decision-making leads to students' actions that go beyond individual and social participation.

**Table 2.** Purposes of civic competences/education in latest Grades 6 and 7 civic education curricula.

| 2012 Kosovo Core Curriculum (Stage 3 – Grades 6 & 7) | 2018 Grade 6 civic education curriculum | 2018 Grade 7 civic education curriculum |
|---|---|---|
| *Learning outcomes associated with civic competence:* | *Purposes of Grade 6 civic education curriculum:* | *Purposes of Grade 7 civic education curriculum:* |
| Student:<br>1. Implements and **respects rules of good behaviour** in the classroom, at school, etc. [...]<br>2. **Expresses the opinion** about the school rules and other rules he/she wants to change [...].<br>3. **Reacts to inappropriate behaviour in school/classroom** and out of it, which impact interpersonal relations [...].<br>4. **Expresses understanding** towards persons that suffered violation of any of their rights [...].<br>5. In different ways of expression, explains the necessity to **respect and implement rules and laws** [...].<br>6. Shows high self-esteem in **taking decisions on actions he/she undertakes, without damaging interests of others**, which contribute to increasing the quality of the activity of the social group or the community.<br>7. **Identifies prejudices** that might exist in school and in the surrounding area and suggests concrete actions to fight them.<br>8. **Takes part in activities that promote tolerance and cultural, ethnic, religious, gender, etc. diversity** at school or in community [...]. (MEST 2012, 23) | Civic education covers issues such as **social relations**, associations and **interactions** of the individual with the group and institutions, rights and responsibilities, **decision-making,** environment and sustainable development.<br>Students of this age group must **understand the relationships with the social context** and reflect on the environment where they live. Therefore, Civic Education assists students to **develop their intellectual, moral, and social potential as well as to think and act responsibly.** [...] Grade 6 civic education cultivates in students the love for people, country, life and the world in general. (MEST 2018a, 146) | Grade 7 civic education covers issues such as **social relations**, people's behaviours and attitudes, connections and mutual impact of nature and society, social, human and civic values, participation in institutional **decision-making**, and environment and well-being.<br>Students of this age group must **understand the relationships with the social context** and reflect on the environment where they live, therefore they must cultivate and practice civic and human values. They must **understand that democratic society is grounded on rule of law, respect of human rights, respect of diversity, equal opportunities, transparency, inclusion, solidarity and respect of human dignity**.<br>Civic education teaches students to become **active and responsible citizens in decision-making**, to be familiar with types of institutions and their functions and responsibilities [...]. (MEST 2018b, 160) |

Adapted from MEST (2012, 2018a, 2018b). Words in **bold** indicate relevant concepts related to conceptions of citizenship.

## Discussion, conclusions, and further research

The findings and results presented above along the lines of main guiding questions that the article addresses highlight a number of issues relevant for a developing context such as Kosovo. First, Kosovo represents a unique case in the recent educational developments and reforms, especially within the European context, in that it has served as an open ground for European education trends. Kosovo deliberately and intentionally tried to break away from its troubled past of conflict and draw near the Western Europe trends. Kosovo is a clear example of 'loud borrowing' as neither 'externalization' nor 'silent borrowing' (Waldow 2009) really capture the policy flow into Kosovo's curriculum reform; rather, local policy makers called for and welcomed curriculum policy proposals offered by the international organisations and consultants deemed to be in line with current Western Europe education trends at the time. In Kosovo's context, loud borrowing indicates the education policy-making process in which national authorities deliberately pursued and locally adopted the 2006 EU recommended policy on key competences.

Also, while Kosovo represents a strong case of convergence in education policy, it is unique for the European context in the sense that international policies arrived in Kosovo through international consultants affiliated with the UNESCO, UNICEF or the World Bank or another organisation from the West – which confirms prior findings in global education policy flows, which usually follow a one-way direction from the West to developing countries (Verger, Novelli, and Altinyelken 2012). As a result, due to the lack of local expertise on the one hand, and political openness and support for anything 'European' or 'international' as a desired benchmark on the other, Kosovo turned into an open educational project to install new curriculum trends, especially through the 2011 reform.

In this regard, 'loud borrowing' might be the more appropriate term instead of borrowing since educational reform was adapted from international organisations to the Kosovo context, although the documents at the end were published under auspices of the local institutions – DES in 2011 and MEST in 2011. This process of 'loud borrowing' allowed local authorities to signal progress towards European education standards as they amplified incoming curriculum policies to the local public and the international community. To illustrate this, the then incumbent Kosovo minister of education stated, in support of the adoption of the 2011 competence-based curricula, that

> The solutions proposed in this document [KCF] take into account the immediate needs for improvement of pre-university education in Kosovo, as well as the present educational trends in developed countries, so that our students are competitive with their peers in Europe and beyond. (MEST 2011, 5)

Ultimately, the curriculum policy reform had to play the dual role of reforming education locally, and signalling the European orientation of Kosovo's leadership and public internationally. As such, loud borrowing indicates an education policy-making process in which national authorities deliberately pursue and welcome external policies for both educational and political ends.

Considering the broader political, social, and economic context of Kosovo then, it is evident why the 2011 reform on competence-based education approaches made it into the Kosovo curriculum. In efforts to show the closeness of Kosovo to Western Europe, the Kosovo government, after declaration of independence in 2008, sponsored international marketing initiatives which branded Kosovars as 'Young Europeans' and Kosovo as the youngest country introduced within the European boundaries (see for example Hapçiu and Sparks [2012]). Adopting competence-based curriculum (CBC) reform based on EC key competences thus served the aspirations of local policy-makers, arguably not because CBC was considered the most appropriate reform, but precisely because it served the larger goal of signalling to the international community the aspiration of Kosovars to be part of the European developed nations.

Turning to civic competences in the 2011 policy, the findings provide explicit evidence of the 'loud borrowing' of education policy, particularly from the 2006 ECRF (OJEU 2006) to the 2011 KCF (MEST 2011), with the key conceptions following primarily the *personally responsible/individualist* definition of democratic subjectivity or good citizenship. Both in EC and Kosovo documents, civic education envisions future democratic citizens who understand the institutional and social contexts and act accordingly by obeying laws and participating in civic and democratic life. From the educational policy perspective then, the new 2011 KCF aims to construct Kosovars as 'Young Europeans' along the same lines that the European Commission recommends to educate all other students across EU member states (for details see Hapçiu and Sparks [2012]). Also, civic education goals in Kosovo's lower secondary core curriculum, and in Grades 6 and 7 provide more evidence of the instrumentalist role of education in producing a specific future democratic citizen who can think rationally and autonomously in Kantian terms and participate in civic life through social interactions in the Deweyan sense. Related to this, the adoption of CBC as an EU-promoted policy assists in overriding local ethnic tensions in Kosovo by offering a European-oriented vision of education and its associated values that contribute towards the newly-promoted identity of 'Young Europeans'. In this sense, Kosovo's civic competences, similarly to prior research in post-conflict societies (Quaynor 2012), avoid local ethnic-related controversial issues, and push for a European identity that builds on internationally-promoted democratic citizenship and civic competences.

Lastly, what is lacking both in the ECRF and Kosovo conceptualizations of civic competences is a more proactive focus on a justice-oriented/political conception of democratic subjectivity in Arendt's (1977, 1958) terms, where students not only *learn for* and *participate in* democracy, but also have the possibility to become democratic subjects by *doing* democracy, which in turn initiates new beginnings of others who take up students' *doing* as a precondition for students to become democratic subjects. Similarly, conceptions of justice-oriented citizens who, as noted by Westheimer and Kahne (2004), critically assess social, political, and economic structures to see beyond surface causes, and seek out and address areas of injustice, are less visible in Kosovo's 2011 civic competences, but are still noted in learning outcomes for grades 6 and 7. It might take sustained efforts in implementing the 2011 civic competences on personally responsible/individualist and participatory/social conceptions of citizenship to build a cohesive democratic and inclusive society. Only then, perhaps, will there be room for more emphasis on justice-oriented/political conceptions of citizenship in a post-conflict context such as Kosovo so that students and future citizens are able to address areas of injustice through democratic means without reverting to past inter-ethnic violence.

### *Implications, limitations and further research*

The idea of loud borrowing as conceptualised in the article has implications for the Kosovo case and the field of comparative education more broadly. Regarding Kosovo, loud borrowing specifies the approach policy-makers have followed in education policy-making since the end of the war in 1999. It reveals how and why competence-based curricula became part of curriculum reform in 2011, and implies that future curriculum reforms in the country can be initiated or adopted either through a similar internationally-driven and locally-welcomed process, or another locally-inspired and locally-developed curriculum reform process based on locally-available educational expertise. Regarding the field of comparative education, loud borrowing exemplifies a unique process of travelling education policies from an external source to a developing context. It implies that for a developing country with certain political aspirations the source of the policy is equally, if not more, important than what the policy contains. As such, future comparative education research might contribute towards a more nuanced understanding of how and why developing countries engage in loud borrowing.

In the light of the findings related to the civic competence curriculum policy in Kosovo, and to respond to the question *What kind of citizens?* (Westheimer and Kahne 2004; Biesta 2008), this article has demonstrated that civic education curriculum in Kosovo offers opportunities for students to learn about the democratic society and democratic institutions they are embedded in, and eventually how to participate in the civic and democratic life in a distant future, i.e. become citizens who are *personally responsible/ individualist* and *participatory/social*. Indeed, the findings are in line with those of Westheimer and Kahne (2004) on the US, and Biesta (2008) on Scotland, where the personally responsible/individualist and participatory/social conceptions of citizenships were dominant. These conceptions have implications for curriculum policy-making and implementation in Kosovo (and Europe more broadly), particularly pertaining to the effects that implementation of competence-based curricula have in diverse contexts. As shown in the analyses here, civic competences as part of a competence-based curriculum in Kosovo and also as promoted at the EU level, seem to be focused on developing and maintaining existing democratic order. If education is to serve a more critical role in advancing democracy and human rights in Kosovo and globally, a turn towards justice-oriented/political conceptions of citizenship will be required in future curriculum reforms/policies.

While the present study fills a gap in the literature on different conceptions of civic competences in developing contexts, one clear limitation needs to be recognised. The study only captures the possibilities that Kosovo students have to develop into democratic citizens relying on the education *for* democracy approach, i.e. the study contributes to a deeper understanding of the curriculum policy context in pursuit of democratic citizenry but the findings are limited in the sense that the study does not capture whether the education *through* democracy approach is present in Kosovo schools. Therefore, future research could examine the institutional and structural context of Kosovo schools in search of presence, or lack thereof, of democratic practices. This would require fieldwork across a number of schools in Kosovo to collect and analyse contextual data on school factors and relationships that promote, or inhibit, the pursuit of democratic purposes of education: first, to examine to what extent the education *for* democracy goals are implemented in schools; and second, and more importantly, to examine if schools in Kosovo are democratic institutions that make education *through* democracy possible?

## Notes

1. This article uses the word *competence* throughout because the definition of competence in Kosovo curriculum documents is aligned with the European Commission key competences, even though the documents themselves use *competency*.
2. The curriculum policy documents examined here are only those produced and adopted by the Kosovo governmental authorities, which only affect Albanians and other communities that recognize and accept Kosovo authorities, but not the Kosovo Serbian community, whose education system is affected by curricula developed and adopted in Serbia. This situation has further implications that cannot be addressed in the present study; however it has already been argued that the divisive situation contributes to ongoing segregation and fragmentation of Kosovo society along ethnic lines (for details, see Horvatek and Tahirsylaj 2017).

## Disclosure statement

No potential conflict of interest was reported by the author(s).

## References

Anderson-Levitt, Kathryn. 2003. *Local Meanings, Global Schooling: Anthropology and World Culture Theory*. New York: Palgrave Macmillan.

Anderson-Levitt, Kathryn. 2017. "Global Flows of Competence-Based Approaches in Primary and Secondary Education." *Cahiers de la Recherche sur l'Éducation et les Savoirs* 16: 47–72.

Arendt, Hannah. 1958. *The Human Condition*. Chicago: The University of Chicago Press.

Arendt, Hannah. 1977. *Between Past and Future: Eight Exercises in Political Thought*. Harmondsworth: Penguin Books.

Assembly of Republic of Kosovo. 2008. "Kosovo Constitution." *Official Gazette of the Republic of Kosovo*. https://gzk.rks-gov.net/ActDetail.aspx?ActID=3702.

Assembly of Republic of Kosovo. 2011. "Law on No.04/L –032 on Pre-University Education in the Republic of Kosovo." *Official Gazette of the Republic of Kosovo* 17. https://masht.rks-gov.net/uploads/2015/06/03-ligji-per-arsimin-parauniversitar-anglisht.pdf.

Biesta, Gert. 2007. "Education and the Democratic Person: Towards a Political Understanding of Democratic Education." *Teachers College Record* 109 (3): 740–769.

Biesta, Gert. 2008. "What Kind of Citizen? What Kind of Democracy? Citizenship Education and the Scottish Curriculum for Excellence." *Scottish Educational Review* 40 (2): 38–52.

Bowen, Glenn A. 2009. "Document Analysis as a Qualitative Research Method." *Qualitative Research Journal* 9 (2): 27–40.

Cohen, Lois, Lawrence Manion, and Keith Morrison. 2011. *Research Methods in Education*. 7th ed. London: Routledge.

Department of Education and Science (DES). 2001. *The New Kosovo Curriculum Framework - Preschool, Primary and Secondary Education* - Discussion White Paper. Prishtina: DES.

Dewey, John. (1916) 1966. *Democracy and Education*. New York: The Free Press.

Galston, William A. 2004. "Civic Education and Political Participation." *PS: Political Science & Politics* 37 (2): 263–266.

Hapçiu, Annea, and John R. Sparks. 2012. "The Internal Effect of the Kosovo: The Young Europeans National Branding Campaign on the Kosovar People." https://library.fes.de/pdf-files/bueros/kosovo/09780.pdf.

Horvatek, Renata, and Armend Tahirsylaj. 2017. "'Small' States Acting 'Big': How Minority Education Models in Post-Conflict Croatia and Kosovo Perpetuate Segregated Societies?" In *Re-reading Education Policy and Practice in Small States: Issues of Size and Scale in the Emerging «Intelligent Society and Economy» (Comparative Studies Series)*, edited by Tavis D. Jules, and Patrick Ressler, 111–131. Frankfurt am Main: Peter Lang.

Hsieh, Hsiu-Fang, and Sarah E. Shannon. 2005. "Three Approaches to Qualitative Content Analysis." *Qualitative Health Research* 15 (9): 1277–1288.

IEA. n.d. *International Civic and Citizenship Education Study*. https://www.iea.nl/studies/iea/iccs.

Kant, Immanuel. (1784) 1992. "An Answer to the Question: What is Enlightenment?" In *Postmodernism. A Reader*, edited by P. Waugh, 89–95. London: Edward Arnold.

Ministry of Education, Science and Technology (MEST). 2011. *Curriculum Framework for Pre-University Education in the Republic of Kosovo.* Prishtina: MEST.

Ministry of Education, Science and Technology (MEST). 2012. *Kosovo Core Curriculum for Lower-Secondary Education (Grades VI, VII, VIII and IX).* Prishtina: MEST.

Ministry of Education, Science and Technology (MEST). 2018a. *Kurrikulat lëndore / planet mësimore: klasa e gjashtë* [Subject Curricula/Teaching Plans: Grade Six]. Prishtina: MEST.

Ministry of Education, Science and Technology (MEST). 2018b. *Kurrikulat lëndore / planet mësimore: klasa e shtatë* [Subject Curricula/Teaching Plans: Grade Seven]. Prishtina: MEST.

Official Journal of the European Union (OJEU). 2006. *Recommendation of the European Parliament and of the Council of 18 December 2006 on Key Competences for Lifelong Learning (2006/962/EC).* http://eur-lex.europa.eu/LexUriServ/LexUriServ.do?uri=OJ:L:2006:394:0010:0018:en:PDF.

Official Journal of the European Union (OJEU). 2018. *Council Recommendation of 22 May 2018 on Key Competences for Lifelong Learning.* https://eur-lex.europa.eu/legal-content/EN/TXT/PDF/?uri=CELEX:32018H0604(01)&rid=7.

Papadimitriou, Dimitris, Petar Petrov, and Labinot Greicevci. 2007. "To Build a State: Europeanization, EU Actorness and State-Building in Kosovo." *European Foreign Affairs Review* 12: 219–238.

Quaynor, Laura J. 2012. "Citizenship Education in Post-Conflict Contexts: A Review of the Literature." *Education, Citizenship and Social Justice* 7 (1): 33–57.

Saqipi, Blerim. 2019. "Understanding the Relation of Policy Discourse and Re-Conceptualising Curriculum: a Kosovo Perspective on a new Meaning of Context." *Center for Educational Policy Studies Journal* 9 (2): 33–52.

Steiner-Khamsi, Gita. 2004. *The Global Politics of Educational Borrowing and Lending.* New York: Teachers' College Press.

Tahirsylaj, Armend. 2018. "Curriculum Reform as a Political Statement in Developing Contexts: A Discursive and non-Affirmative Approach." *Transnational Curriculum Inquiry* 15 (2): 38–49. https://ojs.library.ubc.ca/index.php/tci/index.

Tahirsylaj, Armend, and Daniel Sundberg. 2020. "The Unfinished Business of Defining Competences for 21st Century Curricula – A Systematic Research Review." *Curriculum Perspectives* 40 (2): 131–145. doi:10.1007/s41297-020-00112-6.

Tahirsylaj, Armend, and Ninni Wahlström. 2019. "Role of Transnational and National Education Policies in the Realisation of Critical Thinking: The Cases of Sweden and Kosovo." *The Curriculum Journal* 30 (4): 484–503.

Torney-Purta, Judith, John Schwille, and Jo-Ann Amadeo. 1999. *Civic Education Across Countries: Twenty-Four National Case Studies from the IEA Civic Education Project.* Amsterdam, The Netherlands: IEA Secretariat.

UNESCO. 2008. The Six EFA Goals. http://portal.unesco.org/education/en/ev.php-URL_ID=53844andURL_DO=DO_TOPICandURL_SECTION=201.html.

Verger, Antoni, Mario Novelli, and Hulya Kosar Altinyelken. 2012. "Global Education Policy and International Development: An Introductory Framework." In *Global Education Policy and International Development: New Agendas, Issues and Policies*, edited by A. Verger, M. Novelli, and H. K. Altinyelken, 3–32. London: Continuum.

Waldow, Florian. 2009. "Undeclared Imports: Silent Borrowing in Educational Policy-Making and Research in Sweden." *Comparative Education* 45 (4): 477–494.

Weinstein, Harvey M., Sarah Warshauer Freedman, and Holly Hughson. 2007. "School Voices: Challenges Facing Education Systems After Identity-Based Conflicts." *Education, Citizenship and Social Justice* 2 (1): 41–71.

Westheimer, Joel, and Joseph Kahne. 2004. "What Kind of Citizen? The Politics of Educating for Democracy." *American Educational Research Journal* 41 (2): 237–269.

Zylfiu, Bahtije Gerbeshi. 2014. "The Students Participation in Democratic Life in Kosovo." *Journal of Educational and Social Research* 4 (1): 309–315.

# Imagining globally competent learners: experts and education policy-making beyond the nation-state

Meg P. Gardinier

**ABSTRACT**
This paper examines competency-based educational policy-making in a global context. Specifically, it explores how the thinking around competency, spearheaded by international organisations and experts, has led to the development and deployment of a particular notion of global competency. Drawing on critical policy research, I examine three international policy events in which experts convened to discuss, debate, and co-construct ideas related to competencies in education. I argue that by structuring the assessment of knowledge and fixing meanings, the OECD, along with networks of experts, has created and diffused a particular social imaginary of a globally competent learner. Given the complexity and uncertainty of the world today, increasing the global and intercultural knowledge and awareness of the world's students is vitally important. Yet, with so much at stake, researchers must critically examine the processes through which educational futures are being imagined while at the same time, pursuing more equitable and inclusive education policy-making within and beyond the nation-state.

## Introduction

2020 has been a year of increased global focus. In terms of education, the Covid-19 pandemic has had an unprecedented impact on schooling, with over 70% of learners in 158 countries impacted by school closures.[1] The global scope of the challenges facing schools underscores the significance of approaching education as a global public good (UNESCO 2015).

Historically, education policies related to curriculum, assessment, and future goal-setting have been addressed on a national or a state-wide basis. Yet over the last two decades, educational goals and strategies in diverse national contexts have increasingly been embedded in policy discourses linking national education priorities with the wider global phenomenon of the knowledge-based economy (Jakobi 2007). In some countries, domestic education strategies have aimed to align with the United Nations' Sustainable Development Goals (SDGs), including SDG-4 to 'ensure inclusive and equitable quality education and promote lifelong learning opportunities for all'.[2] In these and other ways, education policy-making has gone global.

As highlighted in this special issue, the adoption of competence-based educational reforms has played a significant role in policy-making across diverse contexts despite the lack of clarity or consensus on the specific meaning of the term. Building on this notion of polysemy, this paper examines how competency has been conceptualised in different ways by international experts. In a narrow sense, students' competency (measured in particular *competencies*), has been envisioned as an outcome of schooling. From a wider perspective, competencies and competency-based reforms have been positioned as a means of orienting and *normatively anchoring* (see OECD 2002) educational goals and policies at different scales. This is especially the case with global competency, which is seen as necessary for students' success in the twenty-first century.

This paper investigates how the general idea of *competency* and the particular concept of *global competency* have become sites of meaning construction in education policy-making. Drawing on comparative education and international relations theory, I argue that by structuring the assessment of knowledge and fixing meanings, the OECD, in collaboration with select experts, has created and diffused a particular social imaginary of a *globally competent learner*. Following Nordin and Sundberg (2016 this issue), the social imaginary serves as a kind of 'coordinative discourse' or logic that, in turn, constructs competency in a way that positions the OECD to provide the necessary data and evidence to solve future education policy problems. By tracing the discursive development of normative and conceptual dimensions of competency-based educational models, researchers can better understand the important role of experts in education policy-making beyond the nation-state.

## Methodology

To examine competency-based educational policy-making in a global context, I draw on the emerging method of network ethnography which 'takes seriously the need to rethink the frame within and scales at which new education policy actors, discourses, conceptions, connections, agendas, resources, and solutions of governance are addressed. In other words, thinking about the spaces of policy means extending the limits of our geographical imagination' (Ball 2016, 549). Furthermore, this approach enables researchers to 'think outside and beyond the framework of the nation state to make sense of what is going on inside the nation state' regarding education policy-making (Ball 2016, 549).

Drawing on this approach, this paper aims to 'follow policy' through select international policy events in which experts convened to discuss, debate, and co-construct new ideas related to competency-based education. This examination shows how various actors bring multiple meanings to their interpretation of competency, key competencies, and global competency. Following policy in this way builds on the notion of epistemic communities as a source of international policy coordination (Haas 1992) and also the role of experts within policy networks (Normand 2010). For Haas (1992), the concept of 'epistemic communities' refers to a 'constellation of beliefs, values and methods shared by members of the same community' (Normand 2010, 408).

Previous research has also demonstrated the significant role of experts in the articulation of education policy problems (Grek 2010) and policy solutions (Barnett and Finnemore 2004). My use of the term 'expert' throughout this paper draws primarily on the work of Barnett and Finnemore (2004) who analyse the relationship between authority and expertise in international organisations. From this perspective, expertise refers to 'specialised knowledge derived from training or experience' in a professional field, which is important because the 'deployment of specialized knowledge is central to the very rational-legal authority that constitutes bureaucracy in the first place' (Barnett and Finnemore 2004, 24). Furthermore, the very knowledge base that defines expertise not only legitimises experts' authority, but it also influences 'what problems are visible to staff and what range of solutions are entertained' by IOs (Barnett and Finnemore 2004, 24). Experts also confer the appearance of both scientific validity and depoliticisation upon the work of the IOs.

Three policy-relevant events in which experts examined the idea of competencies were selected as instances of meaning-making in educational policy and planning. The first brief case examined is the 1996 final symposium of the Council of Europe's project on the topic of *Key Competencies for Europe* in Berne, Switzerland. The next case examined is the OECD DeSeCo Project (*Definition and Selection of Competencies: Theoretical and Conceptual Foundations*) which took place during 1997-2003. The aim of the DeSeCo Project was 'defining and selecting key competencies necessary for individuals to lead a successful and responsible life and for society to face the challenges of the present and near future' (Rychen 2001, 7). The third case examined is the launch of the OECD PISA Global Competence assessment framework which took place in 2017 at the Harvard Graduate School of Education. The case of the PISA Global Competence assessment was selected because in addition to being the first international large-scale assessment of students' global competence, it also represents an interesting and timely example of the role of experts in the process of generating key policy ideas in meetings convened by supranational organisations (see also Ledger et al. 2019).

In each of the three cases, key publications, documents, and video presentations were analysed with a view towards understanding the role of experts in constructing meaning around competences in education. Taken together, these three policy-relevant events illuminate how international organisations such as the OECD have played a pivotal role in normatively anchoring the meaning of competency in education.

### Research questions

Data from these expert-led events enabled the author to 'follow policy' (Ball 2016) in order to address the following inquiries:

(1) How has the notion of *competency* been conceptualised by education experts at international policymaking events?
(2) How has the particular concept of *global competency* been defined by leading international experts?
(3) From a theoretical perspective, how have these conceptualisations of competencies enabled policymakers and experts to imagine and begin to construct new educational futures for learners in the twenty-first century?

To address these questions, the paper is structured in three main sections. The first section presents a review of literature on educational policymaking from global and post-national perspectives. The second section describes and analyses the three cases in which experts worked to envision, define, and articulate key competencies for education in Europe and global competency for learners throughout the world. The third section discusses the results of this analysis and concludes with a discussion of implications for understanding future competency-based and global competency-based discourses in education policy and practice.

## Theoretical and conceptual frames

Exploring how education experts engage in conceptualising competencies is particularly timely and instructive as competency-based educational discourses continue to pervade education policy-making debates. As research cited in this special issue has shown, *competency* has been envisioned as a construct that is measurable, assessable, and seen as a desirable outcome of students' learning. With the release of results from the 2018 PISA Global Competence assessment, the concept of *global competence* is also gaining traction, though not without some critique and contestation. For example, from a measurement perspective, Engel, Rutkowski, and Thompson (2019) deem the OECD's global competence an 'amorphous construct' (118) for which there is a 'lack of a universal international definition', thus posing a challenge for an ILSA (122). Grotlüschen (2017) questions whether the OECD PISA Global Competence assessment includes, or effectively ignores, the global South. Cobb and Couch (2018) critically analyse the implications of the assessment for teacher education, concluding that the OECD has used the PISA Global Competence assessment as a 'new form of global pedagogic governance' (45). Auld and Morris (2019a, 17) critically examine the silences and inconsistencies of the PISA Global Competence assessment, arguing that 'the OECD's view of a globally competent student is one that is rooted in an elite western liberal tradition that privileges the privileged'. Similarly, Ledger et al. (2019, 27) critique the legitimacy of the instrument when the OECD's 'power to operationalise global competency rests within an international community of experts that hail from OECD nations with some of the past's largest colonial footprints'. Taken together, these critiques raise the question of whether there exists 'a truly global conception of global competence and if not, whose global competence is prioritised and who benefits from such an international measurement' (Engel, Rutkowski, and Thompson 2019, 123). Given these critiques, it is particularly timely and instructive to examine how competence in general, and global competence in particular, have been conceptualised.

### Education policymaking as a post-national endeavour

Over the past decade, research in the field of global education policy (GEP) has facilitated a theoretical pivot away from the nation-state as the predominant unit of analysis in comparative education research. This shift is due in large part to the increasingly significant role of supranational organisations in education policy debates. For example, Rizvi and Lingard (2010, 16) argue that 'education policymakers within the state are also networked with policymakers in agencies beyond the nation, including international organisations such as the OECD, UNESCO and supranational organisations such as the EU, resulting in the creation of an emergent global education policy community'.

Through a more neo-institutionalist sociological lens, Ramirez and Meyer (2012) infused a post-national perspective into their research on global citizenship education.

Based on an analysis of textbooks from nearly 500 secondary schools in 70 countries between the years 1970-2008, Ramirez and Meyer (2012, 12) concluded that 'a nationalist world may also be shifting toward a more post-national one, characterised by a variety of social movements that highlight global issues, call for transnational activities, and pave the way to new forms of solidarity and identity [...]– in an imagined world community'.

Ramirez and Meyer (2012) draw on the work of Saskia Sassen (2002, 280) who argues that 'the growing prominence of the international human rights regime has played an important theoretical and political role in strengthening post-national conceptions'. These theorists collectively emphasise a key idea in their post-national framing: *interdependence*. For Ramirez and Meyer (2012, 21), 'Instead of the model of the independent national state, we now have models of an interdependent world, economically, politically, culturally, and ecologically'. For Sassen (2002, 282), forces such as climate change, economic globalisation, and global social media 'create structural interdependencies and senses of global responsibility'.

This post-national shift has important implications for emerging ideas of global citizenship and global competence in education policy. As Ramirez and Meyer (2012, 13–14) assert, 'These changes may be thought of as reflecting a paradigm shift in both what counts as knowledge and how students are imagined as learners. This paradigm shift celebrates active learning in knowledge societies that themselves seem to be imagined in ways not limited to the territorial nation-state. To be sure, education for national development and citizenship persists. But in a globalised world the scope of the problem expands'.

Through these insights, the question of students' membership and belonging within an increasingly post-national environment of an imagined world community becomes central. Post-national research has shown how local issues are increasingly approached within a global frame of reference. Along similar lines, as discussed below, the OECD PISA Global Competence assessment also reflects the notion that globally competent learners are able to demonstrate the ability to conceptually link their local educational experiences with wider global issues. This shift from education that exclusively promotes national identity to learning that fosters a sense of students' post-national membership and belonging, has important implications for how we think about education policymaking within and beyond the nation-state.

### *The role of international organisations (IOs) in constituting 'the global'*

In response to growing attention to the relationship between globalisation and education, comparative and international education researchers have increasingly sought to 'theorize the global'. For example, Robertson (2018, 37) theorises that the term *global* 'features in education policy in somewhat different, though related, ways, as a 'condition of the world', 'discourse', 'project', 'scale' and 'means of identifying the reach of particular actors''. Each of these uses introduces a different pathway for understanding the place of 'the global' in education policy. When applied to models of competency-based education, the concept of the *global* evokes an imagined community, a new space of post-national citizenship, an over-generalized ideal, and/or a complex, volatile, and uncertain context. Following Appadurai (1996, 31), theorising the global also invokes new cultural processes that position *the imagination as a social practice*.

Yet despite these diverse meanings attributed to globality, for purposes of assessment, competencies (however global they may be), must be concrete and measurable.

Along these lines, Kamens and McNeely (2010, 14–15) assert that, 'The growth of both national assessments and international testing can be seen as part of an international movement to rationalise – and standardise – educational systems'. This process has largely been facilitated by IOs such as UNESCO and the OECD that serve as 'agents of diffusion' (Kamens and McNeely 2010, 14). More recently, scholars of international assessment have critiqued the processes through which the OECD, primarily an international economic policy organisation, has led the charge for cross-national measurement in education (Engel, Rutkowski, and Thompson 2019). Similarly, comparative education scholars have argued that international organisations have played a central role in influencing education policy-making by promoting multilateralism (Mundy 2007), structuring epistemological debates (Lingard and Sellar 2016), and deploying forms of global governance in education (Leibfried et al. 2007; Wiseman and Taylor 2017).

Complementing these perspectives, international relations scholars offer key insights on the role of international organisations in diffusing policy ideas such as those embedded in competency-based educational reforms. For example, Barnett and Finnemore (1999, 710) show how IOs such as the OECD actively 'structure knowledge' as they engage in practices that '(1) classify the world, creating categories of actors and action; (2) fix meanings in the social world; and (3) articulate and diffuse new norms, principles, and actors around the globe'. Similarly, Haas (1992, 2–3) argued that through 'networks of knowledge-based experts-epistemic communities', IOs play a key role in 'helping states identify their interests', 'framing issues for collective debate', and exerting 'control over knowledge and information' – all of which empower IOs in the international system.

In this paper, I draw on these theoretical perspectives to examine the ways in which policy-relevant thinking around *competency*, spearheaded by networks of experts, has led to the development and deployment of a particular notion of *global competency*. I argue that by structuring the assessment of knowledge and fixing meanings, the OECD, alongside a select group of experts, has created and diffused a particular social imaginary of a *globally competent student* while perhaps excluding other possibilities. Given the complexity and uncertainty of the world today –with the global pandemic, climate crisis, and rising nationalism– increasing the global awareness and intercultural knowledge, skills, and attitudes of students is vitally important. Yet, with so much at stake, we must critically evaluate whether the processes through which new futures are being imagined are as equitable and inclusive as they could be. Towards this goal, the cases examined below aim to illuminate how experts engaged in policy-relevant processes of meaning-making and contestation as they conceptualised competencies for education in Europe and the world.

## Conceptualising competencies: case studies

### Case 1: imagining key competencies for Europe: the challenges of politics and polysemy

During March 27-30, 1996, the Council of Europe's Council for Cultural Cooperation (CDCC) convened a symposium to examine the topic of 'Key Competencies for Europe' in Berne, Switzerland. A report on this event, compiled by Mr. Walo Hutmacher (1997) who worked with the OECD on the INES (International Educational Indicators) project, provides important insights into the role of competencies in the development of a pan-European approach to education. The symposium brought together approximately 50 participants including teachers, school managers, officials, and education experts from European countries including OECD member countries and representatives from 'transitional democracies' such as Albania, Bulgaria, and the Former Yugoslav Republic of Macedonia.

Two interesting and relevant findings emerge through a review of Hutmacher's (1997) report. First, Hutmacher noted that the lack of a uniform and common understanding of key competencies was largely due to the cultural and linguistic differences among symposium participants. He noted, 'In every language, there are a profusion of terms, and polysemy' (Hutmacher 1997, 4). Furthermore, his observation of participants' varying political and economic experiences led Hutmacher (1997, 15) to conclude the following: 'the symposium also confirmed what the earlier lists [of competencies] had already shown: problems and priorities differ noticeably between the countries with a long tradition of democracy and a market economy, and the countries in transition'. For example, Hutmacher (1997, 15) noted that in contrast to representatives from longstanding democracies who seemed to take their experience for granted, several representatives from newer democracies stressed that '"everything is still to be done' to build a stable democratic order'.

A second insight gained through an analysis on the Berne symposium report relates to the importance of context in the conceptualisation of key competencies. During the symposium, participants were asked to categorise and rank different competencies for 'young Europeans' and for 'the building of Europe' (Hutmacher 1997, 14). After completing this exercise, participants concluded that, 'the determination of priorities will depend on a balancing of interests, which must be a political matter' (Hutmacher 1997, 14). Drawing on his observations of this exercise and the symposium as a whole, Hutmacher (1997, 11) noted, 'There is no doubt that the choices and priorities are heavily influenced by the views of whoever defines the key competencies and of the persons for whom they are defined, and by the contexts in which they are implemented'. Thus, in addition to being primarily a political task, defining and selecting priorities for European education in the form of key competencies is also quite subjective in that it draws extensively on the contexts which are most familiar to the educators and policy-makers involved.

### Case 2: defining, selecting, and conceptualising key competencies: insights from the OECD DeSeCo Project

In 1997, the OECD also initiated a consultative process to examine the role of key competencies for education. The DeSeCo Project (*Definition and Selection of Competencies: Theoretical and Conceptual Foundations*) was an interdisciplinary and policy-oriented research programme carried out under the leadership of the Federal Statistical Office of Switzerland with 'considerable support' from the U.S. Department of Education, National Center for Education Statistics (Rychen, Salganik, and McLaughlin 2003, 15). Through a series of interactive workshops and symposia, experts from different academic disciplines, international organisations, stakeholders from multiple sectors, and participants from at least 12 countries[3] aimed to clarify the concept of competency and articulate disciplinary perspectives on the following question: *What competencies do we need for a successful life and a well-functioning society?*

As in the Berne Symposium, the starting point for the DeSeCo project was attempting to clarify the definition of competency; yet this proved to be difficult. Amidst much ongoing debate among participants, a working definition was adopted and has been noted in some of the papers in this special issue. DeSeCo participants 'acknowledged diversity in values and priorities across countries and cultures, yet also identified universal challenges of the global economy and culture, as well as common values that inform the selection of the most important competencies' (OECD 2005, 5). Furthermore, the DeSeCo experts echoed some of the same ideas captured in the Berne Symposium report on the subjective and contextual aspects of defining key competencies for education in Europe and beyond. They noted, for example, that (OECD 2001, 3):

> The underlying assumption of the DeSeCo Program is that defining and selecting key competencies relevant for individuals and societies is at the same time an ethical, a scientific, and a political issue. First, no frame of reference is neutral. One's underlying vision of the world, including assumptions about society and individuals and about what a successful life implies, affects the identification of key competencies.

This statement is profound because DeSeCo ultimately provided the conceptual foundation for establishing the OECD's main competency-based assessment, Programme for International Student Assessment (PISA). Recognising the inherent lack of neutrality behind identifying key competencies seems to diverge from PISA's claims of universal and objective validity. Nonetheless, in these early days, DeSeCo participants aimed to apply a diverse set of theoretical approaches and analytical tools to a common project while recognising that competencies needed to be contextualised because 'individual characteristics such as gender, age, and social status, and aspects of the social environment such as culture and national context influence the forms that key competencies described at the abstract level take in specific contexts' (OECD 2001, 3–4).

Despite the inherent complexity of the task, DeSeCo ultimately found a 'common denominator' (Rychen 2001, 11) in the following 'three broad categories' of key competencies: '(1) to act autonomously and reflectively; (2) to use tools interactively; and (3) to join and function in socially heterogeneous groups' (Rychen 2001, 12). In addition to establishing this common framing of key competencies, the OECD DeSeCo Project holds further significance in that by defining and selecting key competencies, DeSeCo experts and stakeholders concurrently began constructing a new social imaginary of a *competent learner*.

Returning then to the question of how the concept of *competency* came to be constructed by experts working with the OECD, we can identify a number of core beliefs in operation. First, *competent learners* were imagined as autonomous individuals who can differentiate themselves from their social identities as well as from their own subjective thoughts in order to develop their ability to be critical, reflective, independent, responsible, and mature (see Perrenoud 2001 and Kegan 2001). Second, key competencies for success in the global economy require the interactive use of tools such as language and technology (OECD 2005). Specifically, *competent learners* must critically reflect on the 'nature of information itself – its technical infrastructure and its social, cultural, and even ideological context and impact' (OECD 2005, 11). In the end, the

DeSeCo Project advocated a set of key competencies based on an imagined ideal learner who is future-oriented, socially mature, goal-oriented, and extremely self-aware.

As in the Berne Symposium, these priorities selected for competent learners reflect the contexts most familiar to the experts who envisioned them. Echoing this point, the former DeSeCo co-director Rychen noted in 2016, 'In most OECD countries individuals are expected to be adaptive and flexible, innovative, creative, open-minded, tolerant, self-directed, and self-motivated, and able to take responsibility for their decisions, behaviour, and actions as lifelong learners, parent, partner, employee or employer, citizen, student, or consumer' (13). These underlying expectations thus continue to inform the OECD's development of competency assessment frameworks, the latest example of which is the 2018 PISA Global Competence assessment discussed below.

### Case 3: imagining globally competent learners: PISA's 2018 global competence assessment

The decision to assess students' global competence through one of PISA's innovative assessments[4] emerged from consultation with key international experts and stakeholders who identified a growing need to evaluate the extent to which young people are prepared for life in increasingly complex and multicultural societies. One such expert was Harvard Professor Fernando Reimers who published several papers on global competency and education during 2008–2013 (see, for example, Reimers 2008, 2009a, 2009b, 2009c). In 2013, Reimers authored a thought piece titled, 'Assessing global education: An opportunity for the OECD' providing a clear rationale for the assessment of global competence through PISA.

Seemingly following Reimers' advice, in 2014, an international and interdisciplinary group of experts 'came together under the auspices of the PISA Governing Board to consider a novel question: can we evaluate, through an international assessment, the global competence of 15-year-old students?' (Piacentini 2017a, 507). The answer, they believed, was yes. The subsequent design of the assessment included multiple choice and open-response questions based on a number of scenarios that addressed the OECD's four key content domains of global competence: 'culture and intercultural relations; socio-economic development and interdependence; environmental sustainability; and global institutions, conflicts, and human rights' (Piacentini 2017a, 509). When asked about the worldwide relevance of the assessment questions, Piacentini stated that in using scenarios as a basis for assessment, the OECD is 'making one big assumption: that you can identify a set of issues that are relevant for students across all countries, no matter where they live' (2017b, 48:37).

Meanwhile, during 2010, two other educational experts were developing ideas about educating globally competent students. Professor Veronica Boix Mansilla of Harvard's Project Zero and Tony Jackson, Director of Asia Society's Center for Global Education (CGE), worked with a task force convened by the U.S. Council of Chief State School Officers (CCSSO) as part of the EdSteps initiative to evaluate 'research and best practices to explore what capacities a globally competent student should embody' (Boix Mansilla and Jackson 2011, viii).

For Jackson and Boix Mansilla, global competence encapsulated the idea of a successful student in the twenty-first century. For instance, in a presentation at Big Ideas Fest in 2009, Jackson advocated for a new approach to education that would 'change the definition of success' by asking 'What does it mean to be globally competent?' (2010, 4:15).

Interestingly, by 'following policy' (Ball 2016) and comparing the transcripts of Jackson's 2009 Big Ideas Fest presentation with a 2017 presentation by Andreas Schleicher, OECD Director for Education and Skills, a clear overlap of ideas on global competence emerges. For example, Jackson (2010, 5:00) noted that 'in our definition of globally competent students, content knowledge matters, and what's even just as important, is that they need to learn how to think in the ways the disciplines call for; they need to *learn how to think like scientists*, and think like historians, and think like artists. But in so doing, they also need to think from a global perspective' (emphasis added).

A few years later, at the launch of the PISA Global Competence assessment framework, Schleicher (2017, 10:25) explained that while knowledge is an important 'ingredient' in the OECD's concept of competency, 'We put much more of a premium on epistemic understanding: *Can you think like a scientist*? Can you think like a mathematician? Can you think like a philosopher? ... And you're going to see that when we talk about the design of global competency' (emphasis added).

The perspectives of the OECD and Asia Society's CGE clearly merge in their joint 2018 publication which defined four main qualities of 'globally competent youth. [They]:

(1) investigate the world beyond their immediate environment by examining issues of local, global, and cultural significance;
(2) recognise, understand, and appreciate the perspectives and world views of others;
(3) communicate ideas effectively with diverse audiences by engaging in open, appropriate, and effective interactions across cultures; and
(4) take action for collective well-being and sustainable development both locally and globally'. (Asia Society/OECD 2018, 5)

Drawing on similar notions of a *successful student*, Boix Mansilla goes one step further in articulating the new social imaginary of the *globally competent learner*. Reflecting on the significance of the PISA Global Competence assessment framework during the launch at Harvard, she shared the following powerful ideas (Boix Mansilla 2017, 2:06:35):

> I think that we are re-framing the notion of the student as a student who is very embedded in the forces that are shaping our world. A student that is in the middle, at the intersection of migratory flows, immigrant students, refugee students, local students receiving others. ... I think that part of the invitation is – let's revise, and refine our notion of who the learner is, and how contextual the learner is, so that we don't leave the world outside, but we bring the world inside.

Thus, with the 2018 PISA Global Competence assessment, a new social imaginary has been constructed and internationally circulated: a *globally competent learner* is a young person that exists at the intersection of local and global, is self-reflective in their globally-mindedness, and consciously acts for the wellbeing of others within and beyond their local and national contexts.

## Analysis of cases

The cases of the Berne Symposium, the DeSeCo project, and the PISA Global Competence assessment framework provide depth and nuance in elaborating how notions of competency and global competency have been developed, defined, and deployed by experts engaged in policy-relevant research and consultation. From the theoretical perspective of 'following policy', these cases illustrate how 'global policy networks are social and human constructions' that are 'always *under construction*' (Ball 2016, 562).

As we compare different expert notions of competency, we can identify areas of overlap and synergy, as well as areas of divergence where certain views were not prominently adopted into policy-relevant frameworks. For example, one key issue is the importance of context in the understanding and assessment of competencies. Although participants at the Berne Symposium and DeSeCo clearly highlighted the importance of context as a factor that informed their understanding of key competencies, the PISA Global Competence assessment framework adopted a more de-contextualised approach in which students' global competence can be evaluated universally through an instrument that seemingly possesses global relevance. This point echoes Auld and Morris's finding that 'the OECD's conception of Global Competence is an ahistorical and depoliticised entity' (2019b, 18). When asked about the international applicability of the assessment framework, Piacentini replied, 'We have set these content domains, but we are not making fine prescriptions on exactly how you frame these issues. And we are just saying that the best way you can do it is to connect these issues to the reality of the students' (2017b, 2:03:48). Yet, according to a growing number of researchers, the assessment framework and related documents provide 'insufficient examples of how schools can promote global competence' (Ledger et al. 2019, 29).

Connecting PISA results back to national-level policymaking, the OECD argues that data from the Global Competence assessment can serve a dual purpose; first, it 'will provide insights on which policy approaches to global education are most commonly used in school systems around the world' (Piacentini 2017a, 510). Next, 'the results of the assessment can also stimulate innovation at the level of individual schools, as schools seek effective approaches to raise their students' global competence' (Piacentini 2017a, 510), although some researchers may question the assertion that PISA results, which are geared toward system-level analyses, could fuel school-level innovations (see, for example, Auld and Morris 2019b and Ledger et al. 2019).

According to Andreas Schleicher, the OECD excels at influencing national education policy-making processes. They do this by increasing 'the cost of political inaction' by 'making visible how big the gaps are' and also by reducing 'the cost of political action' by showing policymakers the data and tools they need to effect change (Schleicher 2017, 1:47:05). Following this logic, with results from the PISA Global Competence assessment, the OECD sees itself as well positioned to provide the evidence-base needed for countries to improve their standing in the world community.

Returning then to the pathway of IO authority and expertise as outlined by Barnett and Finnemore (2004), the OECD, relying on input from select experts, has defined the need and disseminated the tools to assess students' global competence worldwide. By defining the issues that give rise to the need for globally competent students, the OECD claims to

CONTEXTUALIZING GLOBAL FLOWS OF COMPETENCY-BASED EDUCATION    141

be well positioned to provide solutions through their analysis of PISA data, which, in sum, 'will help education systems identify what is working and what needs to be implemented more intentionally and systematically to ensure all students develop global competence' (Asia Society/OECD 2018, 4). Yet with the lack of a 'global consensus' on the construct itself (Engel, Rutkowski, and Thompson 2019,), and with increasing concern over the processes through which the assessment was constructed, questions remain about the potential impact of the PISA Global Competence assessment results.

### *Is the future of competency global? Education 2030 and DeSeCo 2.0, UNESCO futures of education*

We can continue to follow policy as the OECD expands their efforts to construct new social imaginaries around the knowledge, skills, and competencies that students will need to succeed in the coming decades. Drawing on the conceptual foundation laid by the DeSeCo Project, the OECD's 'Future of Education and Skills 2030 Project' asks once again, 'What knowledge, skills, attitudes, and values will today's students need to thrive in and shape their world? How can instructional systems develop these knowledge skills, attitudes and values effectively?' (OECD 2019, 4). The OECD Learning Compass 2030 seeks to answer these questions through the development of *future competencies* in which students are imagined 'to be ready and competent for 2030' by being 'able to use their knowledge, skills, attitudes and values to act in coherent and responsible ways that change the future for the better' (OECD 2019, 6). Once again, this project 'reconceptualises' DeSeCo's work on competencies for the 2030 context and beyond (OECD 2019, 19), and in effect, demonstrates how the OECD is able 'to define problems for other actors', 'specify which actors have responsibility for solving those problems, and use their authority to identify the right or appropriate kind of solution' (Barnett and Finnemore 2004, 34).

## Conclusion

This paper has outlined a theoretical analysis of competence-based education as an example of meaning-making in education policymaking beyond the nation-state. By looking closely at the work of international organisations including the Council of Europe and the OECD on competencies in education, we can trace Barnett and Finnemore's (2004) arguments regarding the interplay of authority and expertise in the international system. Specifically, the three cases demonstrate how experts initially grappled with the meaning of key competencies in education and contested efforts to create a uniform meaning, yet eventually advocated a shared conceptualisation that was then deployed through the implementation of an international assessment and the dissemination of policy-relevant data and reports.

By constructing the social imaginaries of the *competent/successful student* and the *globally competent learner*, the OECD, along with select experts, defined and solidified parameters of meaning. Furthermore, while emphasising the need for global competence, the OECD concurrently set out to collect the evidence base with which they will assist national policy-makers in addressing their students' learning gaps. Through these processes, international organisations like the OECD are becoming increasingly dominant in establishing and circulating the normative frames in which local and national education policy-makers operate.

Due to the space limitations, it has not been possible here to delve more deeply into the specific processes through which the PISA 2018 Global Competence assessment framework was constructed, nor to investigate the role that diverse stakeholders such as education ministers from non-OECD countries, corporate multinational test-makers such as Pearson and ETS, or local teachers and youth played in developing the assessment framework, test and questionnaire items, or the scenarios that were used to assess and evaluate students' global knowledge, skills, and attitudes. Several recent publications delve into these and other facets of the PISA 2018 Global Competence assessment (e.g. Auld and Morris 2019b; Engel, Rutkowski, and Thompson 2019; Ledger et al. 2019; Simpson and Dervin 2019) and begin to shed light on critical questions such as the following:

- How inclusive and/or representative are the OECD's assessment frameworks and implementation strategies?
- What underlying values are being articulated and normalised through the OECD PISA Global Competence assessment framework?
- What alternatives to this framework exist, or should be developed, to enable a broader set of normative commitments in education to be included as part of the meaning of global competence?
- Finally, who else should be leading and informing this work?

These questions are important to consider, for, as discussed in this article, education policies (which may draw on the OECD's data and expertise) not only aim to shape the technical dimensions of teaching and learning in diverse contexts; they have also become a means through which key actors simultaneously imagine, debate, and co-construct educational futures for the world's youth. Along these lines, imagining education for a preferred future is no longer the exclusive purview of national leaders and policy-makers. As this paper shows, through the work of international organisations and networks of experts who operate as a supranational epistemic community, meaning-making in education policy increasingly occurs beyond the confines of the nation-state.

## Notes

1. https://en.unesco.org/covid19/educationresponse.
2. https://sustainabledevelopment.un.org/sdg4.
3. According to a summary of the DeSeCo project activities (OECD 2005, 18), the first international symposium included reports from the following countries: Austria, Belgium, Denmark, Finland, France, Germany, the Netherlands, New Zealand, Norway, Sweden, Switzerland, and the United States. Based on Rychen and Salganik (2001), the following academic experts and practitioners contributed to the DeSeCo Project: John Carson (USA), Franz Weinert (Germany), Monique Canto-Sperber and Jean-Pierre Dupuy (France), Helen Haste (UK), Philippe Perrenoud (Switzerland), Frank Levy and Richard Murnane (USA), Jack Goody (UK), Robert Kegan (USA), Cecilia Ridgeway (USA), Jacques Delors and Alexandra Draxler (UNESCO), Bob Harris (Education International), and Carlo Callieri (Italy). Also acknowledged in the DeSeCo (2001) text are the following individuals and experts: John Martin, Tom Alexander, Eugene Owen, Marilyn Binkley, Norberto Bottani, Helmut Fend, Walo Hutmacher, Barry

CONTEXTUALIZING GLOBAL FLOWS OF COMPETENCY-BASED EDUCATION 143

McGaw, Scott Murray, Jules Peschar, George Psacharopoulos, Andreas Schleicher, Judith Torney-Purta, Albert Tujinman, and Leonardo Jose Vanella.

4. The innovative assessment domain for each PISA cycle is either a cognitive assessment (e.g. the assessment of problem-solving competencies in 2003, 2012 and 2015), an assessment of non-cognitive dispositions (e.g. student attitudes towards science in 2006), or some combination of the two. PISA's innovative assessment domain is usually considered to be cross-curricular.

## Acknowledgements

Many thanks to Kathryn Anderson-Levitt, Elena Aydarova, and Armend Tahirsylaj for helpful feedback on drafts of this manuscript.

## Disclosure statement

No potential conflict of interest was reported by the author(s).

## References

Appadurai, A. 1996. *Modernity at Large: Cultural Dimensions of Globalization* (Public Worlds, Vol. 1). Ninth Printing ed. University of Minnesota Press, Minneapolis.

Asia Society/OECD. 2018. *Teaching for Global Competence in a Rapidly Changing World*. New York: OECD Publishing, Paris/Asia Society.

Auld, E., and P. Morris. 2019a. "Science by Streetlight and the OECD's Measure of Global Competence: A New Yardstick for Internationalisation?" *Policy Futures in Education* 17 (6): 677–698. doi:10.1177/1478210318819246.

Auld, E., and P. Morris. 2019b. "The OECD's Assessment of Global Competence: Measuring and Making Global Elites." In *The Machinery of School Internationalisation in Action: Beyond the Established Boundaries*, edited by Laura C. Engel, Claire Maxwell, and Miri Yemini, 17–35. New York: Routledge.

Ball, S. J. 2016. "Following Policy: Networks, Network Ethnography and Education Policy Mobilities." *Journal of Education Policy* 31 (5): 549–566.

Barnett, M., and M. Finnemore. 1999. "The Politics, Power, and Pathologies of International Organizations." *International Organization* 53 (4): 699–732.

Barnett, M., and M. Finnemore. 2004. *Rules for the World: International Organizations in Global Politics*. ITHACA, LONDON: Cornell University Press.

Boix Mansilla, V. 2017. *Preparing Our Youth for a Better World: OECD PISA Global Competence Framework Launch*. Discussion points presented at the Launch of the PISA Global Competency Assessment hosted by Harvard Graduate School of Education on December 12, 2017. Accessed from: https://www.youtube.com/watch?v=puYx83MSOgc.

Boix Mansilla, V., and A. Jackson. 2011. *Educating for Global Competence: Preparing Our Youth to Engage the World*. Published by Asia Society Partnership for Global Learning in collaboration with the Council of Chief State School Officers (CCSSO) and EdSteps Global Competence Task Force.

Cobb, D. J., and D. Couch. 2018. "Teacher Education for an Uncertain Future: Implications of PISA's Global Competence." In *Teacher Education In and For Uncertain Times*, edited by Deborah Heck, and Angelina Ambrosetti. https://doi.org/10.1007/978-981-10-8648-9_3.

Engel, L. C., D. Rutkowski, and G. Thompson. 2019. "Toward an International Measure of Global Competence? A Critical Look at the PISA 2018 Framework." *Globalisation, Societies and Education* 17 (2): 117–131.

Grek, S. 2010. "International Organisations and the Shared Construction of Policy 'Problems': Problematisation and Change in Education Governance in Europe." *European Educational Research Journal* 9 (3): 396–406.

Grotlüschen, A. 2017. "Global Competence – Does the New OECD Competence Domain Ignore the Global South?" *Studies in the Education of Adults*. Informa UKLimited, trading as Taylor & Francis Group.

Haas, P. 1992. "Epistemic Communities and International Policy Coordination." Special Issue on Knowledge, Power, and International Policy Coordination, *International Organization* 46 (1): 1–35.

HGSE (Harvard Graduate School of Education). 2017. *Preparing our Youth for a Better World: OECD PISA Global Competence Framework Launch*. Held at Harvard University, accessed at: https://youtu.be/puYx83MSOgc.

Hutmacher, W.1997. *Key Competencies for Europe. Report of the Symposium* (Berne, Switzerland, March 27–30, 1996). A Secondary Education for Europe Project. Council for Cultural Cooperation, Strasbourg, France. REPORT NO DECS/SE/Sec-(96)-43. Accessed from https://files.eric.ed.gov/fulltext/ED407717.pdf.

Jackson, T. 2010. *Matching Design to Outcomes: Teaching Global Competencies in a Changing World*. Talk presented at the Big Ideas Fest, hosted by Asia Society, December 6–9, 2009: https://www.youtube.com/watch?v=yhPA_AQWLjo.

Jakobi, A. P. 2007. "The Knowledge Society and Global Dynamics in Education Politics." *European Educational Research Journal* 6 (1): 39–51.

Kamens, D. H., and C. L. McNeely. 2010. "Globalization and the Growth of International Educational Testing and National Assessment." *Comparative Education Review* 54 (1): 5–25.

Kegan, R. 2001. "Competencies as Working Epistemologies: Ways We Want Adults to Know." In *Defining and Selecting Key Competencies*, edited by Dominique S. Rychen and Laura H. Salganik, 192–211. Seattle, Toronto, Bern, Gottingen: Hogrefe and Huber Publishers.

Ledger, S., M. Thier, L. Bailey, and C. Pitts. 2019. "OECD's Approach to Measuring Global Competency: Powerful Voices Shaping Education." *Teachers College Record* 121 (8), 1–40.

Leibfried, S., A. Rusconi, K. Leuze, and K. Martens, eds. 2007. *New Arenas of Educational Governance: The Impact of International Organizations and Markets on Educational Policy Making*. New York: Palgrave Macmillan.

Lingard, B., and S. Sellar. 2016. "The Changing Organizational and Global Significance of the OECD's Education Work." In *The Handbook of Global Education Policy*, edited by Karen Mundy, Andy Green, Bob Lingard, and Antoni Verger, 357–373. Oxford, UK: Wiley Blackwell.

Mundy, K. 2007. "Educational Multilateralism – Origins and Indicators for Global Governance." In *New Arenas of Educational Governance: The Impact of International Organizations and Markets on Educational Policy Making*, edited by S. Leibfried, A. Rusconi, K. Leuze, and K. Martens, 1939. New York: Palgrave Macmillan.

Nordin, A., and D. Sundberg. 2016. "Travelling Concepts in National Curriculum Policy-Making: The Example of Competencies." *European Educational Research Journal* 15 (3): 314–328.

Normand, R. 2010. "Expertise, Networks and Indicators: The Construction of the European Strategy in Education." *European Educational Research Journal* 9 (3): 407–421.

OECD (Organisation for Economic Co-Operation and Development). 2001. "Definition and Selection of Competences: Theoretical and Conceptual Foundations (DeSeCo): Background Paper." OECD/SFSO/DeSeCo: Accessed at: http://www.oecd.org/education/skills-beyond-school/41529556.pdf.

OECD (Organisation for Economic Co-Operation and Development). 2002. "Definition and Selection of Competences (DESECO): Theoretical and Conceptual Foundations: Strategy Paper." DEELSA/ED/CERI/CD(2002)9: 1–27.

OECD (Organisation for Economic Co-Operation and Development). 2005. "The Definition and Selection of Key Competencies: Executive Summary." Paris: OECD. Accessed at: http://www.oecd.org/pisa/35070367.pdf.

OECD (Organisation for Economic Co-Operation and Development). 2019. *Future of Education and Skills 2030: Conceptual Learning Framework. Concept Note: OECD Learning Compass 2030.*

Perrenoud, P. 2001. "The Key to Social Fields: Competencies of an Autonomous Actor." In *Defining and Selecting Key Competencies*, edited by Dominique S. Rychen and Laura H. Salganik, 121–149. Seattle, Toronto, Bern, Gottingen: Hogrefe and Huber Publishers.

Piacentini, M. 2017a. "Developing an International Assessment of Global Competence." *Childhood Education* 93 (6): 507–510. doi:10.1080/00094056.2017.1398564.

Piacentini, M. 2017b. *Preparing Our Youth for a Better World: OECD PISA Global Competence Framework Launch.* Keynote talk presented at the Launch of the PISA Global Competency Assessment hosted by Harvard Graduate School of Education on December 12, 2017. Accessed from: https://www.youtube.com/watch?v=puYx83MSOgc.

Ramirez, F. O., and J. W. Meyer. 2012. "Toward Post-National Societies and Global Citizenship." *Multicultural Education Review* 4 (1): 1–28. doi:10.1080/23770031.2009.11102887.

Reimers, F. M. 2008. "Preparing Students for the Flat World." *Education Week* 28 (7): 24–25. https://www.edweek.org/ew/articles/2008/10/08/07reimers.h28.html.

Reimers, F. M. 2009a. "'Global Competency' Is Imperative for Global Success." *Chronicle of Higher Education* 55 (21): A29. Publisher's Version.

Reimers, F. M. 2009b. "Educating for Global Competency." In *International Perspectives on the Goals of Universal Basic and Secondary Education*, edited by J. Cohen and M. Malin, 183–202. New York: Routledge Press.

Reimers, F. M. 2009c. "Leading for Global Competency." *Educational Leadership* 67 (1), ASCD. http://www.ascd.org/publications/educational-leadership/sept09/vol67/num01/Leading-for-Global-Competency.aspx.

Reimers, F. M. 2013. *Assessing Global Education: An Opportunity for the OECD.* http://search.oecd.org/pisa/pisaproducts/Global-Competency.pdf.

Rizvi, F., and B. Lingard. 2010. *Globalizing Education Policy.* Routledge Publishing.

Robertson, S. L. 2018. "Researching Global Education Policy: Angles in/on/out." In *Global Education Policy and International Development: New Agendas, Issues, and Policies*, 2nd ed., edited by Antoni Verger, Mario Novelli, and Hulya K. Altinyelten, 35–54. London: Bloomsbury.

Rychen, D. S. 2001. "Introduction." In *Defining and Selecting Key Competencies*, edited by Dominique S. Rychen and Laura H. Salganik, 1–15. Seattle, Toronto, Bern, Gottingen: Hogrefe and Huber Publishers.

Rychen, D. S. 2016. "E2030 Conceptual Framework: Key Competencies for 2030 (DeSeCo 2.0) Working Paper," Directorate for Education and Skills Education Policy Committee, EDU/EDPC (2016)23/ANN1.

Rychen, D. S., and L. H. Salganik, eds. 2001. *Defining and Selecting Key Competencies.* Hogrefe and Huber Publishers.

Rychen, D. S., L. H. Salganik, and M. E. McLaughlin, eds. 2003. *Contributions to the Second DeSeCo Symposium.* Geneva, Switzerland, 11-13 February, 2002. Neuchatel: Swiss Federal Statistical Office. Accessed from http://www.oecd.org/education/skills-beyond-school/41529505.pdf.

Sassen, S. 2002. "Towards Post-National and Denationalized Citizenship." In *Handbook of Citizenship Studies*, edited by Engin F. Isin, and Bryan S. Turner, 277–292. London: SAGE Publications Ltd. doi:10.4135/9781848608276.n17.

Schleicher, A. 2017. *Preparing Our Youth for a Better World: OECD PISA Global Competence Framework Launch.* Keynote talk presented at the Launch of the PISA Global Competency Assessment Framework hosted by Harvard Graduate School of Education on December 12, 2017. https://www.youtube.com/watch?v=puYx83MSOgc.

Simpson, A., and F. Dervin. 2019. "Global and Intercultural Competences for Whom? By Whom? For What Purpose?: An Example from the Asia Society and the OECD." *Compare: A Journal of Comparative and International Education* 49 (4): 672–677. doi:10.1080/03057925.2019.1586194.

UNESCO United Nations Educational, Scientific and Cultural Organization. 2015. *Rethinking Education: Towards a Global Common Good?* UNESCO Publishing. https://unevoc.unesco.org/e-forum/RethinkingEducation.pdf.

Wiseman, A., and C. S. Taylor, eds. 2017. *The Impact of the OECD on Education Worldwide.* International Perspectives on Education and Society, 31. Emerald Publishing Limited.

# Index

Note: Page numbers followed by "n" denote endnotes.

actors 10–11, 21, 22, 36, 53, 55, 59, 99, 101, 102, 135, 141
Anderson-Levitt, Kathryn 22, 30, 31n1, 39
Appadurai, A. 134
Arendt, Hannah 126
articulation method 69, 77
Assessment and Teaching of Twenty-first Century Skills (ATC21S) 23, 24, 26
Auld, E. 133, 140
Aydarova, Elena 11

Barnett, M. 131, 140, 141
Berne Symposium 137, 138, 140
Biesta, Gert 116–119, 121, 123, 127
Bonnéry, Stéphane 22, 31n1
Bordoli, Eloísa 9, 13

China 5, 7, 11, 83–88, 90–93; key competencies framework 86
citizens 4, 13, 45, 87, 100, 115–117, 126, 127, 138
civic competences 43, 116–119, 121–123, 125–127
civic education 117, 119, 122, 123, 125; curriculum 119, 121, 123, 127
Clément, Pierre 10, 13
Cobb, D. J. 133
Common Core State Standards 7, 91, 99, 100, 103, 106
competence-added curriculum 27, 29, 30; framework 29–30
competence-based curriculum/curricula (CBC) 29, 120, 125, 127
competence movement 22, 30
competences/competencies 2–4, 7–10, 51, 56, 76, 91, 100, 105, 107, 108, 131, 132, 136, 137, 141; conceptualising 135–136; curricular design for 67–78; managerial roots of 38–39; pedagogy and management 39–40; productive plasticity of 3–4; reforms 10, 102; translation of 43–44; vs. scholasticism 38

competency-added reform 99, 105, 107, 109
competency-based approaches 4, 12, 13, 51, 52, 56, 60, 62
competency-based reforms 2–5, 8–10, 12, 13, 99–102, 108, 110
competent learners 130, 131, 134, 137–139, 141
compulsory school curriculum 35–47
compulsory schooling 12, 27, 28, 36, 37, 41, 45–47
compulsory school syllabuses 43, 46
conceptual frames 133
conservatism 44
contingencies 3, 10
convergence 11, 12, 20, 100, 116, 125
Couch, D. 133
Cullen, Carlos 76
culture 30, 44, 45, 63, 67, 85, 93, 94, 137–139
curricular design 84, 85, 90; elaboration process 73–75
curricular policies 77, 78
curricular universalisation 71–72
curriculum policy reform 119, 125
curriculum reforms 20, 27, 28, 36, 86, 109, 115, 116, 118, 120, 126

Debord, Guy 52, 53, 59, 64
democratic/democracy 26, 90, 100, 117–119, 122, 123, 126, 127, 136; citizens 116, 125–127; citizenship 119, 122; society 4, 116, 117, 120, 122, 127; subjectivity 117, 118, 125, 126
Deng, Li 9, 12
digital learning 103
disciplinary knowledge 29, 74, 93, 103
disciplinary skills 75, 100, 104
discursive hybridity 29
discursive interactions 21, 22
documents' internal logics 75–77
domestic contingencies 109

economic development 51, 55, 92, 93
educational approaches 60–62

## INDEX

educational reforms 43, 51, 52, 62, 63, 92, 118, 125
educational systems 39, 52–55, 59, 60, 63, 64, 71, 135
education experts 87, 132, 133, 136
education policy 44, 84, 85, 94, 125, 130, 133, 134, 142
education policy-making 130–142
education reforms 54, 93, 118
Engel, Laura C. 133
epistemic communities 8, 11, 21, 131
ethnographic engagement 54
European Key competencies 42–43
experts 8, 11, 12, 54–57, 60, 131–133, 135, 138, 140, 141

Fadel, Charles 87
Fichtner, Sarah 22, 31n1
Finnemore, M. 131, 140
France 8, 10, 11, 35–41, 43, 46, 47
Freire, Paulo 75
French education system 37, 38, 41
French genealogy 37

Gardinier, Meg P. 8, 11
Giroux, Henry 75
global competence/competency 2, 5, 131–135, 138–142; assessment 10, 138
global education policy (GEP) 133
globally competent learners 130–142
global policies 20, 21, 30
goals 26, 27, 104–108, 116, 117, 121, 122, 125
Grotlüschen, A. 133

Haas, P. 21, 131, 135
Halász, Gábor 92
higher education 2, 54, 58, 60, 63
higher-order thinking 3, 4, 100, 107, 109
high-order skills 87, 88, 93, 94
Hirsch, E. D. Jr. 93
Howarth, David 69, 77
Hutmacher, W. 136
hybrid competences 27–28; discourse 31
hybridity 3, 7, 9, 10, 12, 35, 47

influential competence frameworks 23–24
international actors 22
International discourses 54–56
international organisations (IOs) 132, 134–135

Kahne, Joseph 116–119, 121, 123, 126, 127
Kamens, D. H. 135
key competences/competencies 12, 13, 22, 24, 26, 27, 37, 55, 56, 84, 86, 90–92, 116, 120–124, 131, 132, 136–138, 140; conceptualising 136–138; frameworks 83–86, 90, 92; for lifelong learning 115

knowledge 23, 24, 28, 29, 38, 40, 43–45, 52, 53, 57–59, 74, 75, 85, 89, 135, 141
Kohn, Alfie 90
Kondakov, Alexander 58, 61
Kosovo 7, 10, 11, 115–121, 123–127; curriculum frameworks 121–123
Kukulin, Ilia 61

learning outcomes 22, 29, 123, 126
Ledger, S. 133
legitimation strategies 10, 29
lifelong learning 22, 38, 88, 115
Lin, C. D. 92
Lyotard, Jean-François 52, 53, 62

Marcuse, Herbert 52, 53, 59
McNeely, C. L. 135
MCRN (*Marco Curricular de Referencia Nacional*) 68, 73–76, 78
Meyer, J. W. 133, 134
Michel, Alain 92
moral priority 83–94
moral values 92, 93
Morgan, Clara 110
Morris, P. 133, 140
motivations 87–88

national curriculum-making 19–31
national pedagogy 75–76
national Swedish curriculum reform 28–29
national transformations 54–56
neoliberal education reform 70–71
new school standards 52, 56, 60, 61
Nordin, A. 131

openness, US actors 109

parallel movements 100–101
pedagogy 39, 44, 56, 61, 62
Peng, Zhengmei 9, 12
PISA Global Competence assessment 11, 13, 132, 133, 138–140
policy-making 19–23, 27, 31, 115, 117, 126, 127, 130, 131; process 10, 116, 124, 125, 140
political conceptions 36, 118
polysemy 3, 8–10, 12, 35–36, 47, 131, 135, 136
post-conflict societies 119, 126
postmodern societies 52, 53
post-national endeavour 133
powerful actors 109
problem-solving skills 85, 105
productive plasticity 3, 4, 10
progressive education 37, 38, 41
progressive & lifelong learning educators 38

quality education 77, 84, 86

# INDEX

Ramirez, F. O. 133–134
Ravitch, Diane 92, 93, 103
Roblin, Natal Pareja 27, 29, 30, 105
Russia 7, 10, 11, 54–59, 61–63
Rutkowski, David 133
Rychen, D. S. 142

Salganik, L. H. 142
Saqipi, Blerim 118
Sassen, S. 134
scandalisation 28
Schleicher, A. 139, 140
secondary education 2, 5, 12, 38, 39, 70
silent reform 99–110
Sivesind, Kirsten 75
skill priority 83–94
Skinner, Burrhus Frederic 22
social constructions 101, 110
social development 88
soft skills 37, 44–46
Steiner-Khamsi, Gita 21
Stroobants, Marcelle 38
subject competencies 56, 58
subject knowledge 24, 26, 28–30, 58, 83, 88, 93
Sundberg, D. 131
Sweden 5, 10–12, 19, 20, 27, 30
Swedish curriculum 21, 27–31; reform 20, 29, 30

Tahirsylaj, Armend 10
Tanguy, Lucie 38
teacher education 2, 94, 133

teacher training 67, 70, 71, 73
teaching communities 68, 70–74, 77, 78
Thompson, Greg 133
transdisciplinary competencies 104
transnational competence frameworks 19–31
transversal competences 27, 37, 43–45
Trilling, Bernie 87
twenty-first century skills 4, 23, 99–105, 107, 109

United States 5, 7, 10, 11, 22, 23, 99–103, 106–109
Uruguay 5, 7, 9–11, 67, 69, 70, 72, 75, 77, 78
US 21st century skills framework 87
US actors 99, 101, 108, 109
US competency movements, international perspective 108
utilitarianism 44

Vatier, Raymond 47n2
Voogt, Joke 27, 29–30, 105

Westbury, Ian 75
Westheimer, Joel 116–119, 121, 123, 126–127
Wheelahan, Leesa 52

Young Europeans 7, 115–127, 136

Zarifian, Philippe 38
Zhao, Yong 94
Zhu, M. J. 90
Zylfiu, Bahtije Gerbeshi 119

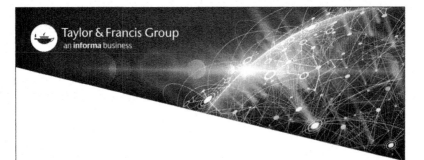